DATE DUE

DE 9 '94			
AP 21 '95			
MY 19 '95			
JY 27 '95			
DE 10 '98			
AP 21 '99			
DE 7 '00			
DE 7 '02			
FE 10 '05			
DE 16 '08			

DEMCO 38-296

Medical Gridlock and Health Reform

**The Eisenhower Center
for the Conservation of Human Resources
· Studies in Health Policy ·**

Medical Gridlock and Health Reform

Eli Ginzberg

Westview Press

BOULDER • SAN FRANCISCO • OXFORD

The Eisenhower Center for the Conservation of Human Resources
Studies in Health Policy

Copyright © 1994 by The Eisenhower Center for the Conservation of Human Resources, Columbia University

Published in 1994 in the United States of America by Westview Press, Inc., 5500 Central Avenue, Boulder, Colorado 80301-2877, and in the United Kingdom by Westview Press, 36 Lonsdale Road, Summertown, Oxford OX2 7EW

Library of Congress Cataloging-in-Publication Data
Medical gridlock and health reform / Eli Ginzberg.
  p.   cm. — (Eisenhower Center for the Conservation of Human
Resources studies in health policy)
  Includes index.
  ISBN 0-8133-2040-2
  1. Health care reform—United States.   I. Series.
RA395.A3M43   1994
362.1'0973—dc20
                                                                        93-46403
                                                                        CIP

Printed and bound in the United States of America

The paper used in this publication meets the requirements
of the American National Standard for Permanence of Paper
for Printed Library Materials Z39.48-1984.

10   9   8   7   6   5   4   3   2   1

To Margaret E. Mahoney,
a friend of many years,
with affection and appreciation

Contents

Tables

Preface

With a few exceptions the chapters that comprise this book have been previously published in health care journals, most of them within the past two years. Accordingly, this volume can be viewed as a follow-up to *The Medical Triangle: Physicians, Politicians and the Public*, which Harvard University Press first published in 1990 and reprinted in paperback in 1991.

The early 1990s saw the U.S. health care system under intensifying pressures and strains because of steeply rising expenditures, an increase in the number of uninsured persons, and a range of other challenges, including increasingly severe pressures on the government and employers, the principal payers for health care. As a consequence of these and other dysfunctional developments, I was encouraged to explore and assess many of these new developments and to make my findings more broadly available by publishing them in various health policy periodicals. They are here reprinted to enable the interested reader to become acquainted with my assessments of the transformations underway in the financing of U.S. health care and in the delivery of services on the eve of an era of major health care reform.

Except for minor changes in wording and an updating of an occasional statistic, the chapters in this volume do not differ from the articles as they were originally published. However, I want to note explicitly that I am indebted to Miriam Ostow (Chapter 16) for agreeing to let me include our joint effort in this collection under my name.

I want to add that my collaboration with Miriam Ostow covers three decades; as head of the health care studies of the Eisenhower Center staff, she has contributed in greater or smaller measure to all of the chapters, not only to the one acknowledged above, and for this collaboration I am deeply in her debt, intellectually and personally.

The Eisenhower Center for the Conservation of Human Resources, Columbia University, which I direct, has been fortunate to have received financial support for research from a number of the nation's leading foundations concerned with health policy. I acknowledge with gratitude the support of The Robert Wood Johnson Foundation, The Commonwealth Fund, The Pew Charitable Trust, and The Josiah Macy, Jr., Foundation.

In the assembling and editing of the chapters I was greatly assisted by my long-term associate, Anna Dutka, who assumed most of the responsibility for taking the discrete pieces and helping to transform them into a book.

For their preparation of the original articles for publication and for overseeing the multiple stages of guiding this volume through the press, I want to express once again my deep appreciation for the splendid assistance that I received from Sylvia Leef and Shoshana Vasheetz, long-term mainstays of the Eisenhower Center staff.

Eli Ginzberg, Director
The Eisenhower Center for
the Conservation of Human Resources
Columbia University

Introduction

About a year ago, Victor Fuchs remarked that from being the nation's leading incrementalist, I had become a leading eschatologist. Fuchs was fully justified in pointing out the radical shift that had occurred in my thinking about the changing U.S. health care system as we entered the early 1990s. As a longtime student of the changing health care scene I had observed, or had read about, many forecasts of radical changes looming on the health policy horizon that time had proven wrong.

Every decade or two the passage of national health insurance appeared to be imminent—it was part of Theodore Roosevelt's platform when he ran for president on the Bull Moose ticket in 1912. Each time the proposal reemerged, the last being in 1976 when Jimmy Carter included it in his successful presidential bid, I was certain that it was no closer to enactment than it had been in 1912, 1935, or the late 1940s.

My reaction to health care cost escalation provided other evidence of my incrementalist approach: In the post–World War II decades, when health care expenditures mounted rapidly, most analysts forecasted that the expenditure trend would inevitably level off once health care outlays, which had amounted to 4.5 percent of gross domestic product (GDP) in 1950, rose to 10 percent, but I saw no reason why such a leveling off should occur. True, President Richard Nixon had issued a national alert in 1969 when current expenditures approached $75 billion (up from $43 billion in 1950 adjusted for inflation) and accounted for 7.5 percent of GDP. In the president's view, a continuation of such expenditure increases threatened the financial stability of the U.S. health care system and even the effective functioning of the U.S. economy. But it seemed to me that the president's warning had been premature and exaggerated. In fact, although health care expenditures continued to accelerate, the health care system continued to function and the U.S. economy did not falter. My incrementalism was reinforced when the ratio of total health care outlays to GDP crossed the 10 percent line in the mid-1980s and kept increasing.

I made some rough projections in 1990 that indicated that if the United States remained on its present course, national health care expenditures would exceed the trillion-dollar mark by mid-decade and the 1.5 trillion-dollar mark not too long thereafter. This was a major shock to my incrementalism.

This arithmetic exercise explains why I altered my approach from incrementalism to one of eschatology. It made no sense to me that the nation was on the way to spending $2 trillion by the year 2000 on health care. It was by no means clear that the payers could find the additional sum; and it certainly made no sense for the United States to devote 21 percent of its GDP to health care. President Nixon was premature in raising his alarm when the ratio approached 7.5 percent, but now that it threatened to be three times as large only a few years hence, it seemed to me that the time had come to warn about serious trouble ahead.

The foregoing abbreviated comments about my "conversion" provides a starting place for introducing the reader to the twenty-one chapters that follow, arranged in four major subdivisions. In my review of the principal themes contained in each of the major sections, I hope to provide the reader with a map of the terrain, which will make the volume more accessible.

Part One: The Changing Health Care Scene—
The Longest View

The five chapters in this section explore the insights that can be gained for a current understanding of health care and its policy directions by a review of relevant events since World War II. Chapters 1 and 2 draw upon my service as Chief Logistical Advisor to the Surgeon General of the Army during World War II. The analysis is based on firsthand knowledge and experience.

The remaining three chapters look briefly at the unique American experience of delivering health care to veterans in a separate hospital system; at how health reform contrasts with other reform efforts in employment, housing, and education; and at how the current and prospective reforms are likely to affect the future of health education.

Part Two: Health Care and the Market

These seven chapters explore many critical dimensions of the current health care system within the context of health care reforms already underway or those looming ahead. Chapters 6 and 7 provide a lengthened perspective on the reform proposals that are now competing for attention. Chapters 8, 9, and 10 deal sequentially with critical dimensions of the extant system: personnel, nonprofit organizations, and high-tech medicine. Chapters 11 and 12 deal with more conceptual issues involved in competition and global budgets.

Part Three: The Poor and the Uninsured

The four chapters in this section single out for evaluation a dominant issue confronting the American people—how to improve the access of the poor and the near-poor to essential health care—and deal seriatim with selected dimensions of the subject. Chapter 13 focuses on current and prospective financing issues connected with improved access for the poor. Chapters 14 and 15 explore briefly the problems of health care access for the poor in New York City and for the nation's Hispanic population.

Chapter 16 seeks to demonstrate that although the introduction of universal health insurance may be a necessary step to assuring health care access to all, it is not sufficient by itself to remove such nonpecuniary barriers as the reluctance of physicians to practice among the poor or the lack of interpreters to facilitate conversation between English-speaking physicians and foreign-speaking patients.

Part Four: Toward Health Reform

These five chapters explore themes critically important to the understanding of the forces impeding or facilitating the transition of the present U.S. health care system to its future contours. Chapter 17 explores the question, Why has health reform been so slow? Chapter 18 reviews the many different interest groups that have a major stake in health reform and provides a partial answer to the question above. Chapter 19, on the future of health care reform, is addressed primarily to physicians to help them recognize major societal forces that are more potent than their professional concerns, even though the latter are still important and will continue to be. The penultimate chapter is a review of recent efforts to seek directions as to where we are and where we should be heading in health reform. The final chapter provides a brief overview of President Bill Clinton's proposals for health reform, advanced in the spring of 1993. It gives a larger perspective and considers what history and analysis can contribute to such an evaluation.

PART ONE

The Changing Health Care Scene:
The Longest View

1

Everything I Know About Health Care
I Learned in the Pentagon
in World War II

A reasonable question to ask is, How did a thirty-two-year-old draft-eligible nonphysician happen to become the Chief Logistical Advisor to the Surgeon General of the Army who had forty-five thousand physicians under his command in World War II? The answer is simple: In 1942–1943 I was working for General Brehan B. Somervell, the commanding general of Army Services Forces (ASF) and the Surgeon General's boss; one of my early assignments was to report on how the Surgeon General's Office (SGO) used resources. My analyses came to the attention of General Raymond Bliss, the assistant surgeon general in charge of operations, who subsequently (summer of 1943) "borrowed" me for the task of developing a reorganization plan that would enable him to prepare effectively for the two-front war. When the plan was ready, the general suggested that I head the new organization, the Resources Analysis Division, whose personnel would report directly to him.

During the course of the next three years I learned a great deal about the planning and administration of the largest medical operation in this nation's experience. At its peak, on a single day it had 600,000 patients occupying hospital beds throughout the world, tended by a work force of over 600,000 nurses, ward personnel, and civilian support staff. Together, patients and workers accounted for approximately one out of every seven persons in the United States Army. What follows are some of the more important lessons I learned that have stood me in good stead in the years and decades since the end of the war.

Lesson One: The Risks of Planning

In developing the reorganization plan, it became clear to me that the SGO was not prepared to hospitalize and treat the large numbers of battle casualties that would be returned to the United States once major invasions had been launched on the European continent and in Japan. Accordingly, the initial task that I faced was to develop a plan to cope with this priority need.

Early reconnoitering disclosed that there were no reliable data to support such a planning exercise. True, Colonel Albert G. Love of the SGO had produced some estimates based on the experience of World War I, but it appeared highly improbable that the invasion of Europe would repeat the pattern of trench warfare used in that war. More recent data were available from the invasion of North Africa, but they were of limited use in calculating the probable casualty rate from a cross-channel operation. By dint of good luck, the other SGO consultants and I had gotten our hands on some information based on the westward push of the Soviet armies, but to our consternation they covered only surgical cases, not medical illnesses. A Russian soldier who took sick had to fend for himself and seek help from the civilian sector; the Soviet Army provided care only for battle casualties.

The absence of a reliable statistical base, however, did not relieve me of the responsibility of carrying through the planning exercise. It was necessary to project the number of general hospitals, specialty services, specialist assignments, and various other requirements of the Army medical system. In the end, my staff and I estimated that on D Day plus six months the system would be responsible for 181,000 patients.

Examining the operating data six months after D Day, I found that we were within half a percentage point of our original estimate. I checked not only the total patient load but also two critical determinants: the number of casualties and the length of time that patients would be hospitalized. It turned out that I had vastly overestimated the number of casualties and vastly underestimated the average length of hospitalization. Clearly, these compensatory errors were my salvation, but what if they had been compounding errors? Lesson: Good planners are more likely to be lucky than smart!

Lesson Two: The Allocation of Limited Tonnage

In the early spring of 1944 General Charles P. Gross, the chief of transportation, called a high-powered conference to review the allocation of tonnage for priority needs. I was the SGO's representative and it was my job to get sufficient tonnage to assure the safe evacuation of the battle-injured. I made my pitch, not once but several times, until General Gross made the trenchant observation that if he deflected tonnage from bringing ammunition in, he could use all of it to move the injured out. Lesson: The availability of medical care is critically important for the morale of troops, but having ammunition to fight the enemy is a higher priority for the Army.

Lesson Three: Physicians Want to Keep Busy

One of the major challenges that faced the senior consultants to the SGO was the need to restrain physicians, especially during the buildup phase of the Army, from doing too much for the patients under their jurisdiction. Every couple of weeks a bulletin was sent to the field, advising physicians not to do procedure A, B, or C because aggressive therapy would probably delay the return of the serviceman to active duty. Hard as it is to believe, circumcision was the most frequently performed surgical procedure during World War II. My preferred explanation for this counterintuitive fact is that even in the absence of monetary gain, physicians wish to keep busy. Lesson: Underemployed physicians will lead to overtreated patients.

Lesson Four: Staff Field Hospitals with Adequate Numbers of Nurses

The only specific "order" that General Bliss gave me during our three year association was to be certain to have the field hospitals, which would be the sites of initial care for battle casualties, well staffed with competent nurses. Bliss was convinced that nurses often made the difference when it came to whether a patient would survive or succumb.

I set about seeking volunteers for overseas duty, and many of those who responded were regular Army nurses with long years of service. Then I ran into an unexpected barrier. The ASF staff told me under no circumstances to send women over the age of forty abroad. Their reason: "You know, they go nuts at that age!" Although I tried hard to dissuade them from this arbitrary interdiction, I lost. They *knew* that older women went berserk! However, I learned an important lesson from the deployment of nurses in the United States Army. Through their proper utilization as patient-care managers rather than as providers of bedside nursing, they were able to make a greater contribution to the quality of hospital care. Civilian hospitals more than forty years later still need to learn this lesson.

Lesson Five: Health Care Versus Morality

The Women's Army Corps (WAC) had over 151,000 enlistments during World War II. It separated about 7.5 percent of the corps because of pregnancy. The policy of the SGO was to provide prenatal, delivery, and postnatal care to WACs who requested it. During the early months that this policy was in effect, the SGO encountered strong objections from the director of the WACs, Colonel Oveta Hobby. The director was hoping to be promoted to general and had concluded that publicity about pregnant WACs would prove counterproductive in the pursuit of her star, which, parenthetically, she never received.

A half-century later, the United States is enmeshed in all sorts of irrational battles about abortion, and many of the key participants appear to be more interested in votes than in proper care for pregnant women and unborn children. Lesson: The boundaries of health care extend far beyond the treatment of the sick and the injured.

Lesson Six: Tensions Between the ASF and the SGO

There were many sources of tension between the senior military of the Army Service Forces and the physicians who headed the Surgeon General's Office. Pressured to commission ever-larger numbers of physicians, the military staff proposed that the United States adopt the Japanese practice of using members of the medical administrative corps (nonphysicians) in various responsible positions, including the command of military hospitals. The SGO was adamantly opposed.

Relatively early in the war, the ASF staff uncovered games that physicians, particularly those assigned to bypassed hospitals in the Pacific, had begun to play. They would convene a medical board, assess the mental status of a physician colleague, and recommend his or her separation on the grounds of "psychoneurosis" or some similar nonspecific diagnosis. In turn, those separated physicians reciprocated the favor before they were sent home. When the ASF staff became aware of what was going on they withdrew the right of the Surgeon General to separate any physician prematurely.

By way of example, it took a lot of convincing to get the ASF to honor a request of Governor Thomas E. Dewey of New York for the early release of Lieutenant Colonel Basil McClean (of Strong Memorial Hospital, Rochester) to head an important new state commission. McClean, an able man with significant accomplishments as a civilian, was a misfit in uniform. As far as the general staff was concerned, however, the request for his separation was just another ploy of the doctors. Lesson: Many people, for good and bad reasons, have developed serious distrust of members of the medical profession.

Lesson Seven: The Japanese Are Different

In late 1945 I accompanied General Bliss and General William Menninger (the Surgeon General Office's chief consultant in psychiatry) on a tour of army medical installations in the Far East. I visited a large hospital for prisoners of war (POWs) on one of the Pacific islands, and on that visit I learned of some unfamiliar practices.

Japanese medical officers refused to operate on their enlisted men until forced to do so by the American officers in charge, literally at the point of a gun. The U.S. staff also reported that many of the amputees who were put on naval vessels, headed for their repatriation on the Japanese mainland, jumped overboard on the voyage home, knowing that their fellow citizens had little tolerance for the severely injured. Lesson: In the absence of detailed knowledge, cross-national comparisons of medical systems are likely to be misleading.

Lesson Eight: The Value of Excess Capacity

In September 1944, some three months after D Day, it looked as if the Allied armies would continue their advance, invade Germany, and win the war before Christmas. Accordingly, General Somervell directed Surgeon General Norman Kirk to explore the possibility of deactivating some fifteen of his sixty-odd general hospitals. Kirk, knowing of my earlier work with Somervell, asked me to accompany him to the critical meeting.

Somervell had been persuaded to consider the optimistic scenario of an early end to the war, but not so unalterably that he refused to listen to a counterargument. I asked him to consider the alternative: Suppose the war did not end. Once the hospitals had been deactivated, it would be next to impossible to reactivate them in time. I suggested that the decision remain moot for ninety days, when the probability of an early end to the war would be clear. Somervell agreed, and the Surgeon General breathed easier. Lesson: Don't cut too close to the bone. There are times when excess capacity makes good sense.

Lesson Nine: Never Underestimate the Power of a Senator

A phone call from the office of Senator Kenneth D. McKeller of Tennessee (chair of the Senate Finance Committee) at 11:15 one morning informed Colonel Albert H. Schwichtenberg, head of the SGO's Hospital Division, and me to be in the senator's office at 1:15 p.m. We were given no clue as to the reason for the summons, nor were we immediately enlightened by the senator, whom we found sprawled silently on his couch when we were ushered in sharply at 1:15. Finally the senator drawled: "I understand you had some ideas of moving the POW hospital out of Tennessee. Forget it. And don't ever think about moving anything in or out without checking with this office first. Good day." Lesson: Don't ever assume that operating effectively and economically is the only important operating principle. Senators are often guided by other criteria.

Lesson Ten: Getting the White House to Act

The Army followed the practice of transferring patients to the Veterans Administration (VA) if, after optimal treatment, they could not be discharged to their homes. But in late 1944 the VA was interposing all sorts of difficulties when we requested transfer beds. These difficulties reflected the VA's limited capacity to respond since its facilities had lost most of their staffs during the preceding years.

To overcome this barrier, I wangled an appointment with the assistant director of the Bureau of the Budget. During our discussion, I pointed out that the president would soon be faced with a national scandal unless the VA underwent a major shake-up. I was summarily told to go back to running Army hospitals and to mind my own business—advice that I had no alternative but to follow. Lesson: Some things can be fixed only by intervention from the top. But many at the top don't like to be bothered with still another problem. Nevertheless, the threat of a scandal can sometimes command attention.

In sum, these are the lessons that I learned about health care during World War II as a result of my duties in the Pentagon:

- Health planning, like all other forms of planning, is to be treated gingerly. The odds are that most plans will turn out to be wrong.
- Medical care is important, but there are situations in which it must take a secondary role.
- Underemployed physicians make for overtreated patients.
- Nurses should be managers of patient-care systems in hospitals.
- Health care and morality are inextricably connected.
- Many lay leaders don't trust physicians.
- Cultures differ vastly in their health perceptions, policies, and modes of treatment.
- Excess hospital capacity may in some circumstances be preferable to operating too close to the margin.
- Don't overlook the power of a senator, especially if he heads the finance committee.
- The threat of a scandal can sometimes spur action for reform.

There are some important long-range forces that helped to shape the evolution of U.S. health care in the succeeding half century that can be traced back to World War II and that warrant at least brief attention.

The most important of these long-term structural transformations affected the future attitudes and behavior of the American public toward health care, led to major shifts in the spending decisions of Congress for biomedical research and hospital construction, and set the stage for the victory of specialism in the training and practice modes of American physicians.

The medical services of the armed forces provided a much higher level of medical care for fifteen million servicemen and some additional millions of their dependents than that to which they had earlier been exposed, thereby helping to raise the public's postwar demand for more and better health care.

This expanded demand was more easily satisfied because of the spectacular growth of private health insurance during and after the war, precipitated by the War Labor Board's 1942 decision that trade unions were free to bargain with employers for health benefits, even in the face of a wage freeze.

The success of the atom bomb and other research breakthroughs during the war set the stage for the radically changed attitude of Congress toward post–World War II federal government funding of biomedical research which increased from $3 million in 1940 to over 10 billion in 1990. Even when the 1940 figure adjusted for inflation, translates into $30 million in 1990 dollars, the enormity of the increase is proof positive that the war left its impact on U.S. medicine. These long-term consequences still dominate our health care system.

2

The Impact of World War II on U.S. Medicine

This chapter is based on the Thirteenth Reynolds Lecture, which, in turn, is based not on archival research but on a reconstruction of my duties in the Office of the Surgeon General of the Army during World War II. I will thus start with one autobiographical reference that relates to health and hospital care in Alabama in the post–World War II era.

Some time in the late 1960s during Governor George Wallace's first term in office, I was invited by the regional hospital planning group to evaluate the governor's plan to respond to the shortage of physicians in the rural areas by building three additional medical schools. My evaluation of the plan was negative in the extreme. It suggested that Alabama needed a beefed-up state department of public health, with some nurse practitioners able to provide first-contact care for the isolated rural population and with transportation chits if the nurses decided that their patients needed hospital care. Alabama got four clinical campuses but not four medical schools, and for that I take some small part of the credit.

It would be not only immodest but also inappropriate if I did not take note right away of three high-ranking physicians in the Surgeon General's Office: Brigadier General Hugh Morgan, chief consultant in medicine; Colonel Michael DeBakey, assistant to Brigadier General Fred Rankin, chief consultant in surgery; and Brigadier General William C. Menninger, chief consultant in psychiatry. They became my teachers and mentors and my close personal friends. Except for their help and support I would never have been able to discharge my responsibilities.

In my approach, three facets are explored. First, selected impacts of World War II on the postwar development of U.S. medical care are highlighted, impacts that have largely escaped evaluation. Second, lessons from World War II that we *should* have learned and applied in the postwar decades but that we ignored, are pointed out. And finally, with the passage of about half a century, I look back in the hope of seeing some new and important long-term influences that I had earlier overlooked.

Under the first rubric of important impacts of World War II on the later development of American medicine, let me call attention to the fact that many millions of servicemen and their dependents had their first contacts with a well-functioning medical care system as a consequence of their military service, a contact that stimulated the post–World War II demand for more and better medical care. This increased consumer demand coincided with the advances in therapy that helped transform U.S. medicine from a caring to a curing system.

The Medical Department of the Army—and also the Navy—developed a splendid record of saving lives during active combat. The Army was able to save 93 percent of all battle casualties that a medical corpsman was able to reach. Of the soldiers who made it into the evacuation system the Army lost only 7 percent. The soldiers knew that they could rely on the Medical Department and this knowledge was critical for their morale as well as their survival.

Few people today realize that large numbers of Americans living in rural areas had very poor medical care during the early decades of the century and through the ten-year depression that began in the 1930s. I recall giving a much-decorated sergeant a lift between Washington, D.C., and Ft. Meade, near Baltimore. In reply to my inquiry about his present assignment, he said I would never believe what he did for many hours each day. He was teaching young men from Appalachia to use soap and water to wash themselves, knowledge that they were first acquiring.

My principal assignment from General Bliss when I came aboard was to prepare the general hospitals in the United States—about sixty-five in total—to provide the highest quality of specialized care for the World War II battle casualties who would be returned to the United States for definitive treatment. That required care in allocating resources, such as medical and, particularly, surgical specialists; providing each specialty service with the requisite equipment and support staff; putting a medical regulatory system in place so that every injured soldier could be sent to a hospital with the necessary specialty capabilities closest to home; and establishing rules and regulations so that each soldier would receive optimal treatment before discharge. On D Day plus six months we had an estimated 181,000 battle casualties in our Zone of Interior general hospitals. The award that I am most proud of is the gold medal for "exceptional civilian service" that the Army awarded me for making this system operational and overseeing it.

The dominance of specialty and subspecialty medicine that came to characterize U.S. medicine in the post–World War II era was the direct consequence of the emphasis that the Army Medical Department placed on specialist care during World War II. This focus on general hospitals' providing definitive care for U.S. battle casualties—and the quality and results of that care—unquestionably contributed to the willingness of Congress in 1946 to make large-scale federal funding to upgrade the hospital plant available to the American people. The passage of the Hill-Burton Act, with conservative Senator Robert Taft in the lead role, indicates that the American people had come to appreciate the importance of quality hospital care. Good hospitals attract good physicians and together they could assure that local populations had access to quality care.

Another lasting impact of the war on the transformation of U.S. medicine resulted from the decision of the federal government to become a major funder of biomedical research. Vannevar Bush's *Science: The Endless Frontier*, written for President Roosevelt but implemented by President Harry S. Truman, set the stage for the new federal role in the support of biomedical research.

It is worth noting that the subcommittee on medical research that reported to Vannevar Bush suggested that the medical schools might be able to make effective use of a budget of $5 to $10 million a year. In 1989 when Anna Dutka and I wrote our book, *The Financing of Biomedical Research*, the annual expenditures of the federal government for biomedical research were approaching the $10 billion level! When World War II got underway total national expenditures were about $45 million. Today the comparable national figure is approaching $30 billion!

One of the by-products of the explosive growth of federal dollars for biomedical research was its impact on American medical education, which despite great accomplishments—witness the University of Alabama at Birmingham—may have had secondary consequences that have not been all for the good. Many have begun to ask whether three out of every four physicians should be trained as specialists or subspecialists. It appears to some of us that a larger number of generalists might be preferable and that physicians-in-training require more than expertise in the biological sciences.

The United States backed into private health insurance during and immediately after World War II as a consequence of the 1942 decision of the War Labor Board to permit trade unions to bargain with employers for health benefits, bargaining that was aided and abetted by the decision of the Internal Revenue Service (IRS) to exempt these payments and benefits from federal income tax. True, the Blue Cross movement had gotten under way in Dallas in 1929, but it is doubtful that private health insurance would have become a potent force without the boost that it received from the war.

Another major impact of World War II on later developments in U.S. medicine relate to psychiatry. At the outbreak of the war, psychiatry dealt almost exclusively with the severely mentally ill, persons who were kept under lock and key for years, even decades, in the back wards of state mental hospitals. But the predominant psychiatric casualties in World War II were upset soldiers suffering from shock, psychoneurosis, and behavioral disorders. Most of them stabilized very quickly once they were removed from the battle zone.

Based on his wartime experiences, in the postwar years William Menninger became a major advocate to increase the appropriations of state legislatures so as to modernize the care of the mentally ill and to expand their access to treatment in ambulatory settings in their own communities. He had considerable success in this public campaign. He also played a leading role in the establishment of the Group for the Advancement of Psychiatry (GAP) which mobilized many of the younger psychiatrists who had seen duty during the war to reorient U.S. psychiatry.

The next lasting impact of World War II on U.S. medicine was the striking transformation of the Veterans Administration. The VA system had been decimated during the war because of the large number of physicians who went into uniform. But the VA had been a weak system for many years previously, for reasons that I only learned by accident. I was told that General Frank T. Hines, the longtime head of the VA, had been a Christian Scientist and therefore had a low opinion of curative medicine. But I do know from personal experience that I ran into a serious problem with the VA when growing numbers of battle casualties who could not be discharged to their homes, such as paraplegics, had to be transferred out of Army hospitals.

Some months later the new VA team was in place—Generals Omar Bradley and Paul Hawley and Dr. Paul Magnuson from Northwestern. The new relationship(s) between the VA and U.S. medical schools represented a major and lasting advance, not only for the medical care of veterans but also for U.S. medical education.

The last major contribution of World War II to U.S. medicine relates to the growth of rehabilitation as a recognized area of medical specialization. Dr. Howard Rusk of the Air Corps was the leader who showed the way, but his path was not an easy one. The Surgeon General, then Norman Kirk, an orthopedist by specialty, had misgivings about Rusk's proselytizing efforts. Moreover, Kirk was fighting a rearguard action to prevent the Air Corps from developing its own general hospitals. This may have clouded his professional judgment about what Rusk was doing. In fact, Rusk was a pioneer who left his mark.

Finally, let us consider lessons from World War II from which we failed to benefit. The Army put medical students into the reserve, paid them a stipend, and saw to it that the medical schools accelerated their programs. I am distressed to see that today four out of every five medical school graduates have debts of over $50,000 on average, much of which has to be paid back at high rates of interest. A colleague recently told me of one of his thoracic surgery residents who is thirty-five and has run up a total debt of about one-quarter million dollars. That is no way for a physician to enter independent practice.

Several years ago Robert Ebert, former dean of Harvard Medical School, and I put forward a plan to ameliorate this situation. We proposed to reduce preparation for first certification from seven to five years by admitting good students to medical school at the end of their junior year in college and by combining the current two years of medical school clerkship with the three years of basic residency training into a shortened four-year, integrated program. We are pleased to learn that some experiments to accomplish this are now under way.

The United States also failed to learn from World War II the advantages of trading public support for medical students for a subsequent period of public service and the correlated advantage of reducing rather than expanding the time to attain the Doctor of Medicine (M.D.) degree and first certification. Both are lessons that we need to relearn.

In yet another arena the military took the lead but civilians failed to follow. The armed forces gave nurses broadened responsibilities as managers of hospital wards and rewarded them by giving them officer status. For the most part, nurses during World War II were provided with an opportunity to make use of all of their skills and energies. They were heavily engaged, and the productivity of the health care system was therefore greatly increased. After the war the United States retrogressed. We have still not regained the ground that we lost since World War II, continue to have repeated shortages of nurses and to suffer from the reduced effectiveness of the health care delivery system.

Closely related to the nursing issue was a practice that the military pioneered—the greater use and deployment of mid-level personnel. Since it was not possible for the military to put a physician on every cargo ship that sailed the seas or at every outpost where a few servicemen were stationed, the armed forces trained a large number of midlevel personnel to provide first-contact care and provided them with communications devices that enabled them to consult with superiors when they faced problems beyond their knowledge and skill. In the past decades we could have used this system as a model for care in many isolated, underserved populations, both rural and urban.

The military also took the lead during World War II to make individual soldiers responsible for protecting and maintaining their own health, particularly in the face of certain risks, such as frostbite or venereal disease. Soldiers were instructed in the procedures they should follow to protect themselves and if they failed to do so, they were subject to punishment.

We are only belatedly coming to recognize that the individual must play a leading role in his or her own health maintenance.

The last lesson that America failed to learn from our experiences in World War II was the danger of "overtreatment." During the war physicians wanted to be busy even if there was no money to be gained and no real patient need for their interventions. I recall vividly the trouble that DeBakey had in sending instructions to the field, ordering physicians not to perform surgery on soldiers suffering from pilonidal cysts because left alone, time would cure most of them. The reason that I have been cautious about repeated postwar efforts to expand the physician supply significantly has been my belief that though a shortage of physicians is undesirable, a surplus can be a real threat, not only to the public's purse but also to its health.

Lessons Learned

Looking back with the advantage of more than forty years of perspective, these are the lessons learned. One can enjoy the benefits of a well-functioning health care system only if the system has ample resources, both human and physical, at its disposal. While there is no question that the Army Medical Department had most of the resources it needed in World War II, resources alone were not enough. They needed to be part of a system in which patients were matched with physicians (specialists) and with appropriate medical centers where the specialists were effectively supported. We were able to do that in World War II because we had control over all staff, facilities, and patients. But that is not easy to replicate in civilian life. Currently we run a costly, duplicative, overexpanded hospital system in the United States, with average bed occupancy in the low 60 percent range.

To make matters more complicated, the United States has never put in place a planning mechanism that balances the production of costly personnel resources, such as specialists, with the evolving needs of the public for more access to generalists. After 1963 Congress put considerable funds into expanding the physician supply, but seven years later the underserved areas were still lacking physicians and six years thereafter (1976) Congress lost interest in the subject and withdrew most of its capitation support.

Our health care system has over nine million employees and cost the nation over $800 billion in 1992. Admittedly, this is not a system that was planned, and it is not easy to control. Government data suggest that we will pierce the trillion-dollar level of expenditures in 1994–1995. The critical question is how long can we maintain such a system. In my view, we cannot remain on such an expenditure trajectory which would require that we find a second trillion dollars by century's end. Such a sum is not extractable from the U.S. economy, nor, in my opinion, would it make much sense (even if the money could be extracted) to spend, on average, close to $30,000 a year for the health care of a family of four.

When I look back, it is clear to me that no large system can be managed without a flow of current data that enables those in a policy role to have a broad perspective about what is going on. I set up such a system for the Surgeon General, and it proved to be very successful. One reason for its success was that we kept it simple. Moreover, we used both the averages and the outliers that emerged from the data only as indicators to determine where further study was needed. For these further probes we relied on the Service Commands. Medical consultants who worked in the field sought to assist their professional colleagues and the hospital commanders to improve their professional and administrative functioning. The primary duty of the consultants was educational, a duty that on balance they performed very well. I have reflected on occasion that it was unfortunate that the faculty of our major academic health centers have not been able to provide similar consultant services in their respective regions.

A final point relates to the growing ambivalence of the American public toward physicians, the most critical resource in any effective system of health care delivery. The basis of effective health care is the establishment and maintenance of a relationship of trust between the physician and his or her patient, and more broadly between all citizens and the members of the medical profession. While physicians make decisions involving life and death, the trust relationship is being weakened even if it has not been entirely eroded. David Rogers once asked me to check the average earnings of a physician at the end of the New Era (1929). I found it amounted to $5,000. A full professor at Columbia at that time earned 50 percent more. Over the decades many physicians have become not only affluent but also wealthy, and that has created substantial public distrust.

I do not believe that our health care system can be protected and improved unless the growing uneasiness among many members of the public about the medical profession is stopped and reversed. Physicians must be in the forefront of the reform of our health care system, and to lead they must have and hold the trust of the American people.

3

The Veterans Administration
in a Vise

It is many years since I last had the opportunity to become familiar with
the problems facing the Medical Department of the Veterans Administration. In the late 1970s I had the occasion to review the Institute of Medicine
report on the VA that advocated the dissolution of the system in favor of
treating veterans in community hospitals. The title of my article in the
New England Journal of Medicine was "How Not to Give Advice to the U.S.
Government."

In preparing the remarks that follow about the status of the VA at the
end of the 1980s, I was greatly assisted by the helpfulness of the VA staff
that provided a great number of studies and reports that enabled me to re-
acquaint myself with the hospital and medical care issues facing the VA
system.

From an outsider's point of view, let me first call attention to the hard
choices that the Medical Department of the VA, the administration, and
Congress will have to make and then let me offer a few suggestions about
strategies and tactics. Since I have had the opportunity to advise a large
number of presidents and have learned that it is easier to offer advice than
to take it, there will be no hurt feelings on my part if you decide not to follow my suggestions.

The first thing that struck me in looking over the materials is that the VA
today accounts for a small part of the federal government's medical expenditures. The VA's approximate $10 billion budget represents some-
thing like 7 percent of the current federal outlays for health care, and it
will most likely decrease to a still smaller fraction because of the inevitable
rise in Medicare's share. The needs of the VA don't really loom large in the
totality of the federal government's health care expenditures and, what's
more, the VA's share is likely to decline further.

The next thing that's clear is that since the federal government faces
continuing large additional expenditures for Medicare, total federal out-

lays for health care can only go up. I interpret this as being "bad for you," because with federal budget constraints, that's where the first claim on new health dollars will go. The declared intention of President George Bush not to raise taxes underscores the difficulties facing the federal budget and the major claimants for more dollars for health. The health expenditures of the VA are far behind Medicare and Medicaid and are not all that much ahead of health expenditures for the armed services and funding for biomedical research and development.

Now let's look at the individual states, because the VA has some relationship to the states—not much, but in terms of older veterans, it does have connections with state nursing homes and related programs. The states, as far as I can read the evidence, have been loath to expand nursing home capacity for fear of increasing their Medicaid outlays, so the VA has less support on that front than it could use. And it is only now beginning to face a significant increase in the older veteran population. If I read the figures correctly, the VA faces almost a 50 percent increase in veterans age sixty-five years and over between now and the end of the century, which is just around the corner. That is bad because the VA is not likely to get much help from the states to provide significant supplemental facilities for caring for older veterans.

But not everything on the horizon is cause for pessimism. Congress took a constructive step a few years ago when it redefined the classes of veterans for whom the VA is required to provide a range of services, and more particularly, those for whom it is not. As I recall the prior situation, the confusion about the VA's responsibility for the medical care of nonservice-connected veterans made it next to impossible for the Medical Department to plan and operate a rational system of health care delivery. Congress went a considerable distance to clean up this particular mess.

Congress has taken other actions in recent years that complicate the VA's task. It has mandated and it has provided incentives for Medicaid to provide more services to women and children in and close to poverty levels, which was, as you will recall, the original intent of Medicaid. Medicaid was not intended to be a program for the elderly. All states have been forced to do more for women and children, and many have also decided to do more than the minimum. That means that they will be able to do less for the elderly, specifically in terms of expanding their nursing home capacity and related programs. These developments will hamper the ability of the VA to respond to the aging veteran population.

We talk a lot about insurance for long-term care, but I don't see all that much happening. I think at best private insurance will come very slowly, if at all. It is by no means clear that long-term care for the elderly is an insurable risk; I am by no means clear how many people really need it. Admittedly, we have a problem with some people being driven into bankruptcy to cover the costs of long-term care, but it may turn out that the best way to deal with this threat is to follow Mark Pauly's suggestion to shore up Medicaid. The recent congressional actions to permit families to protect some of their assets may be the preferred way to go.

We also need to look carefully at the trend in health care expenditures. President Nixon had warned that the nation faced a crisis because the United States was spending so much money on health care. In point of fact, we spent about $75 billion the year that Nixon alerted the nation. We will have spent about $550 billion in 1988! We have been talking a big game of cost containment. As a matter of fact, the only cost containment that I have seen in the whole health care arena is that which concerns the VA. Congress has not been giving it more money. That's effective cost containment, but nowhere else do I find cost containment.

The reason I mention this question of what's going on in health care financing is my belief that the private insurance system in the United States may be starting to break down. Everyone talks about the uninsured; I don't think that's the whole or even the nub of the problem. Admittedly, 35 to 40 million people with no insurance and another 35 to 40 million with inadequate insurance results in 80 million out of 245 million people being at risk or one out of three people. After sixty years of private insurance, that doesn't seem to be an outstanding record.

Looking beneath the surface, I think American corporations are reaching the point at which they may decide that they don't belong in the health insurance business. There's no reason that General Motors, Ford, Chrysler, American Telephone and Telegraph, General Electric, and other very large corporations should be struggling to figure out what's happening to their health benefit dollars through preadmission and utilization reviews. It is simply not their business. And I think one of these days— sooner rather than later—they may finally wake up to this reality and give the responsibility to the federal and state governments, where it belongs. They will surely agree to pay their share of the taxes, but they will want out of the health business. If that happens—and I think it's likely to happen—we'll be in for some big changes.

Having reviewed some of the major social and economic forces at work in the national health care scene, it is clear to me that there is little if anything that justifies optimism. Health Care Financing Administration figures for 1995 take us from a half-trillion dollars of 1989 expenditures to a trillion dollars by 1995, and point to a trillion and a half dollars for health care in the year 2000. I question whether that amount of money will be forthcoming from the American people, and these projections may even prove to be on the low side.

The American people want more and better care. They believe that they are entitled to it. In more than one way, excessive expectations are the nub of our dilemma. Veterans, Congress, and the VA staff have expectations in terms of scale, depth, and quality of services that are far in excess of the resources the Congress has actually given or is likely to give the Veterans Administration. What follows from this dilemma?

In my shorthand, the VA is in a vise. I have earlier mentioned that it faces a sizable increase in the number of elderly veterans; between now and the year 2000, the VA will have to deal with three million additional veterans over the age of sixty-five. Since there are about five million such veterans at present, an increase of three million is substantial. With the increase in the post-sixty-five year veteran group, the VA will be confronted by a much-increased demand for nursing home care, as well as more demands for community-based services for those who can be kept out of nursing homes. Moreover, since the elderly experience more psychiatric difficulties, the demand for more mental health care is certain. Additionally, the number of homeless people—including homeless veterans—continues to increase. In short, the aging of the veteran population will lead to increased demand for a great number of health care and related services.

On the basis of my review of the rich materials that the VA forwarded to me, I have reached the unequivocal conclusion that the VA has become the patsy of Congress. I appreciate, of course, that the VA's Department of Medicine and Surgery does not deal with Congress without instructions from the administration of the VA, the Office of Management and Budget (OMB), and the president, but whoever is responsible, the fact remains that every time Congress asked it to meet a new medical need—and gave it nothing or a pittance to cover the new need—it accepted the assignment. Sooner or later, it was inevitable that the Medical Department would find itself in an impossible position. I assume that you agree with my formulation. The question that those in the Department of Medicine and Surgery ought to ask themselves is how they got themselves into such a mess. The fact that an outsider like myself had relatively little trouble recognizing the mess suggests that it is likely to be a serious one.

Perhaps one will now understand my earlier statement that the VA is in a vise. It cannot maintain a quality health care system with as many missions as it now has and with the dollars that Congress is currently giving it. What can the VA do about this untenable situation? I would suggest that, sooner rather than later, the VA should explore how it can mount a strategic retreat. If the VA doesn't put the task of downscaling at the top of its agenda, then, before too long, it may be forced into a rout.

I realize that during the last few years the VA Medical Department received some dollars for new construction but it can't afford to operate additional beds. Congress is always partial to appropriating money for a new hospital, but it doesn't make sense to do so given the predicament in which the VA finds itself. It has too many hospitals and too many empty beds. Given the VA's resources, it is seriously overexpanded. If Congress wants to give the VA some additional dollars for construction, the Medical Department should try to persuade it that the VA needs to use the money for modernization or conversion of existing hospitals. It must do everything possible not to thin out the VA's resources still further; this is the wrong way to go.

Moreover, the VA must face the fact that this country has about a quarter-million too many hospital beds. It makes no sense for Congress, in the face of this large surplus, to appropriate funds to build new VA hospitals. A minor suggestion dealing with semantics: If the VA has a construction division, as I assume it does, I would act quickly to change its name to "remodeling and conversion division," or some similar words to underscore that new hospitals are no longer high on the VA's agenda. My guess is that if Congress, with a little prompting from the VA, doesn't catch on that the construction of new VA hospitals should be put on the shelf, community hospitals around the country, which are facing more and more empty beds, will help to get the message across.

The recent addition of catastrophic insurance for Medicare patients, had it not been repealed, would go some distance—how far I am in no position to judge—to ease the demand for inpatient acute-care services for the VA's growing elderly population. To the average citizen, it must appear that the VA system and Medicare, with catastrophic coverage added, represent overlapping entitlements for eligible veterans.

To complicate things further, there are many indications that, over the next few years, Congress and the administration will seek to lower the indirect costs for graduate medical education. Since the VA's Department of Medicine and Surgery is associated with 120 or so academic health centers that have always placed a high value on the VA's money—and now that they are going to be poorer, they will be even more interested in the VA's money—I suspect that they will balk at any efforts to reallocate funding arrangements with them.

We now come to the major question: What can the Medical Department do about all of this? If VA physicians don't want to look for other jobs, they must find the answers to four basic challenges that I offered earlier and that I now want to focus on once again.

The first one relates to the near- and longer-term consequences for the VA, now that catastrophic Medicare coverage has been added. Of course, if it is rescinded, that will be a definitive answer.

Second, the VA has to consider in all of its planning the fact that, with the exception of New York City, this country, as mentioned above, has a great many surplus beds. We have an acute shortage of hospital beds in New York City, but most other cities have more beds than they can possi-

bly use. The surplus of acute-care beds, an important point, should be a
key consideration in the VA's ongoing planning.

Third, the VA must proceed on the premise that the dollars that the federal government will have available to spend on health care in the future
will go in the first instance to Medicare and only secondarily to Medicaid.
The VA is not likely to get many additional dollars out of Congress.

That brings us to the fourth point: The major challenge that the VA faces
is how it can reconfigure its system effectively. What can it do best for
those veterans with priority claims on federal assistance? The VA Medical
Department cannot possibly deal with all veterans and it is no longer expected to do so. Fortunately, Congress cleared that up a while ago. At
long last the VA has a commitment to some, but not to all veterans. Unless
the VA reconfigures its system radically, however, I don't believe that it
will be able to meet adequately its commitments to those who have high
claims on its system, or that the VA will be able to respond to the new demands arising from the aging of the veteran population it serves.

It may be more than a little presumptuous for me to sketch out how I
would approach the difficult dilemmas the VA faces from overextended
missions and inadequate appropriations. But presumptuous or not, here
are my suggestions. What is it that the VA can do better than others?
Which groups of veterans have specialized needs that the country cannot
afford to disregard? My simplistic answer is that the Medical Department
must give high, if not the highest priority, to the care and rehabilitation of
veterans injured in the line of duty. Further, I have long believed that one
of the strengths of the VA system has been its concern and caring for considerable numbers of homeless, socially disorganized, mentally disturbed
veterans. We know that the states have seldom evidenced any serious
concern for these groups, and the deinstitutionalization of patients from
state mental hospitals has worsened the situation appreciably. In short,
the elderly, psychiatrically impaired veteran group is clearly a high claim-
ant for services.

Even if it wanted to, the VA could not walk away from its affiliation
contracts, but it might seek to modify some of them by placing more emphasis on geriatrics training and services. With five million older veterans, increasing to eight million, the VA is in a potentially strong position
to advance the care of geriatric patients, but it will be able to do so only if it
can make some of its present dollars fungible—unless the VA believes in
miracles and looks to new appropriations from Congress.

The one thing that it can't afford to do, at least not in my book, is to keep
on doing what it has been doing these last years—be polite and keep saying "Yes" to Congress. You want us to take care of AIDS patients? You
want us to care for veterans with posttraumatic stress disorder? The Veterans Administration can no longer play patsy and say, "Yes, we will take

care of all of them." The VA will not meet its obligations to the veterans, to Congress, to the president, or to itself unless it figures out and convinces others, who need to be convinced, of changes that the VA must make to provide the most and best care for the budget that it has to work with. That is the overriding task the VA faces, and nobody but the VA can provide the answers.

4

Health Reform:
Lessons from Employment,
Housing, and Education

The daily press is a potent reminder that for a number of years the United States has been engaged in fruitless discussions about how to reform its health care system, discussions that are likely to continue for some time to come. One facet of these discussions is the growing reference to the health care systems of Western Europe, Canada, and even Japan as models that the United States can follow to put in place a system of universal coverage at a cost that does not risk national bankruptcy. This chapter points to a more promising alternative, one that builds upon our own experiences in related areas of societal reforms, particularly employment, housing, and education, which may help us to obtain a deeper understanding about the dilemmas we face in improving the United States health care financing and delivery system.

A search for clues and answers closer to home derives from the growing appreciation among most scholars that every nation's health care system is embedded in its cultural, political, economic, ideological, and social institutions, which serve as points of departure for any meaningful exploration of health care reform. To ignore the lessons of history in favor of scholastic models, no matter how elegant their analytic apparatus, is certain to lead to frustration and bankruptcy. Two illustrations will make this clear. In 1977, Professor Alain Enthoven of Stanford sent a memorandum to Secretary Joseph Califano, Jr., proposing a consumer health plan that would require the following adjustments and adaptations in the status quo: Hereafter, physicians would practice in prepaid health plans and would compete on the basis of annual risk contracts; employers would establish a ceiling on their employee health benefits that did not provide greater reimbursement for workers who continued to select fee-for-service coverage; the federal government would place a ceiling on the tax-free benefits that employers could deduct from their taxable incomes and on the amounts of health benefits that employees could ignore in calculating their incomes. Finally, the states would have to provide health insurance coverage for persons not covered by private employers.

More than a decade and a half later the record discloses this: Most physicians continue to avoid practicing as members of prepaid plans; employers have altered their health care benefit systems' payment structures to reduce and eliminate most of their earlier discrimination against prepaid plans—in fact they now favor such plans. Despite support from various administrations, and even from the tax-writing committees of the Congress, no ceiling has been placed on tax benefits from employer health care coverage. Of our fifty states only Hawaii has a plan that approaches universal coverage, although the most recently covered vulnerable population is entitled to no more than five days of hospital care per year.

In 1977 when Enthoven submitted the draft of his plan, the United States spent $170 billion for national health care. The most recent data from the U.S. Department of Health and Human Services show total outlays for calendar 1991 at just under $740 billion. After allowing for the depreciating value of the health care dollar and the increase in population, the per capita outlay in constant dollars rose from $1,296 in 1977 to $2,172 in 1991.

Although the Carter administration was looking desperately for a health reform plan, it ignored Enthoven's proposal. Enthoven has refined his original proposal several times in the intervening decade and a half. The plan's greatest "success" to date has been its influence on the current reforms of the National Health Service in Great Britain.

A more contemporaneous illustration of a scholastic exercise in health care reform was outlined by Nobel laureate Milton Friedman in the *Wall Street Journal* (November 12, 1991) this way: Since the end of World War II, outputs have been lagging inputs into the American health care system by wide margins, particularly since the passage of Medicare and Medicaid in 1965. The real problem, Friedman observes, is output. How does he measure this? By "length of life"—but then he adds that "the quality of life is as important as its length." He quickly appends that he does not know how to measure quality. Nevertheless, he offers a threefold solution: End both Medicare and Medicaid, force every family to buy a major medical insurance policy with a deductible of $20,000 or 30 percent of the unit's income during the previous two years, and end the tax exemption on employer health care benefits that employees receive. Consider the following obiter dictum:

> I conjecture that almost all consumers of medical services, and many providers, would favor a simple reform that would privatize most medical care. ... There is only one thing wrong with this dream. It would displease ... the

large number of people who are now engaged in administering, studying and daily reviewing the present socialized system. ... They are sufficiently potent politically to kill any such reform before it could get a real following.

There are other problems, not the least of which are the tens of millions of employees who will fight to keep the tax benefits of their current health insurance coverage; the thirty million plus members of the American Association of Retired Persons (AARP) who would oppose demolishing Medicare; and the many Americans who would balk at a $20,000 deductible health insurance policy. Friedman made some serious errors in estimating consumer support for his plan.

Enthoven is a sophisticated health care analyst and Friedman won the Nobel Prize in economics. What's wrong, very wrong, with their respective health care reforms? Neither Enthoven nor Friedman has taken the time and trouble to assess the U.S. health care system within the fabric of American society as it is—not as they want it to be. Moreover, Friedman's aside that our "medical system has become in large part a socialist enterprise," and "our socialized postal system, our socialized schooling system, our socialized system of trying to control drugs, and indeed our socialized defense system provide clear evidence that we are no better at socialism than countries that have gone all the way," is open to serious question.

A closer look at the U.S. experience with employment, housing, and education policy may prove illuminating and instructive for health reform if we do more than hide behind the term "socialism" or even "consumer choice." At least the effort is worth a try. The way in which a society, American or other, deals with critical issues such as employment, housing, and education reflects basic preferences and prejudices that will condition its thinking and action in the provision of health care.

Employment

In our predominantly, though by no means exclusively, market economy, much of a person's (and a family's) existence is determined by the type of job held, the income earned, the housing and the neighborhood in which they can afford to live, the quality of education to which their children have access and, not surprising, the health care services available. Admittedly the sequence also runs, at least partially, in the other direction. The level of education an individual achieves is the single most important determinant of the later level of income, which in turn determines so many other dimensions of a person's life.

Since most Americans make a sharp distinction between individual responsibility and governmental action, it is important to remind the reader how far government has extended its role into the employment area. In quick review: (1) government has established the minimum age at which young people are permitted to work; (2) it has limited the number of hours of work; (3) it has established rules and regulations governing the health and safety risks to which employees can be exposed; (4) it has established a minimum wage; (5) it has legislated the rights of workers to join unions; (6) it has a Social Security system in place to provide workers and their families with alternative sources of income in the event that they lose their jobs or reach the age of retirement; (7) it has passed antidiscrimination laws and regulations that have gone a fair distance to lower, even to remove, the preexistent barriers against minorities and women in both initial employment and later promotion.

Despite these many interventions, government has stopped short of establishing a right for every adult, able and willing to work, to do so. But that does not mean that government has no role in establishing and maintaining a high level of employment. Since the passage of the Employment Act of 1946 the federal government has just such an obligation, and though it has not been able to prevent the recurrence of various short and long recessions, it has been able to avoid bringing on, or contributing to, a major depression, such as engulfed the U.S. economy in the early 1930s. The federal government has also provided special assistance to major employers at risk of bankruptcy, such as Lockheed and Chrysler; more broadly, it has taken repeated actions to bail out major banks and financial institutions whose possible collapse threatened massive losses of jobs and income.

It is one of the better-kept secrets that a leading Republican ideologue, Arthur F. Burns, the former chairman of the Council of Economic Advisors under President Dwight D. Eisenhower and chairman of the Federal Reserve System under Presidents Richard Nixon and Gerald Ford, proposed in the mid-1970s that the federal government become the employer of last resort, offering a job at 10 percent below the minimum wage to every person able and willing to work. Hubert Humphrey, the leader of the liberal wing of the Democratic party and a strong advocate of a full-employment policy, complimented Burns for his forward-looking contribution, but, Humphrey aside, the intensifying inflation resulted in the stillbirth of Burns's proposal.

By far the most important interrelationships between the employment and health care sectors grew out of the fact that the United States backed into private health insurance provided primarily by employers as a result of the War Labor Board decision made during World War II, which permitted unions to bargain for such health benefits without violating the existing wage stabilization policy. The federal government encouraged such bargaining by providing tax advantages to both employers and employees. The fact that now, in the early 1990s, about fifteen hundred private companies sell health insurance policies and provide administrative surveillance of employer expenditures for health care is further evidence of the commingling of the private-public sectors in the financing, administration, and delivery of health care.

Another type of linkage goes back to shortly after the end of World War II. The federal government then began sustained financing for biomedical research. In 1991, this exceeded $10 billion of federal outlays, and it is a major factor in the continuing rapid growth in national health care expenditures. The existence of established pharmaceutical companies and medical supply companies and the launching of many new companies to exploit the enlarged pool of knowledge and technique helped to assure the leadership of the United States in high-tech medicine and contributed greatly to the growth and profitability of these private sector companies.

In the early 1990s, employment in the health care sector now tops nine million. This equals about one out of every thirteen workers. Between 1988 and 1990, in a period of marked slackening of total employment growth, employment in the health sector grew by 600,000 jobs. With substantial overcapacity in the nation's fifty-five hundred acute-care hospitals, a major challenge that all levels of government will face for the remainder of this decade will be assessing the effects on local employment of reducing the nation's over-expanded hospital plant.

Housing

A century or more ago, any physically competent adult male could head west, obtain a land grant from the federal government, and, with help from his neighbors, build a home for his family. Since then the United States has become an overwhelmingly metropolitan society, and about four in five persons reside in metropolitan areas. Most Americans rely on the marketplace to buy or rent.

Since the late 1930s the federal government, cognizant of the difficulties many low-income persons face in obtaining an apartment or a house on the private market, has pursued a range of subsidy policies. Various state, and even local, governments have also resorted to tax subsidies to expand the housing stock for low-income families. In recent years, a substantial spurt of investment from the voluntary sector, with governmental assistance, dedicated not only to improved housing but also to neighborhood improvement, has occurred. If one asks how successful these governmental subsidy efforts have been, the answers will range from quite successful to total failure, such as the forced demolition of the deserted and uninhabited public-housing units in the Pruitt-Igoe complex in St. Louis, Missouri.

Responding to the desire and interest of the veterans returning from World War II to become homeowners, the federal government initiated a substantial Veterans Administration loan program and followed it with an important tax benefit. Homeowners could deduct from their federal income tax liability both the interest costs of their mortgages and local and state real estate taxes. This tax expenditure benefit has been estimated at about $70 billion annually, exceeding the tax expenditure benefits for private health insurance.

Since most purchasers of a new home must obtain a substantial mortgage to finance their acquisition, the ability and behavior of the financial intermediaries become a critical consideration. The recent collapse of so many savings and loans associations (S & Ls) left the federal government with few options other than a large-scale rescue operation that is estimated to cost the taxpayers several hundreds of billions of dollars before the S & Ls and the banks return to solvency.

Clearly, the broad access that Americans have had to desirable housing was greatly influenced by government actions at all levels—federal, state, and local. Governments have used public funds, tax benefits, antidiscrimination laws, land-use standards, and a great many other public sector policies and interventions to expand the supply of available housing. As is so often the case with governmental interventions in the United States, for the most part the major beneficiaries have not been the poor but the middle- and upper-income classes.

One specific link between housing and health care is the growing number of the urban homeless. Most experts see the roots of this problem in the unthoughtful and indiscriminate release over time of almost 400,000 mentally ill persons from state mental hospitals, without adequate alternative housing for the many who had no families able and willing to care for them and who were unable to care for themselves.

A second important linkage between housing and health is mirrored in the great difficulties that state and local governments have in locating special facilities for AIDS patients, drug addicts, and other seriously ill persons in middle-class neighborhoods because of the NIMBY (Not in My Backyard) syndrome—which impedes treatment and amelioration of their illnesses and impedes recovery. As a consequence, the government is forced to locate more and more of these facilities in the most depressed neighborhoods, thereby assuring their further decline.

The concentration of ever-larger numbers of seriously disadvantaged, low-income persons in a limited number of inner-city neighborhoods makes the challenge of assuring their continuing access to essential health care services much more difficult because most physicians shun establishing or maintaining a practice in such areas. Voluntary hospitals, faced with ever-larger numbers of the uninsured and underinsured, cannot long survive without restricting the amount of charity care they provide. Public hospitals tend to be few and underfunded. Many of the most vulnerable persons in our society, adults and children alike, are likely to be seriously underserved when it comes to basic preventive and therapeutic care. This is, in considerable measure, a consequence of where they live or as a result of their being homeless.

The federal government has sought to assist localities to provide shelter for the homeless, as many courts have mandated. But the discrepancy between supply and need remains so great that many of the homeless continue to opt for the streets rather than use the overcrowded and dangerous shelters. One conclusion is unequivocal: The United States has not committed itself, much less taken action, to providing adequate shelter for every citizen.

Education

Unlike employment or housing, which the individual is expected to obtain through his or her own efforts (the welfare population and the institutionalized excepted), public education has been a governmentally mandated, long-established service available to everybody between the ages of six and eighteen, and, selectively, for children as young as three and four (Headstart). Further, access to continuing education is broadly available for qualified high school graduates in community colleges, state colleges, and universities. A variety of second-choice, remedial programs are available for urban high school dropouts.

Since World War II, the states and the federal government have taken a number of initiatives directed at improving the quality of public education from kindergarten through high school. The barriers to higher education have been substantially lowered for large numbers of qualified young people who in earlier times would have been prevented from continuing their educations because of lack of finances.

Prior to World War II, revenues for public education were raised primarily by local taxing authorities via the property tax, a system of financing that made it very difficult, if not impossible, for residents of low-income neighborhoods to provide an adequate educational experience for their children. Consequently, state aid for public education became the norm, and in less than two decades—between 1970 and the end of the 1980s—the proportion of state funding increased from rough equality with local funding to more than half again as much. Since 1965, the federal government has made some modest contributions to public education. In the late 1980s, the federal contribution was approximately 8 percent of the total outlays for education. But the federal government's primary impact on education was via the U.S. Supreme Court decision in *Brown v. Board of Education* in 1954 and the subsequent implementation of desegregation orders. Desegregation of public schools in metropolitan areas was vitiated to a marked degree by the ability of many middle-class, white families to relocate to suburban areas. During the postwar decades, large-scale expansion of higher education was underwritten by both the states and the federal government and resulted in the establishment of new, and the expansion of existing, state colleges, universities, and community colleges. The expansion was furthered by extensive student loan programs in which the federal government took the lead.

There has been much handwringing in the 1980s and early 1990s about the poor quality of American education, particularly the shortcomings of junior and senior high schools. The schools have been held responsible for the retardation in the international economic position of the United States. However, in theory, the link between poor schooling and the loss of U.S. competitiveness has not been established. It is true that schools in low-income, disorganized, urban neighborhoods are often dysfunctional to a point that many young people drop out of school. Lacking skills and competences, they encounter great difficulties in getting regular jobs, and many resort to illicit and illegal activities.

With the advantage of a lengthened perspective gained from the involvement of government in providing access to basic education for children and young people for over a century and a half, we must conclude that the results have been mixed. At the time of World War II, when the minimum standard for induction into the Army was the equivalent of a fourth-grade education, over a million young men were rejected for what was labeled "mental deficiency" but which should have been coded "lack of educational achievement." In South Carolina about 250 young black men per 1,000 were rejected. The proportion of whites rejected in some of the more rural Southern states was in the 60 to 70 per 1,000 range. John Fischer, the former president of Teachers College, Columbia University, once observed that public education has served the American people well, except for poor whites and minorities. This judgment has not lost its edge, even in the 1990s.

Lessons for Health Care Reform

Increasing numbers of domestic and foreign observers of our health care system are at a loss to understand why the United States is taking so long to adopt a series of reforms to achieve justice, equity, and efficiency.

Universal Coverage

What are the impediments to the United States following in the footsteps of most advanced nations and acting expeditiously to provide health insurance coverage for the thirty-five million persons who currently lack coverage? The United States continues to expect individuals to find jobs and earn incomes that will enable them to secure housing and other essentials for themselves and their dependents. The only governmental commitment that exists to deliver a basic service to the public is that of providing schooling for all children and young people up to age eighteen, a commitment that up to the present has carried with it little accountability about how well government meets its responsibility.

True, government has moved a considerable way to put in place "safety nets" for persons unable to work, the unemployed, low earners, and many more who are not capable of supporting themselves. Although existing social welfare supports are not responsive to all, or even to most, of the poor, most Americans balk at expanding the role of government in providing jobs, housing, and a quality education for all. Since our society has a number of health care safety nets in place, such as public health clinics, public hospitals, Medicaid, and charity care funded by nongovernmental hospitals, the political energy to move toward universal coverage is limited. The partial failure of public education after a century and a half of responsibility adds a healthy dose of skepticism to the presumed benefits that would flow from a system of universal health care coverage.

Neither justice nor equity have commanded top-ranking positions in the nation's value scale. Many politicians continue to rail against "welfare cheats." Though we have made considerable progress on the discrimination front since the early 1950s, racism continues to pervade every sector of American life.

Cost Containment

Anybody who has looked even superficially at the expenditure trends in the American health care system is startled by the fact that the share of gross national product (GNP) devoted to health has increased from about 4.5 percent to 14 percent since World War II and shows no sign of leveling off. The principal payers (other than households) in descending order of importance are (1) employers and private health insurance (PHI), (2) the federal government, and (3) state governments. Together they account for about three out of every four dollars of health care expenditures. For the better part of the last two decades, each of these three payers has made valiant efforts to curtail its outlays, but with limited success.

Clearly, the difficulties are considerable and are likely to remain so, as long as each payer continues to go its own way. But most employers, despite unease with steadily rising health costs, are not about to enter into a partnership with the federal government to control these costs. They prefer to keep their distance. And the federal government, facing a deficit of $300 billion, is not looking for new responsibilities.

Talented economists have no difficulty in modeling the structure and interactions of an "efficient" health care system, but their models lack the incentives and the specifications that would lead to the cooperation of key decision makers—physicians, voluntary hospitals, private health insurance companies, and the other interested parties—in putting into practice what these analysts have designed. Government may be willing to intervene in the critical areas of employment and housing to moderate the shortfalls in the operation of the market, but only up to a point. Government was careful not to assume responsibility for the economic efficiency, much less for the social justice, in the production and distribution of the nation's housing stock.

Administrative Waste

All analysts of our current health care system agree that administrative costs are out of control. They differ only about the outer range of their estimates, but few would set the figure below 15 percent. If malpractice and defensive medicine were included, the figure could easily approach 25 percent, or even more. Here is a major opportunity for reform. We have fifteen hundred private sector companies selling basic health care insurance; the Canadians have none. But eliminating administrative waste is more complicated than it seems. The history of the U.S. Department of Housing and Urban Development (HUD) shows weakness in terms of financial probity and a neglect of administrative competence. As chairman of the National Commission for Employment Policy in the 1960s and 1970s, I was in a good position to watch the expenditure of $85 billion of federal funds to underwrite the training and employment of the hard-to-employ. Although most of the money went to the poor and unskilled, only a small percentage of the trainees, possibly as few as 10 to 20 percent, achieved the goals of the program by obtaining and keeping a regular job. Most seriously, the educational establishment has been charged with permitting the additional dollars flow into overhead instead of into expanded and improved services to students.

No informed person will argue against taking action to reduce the excessively high costs that characterize our current health care system. The difficulty arises when one looks for specific remedies. It is not easy for the federal and state governments, which are committed to the competitive market as the preferred instrument for distributing scarce resources, to move individually or jointly to outlaw private health insurance companies, which are the critical players in providing coverage for most Americans under the age of sixty-five.

Quality Control and Efficiency

Despite the unflattering comments made earlier about the efficiency of governmental operations in employment, housing, and educational programs, all is not bleak. The Social Security system mails out about thirty million checks monthly, involving over $250 billion annually, with relatively few snags or complaints. This gives us some ground for believing that the federal government can play a constructive role in reducing administrative waste in the health care sector as long as its responsibilities are tied to check-writing, not micromanagement of service delivery.

Conviction is growing among leaders of American medicine and health services research that many diagnostic and therapeutic interventions are of questionable, if not negative, value. Medical and surgical procedures can lead to permanent injury or premature death. Small wonder that "outcomes research" has attracted increasing attention of late, including increased, if still modest, funding from Congress. The aim of this new effort is to learn more about untested interventions in the hope and expectation of developing "practice guidelines" for physicians to inform and improve patient treatment. Some analysts look to outcomes research not only as a way to improve quality but also to lower costs.

Here, too, as in the arena of administrative waste, many opportunities beckon, but expectations should be restrained. One of the key proponents of outcomes research, Paul Ellwood, has set ten years as the time required before useful results will emerge. Pessimists point out that in a dynamic biomedical environment, practice guidelines will always lag behind new therapeutic breakthroughs and advances.

Several lessons emerge from our earlier discussions of employment, housing, and education. Employment and training programs showed a serious shortfall between congressional expenditures and the ability of the prime sponsors to deliver efficient and effective training services to the hard-to-employ. Some did a good job, but they were in the minority. In the case of public housing, the demolition of the Pruitt-Igoe houses in St. Louis is a potent reminder of how a large gap can develop between plan and execution. Admittedly the St. Louis failure was extreme. More relevant are the continuing shortfalls in quality control and accountability in public education, where even today no agreement exists about how well or poorly the system is performing.

The scope of the challenge facing medicine is revealed by the fact that during the course of a year patients make about 1.3 billion visits to physicians. Physicians are licensed by state governments, and most large hospitals operate with a closed staff. The medical specialty societies are heavily involved in providing continuing educational opportunities for their members. The improved control over quality and efficacy is highly desirable, but it will remain an open-ended endeavor.

There is no question that the state of our health care system calls for major reforms directed to providing universal coverage, cost containment, the elimination of administrative waste, and quality improvement. But before we go any further, it is important to point out that two out of every three Americans are reasonably satisfied with the quality of medical care to which they have access, and they are unlikely to support major reforms unless they become worried about the prospective erosion of their present coverage. That leaves one out of every three Americans at risk in obtaining access to the health care system or in obtaining essential health care services, preventive, therapeutic or rehabilitative. But this shortcoming must be placed in perspective. The American public has repeatedly demonstrated its unwillingness to make more than marginal adjustments to broaden opportunities for the unemployed to obtain jobs, for the homeless to obtain shelter, for many poor children to obtain a suitable education.

Our recent presidents have opposed the expansion of government programs that would serve the unemployed, the homeless, and the illiterate. They have railed against higher taxes, although Americans carry a lower tax burden than the citizens of any other advanced country, but they have been silent about our historical commitment to "equality of opportunity" for every American child and adult. Significant health reforms are unlikely to be implemented until the nation remembers *e pluribus unum*, the words on the Great Seal of the United States.

5

The Reform of
Medical Education

Although the Flexner reforms, introduced at the beginning of the second decade of this century, have shaped American medical education over the past eight decades, there have been several major structural changes that have altered the nature of the profession during that time. One has been the elongation of professional training from four years of medical school and one year of internship to a minimum of seven years of training, with many residents, especially those in the surgical subspecialties, continuing for another seven years, if we include their fellowship training.

Another change has been the evolution of biomedical research as the critical mission of the leading medical schools, which began with the inauguration of large-scale federal financing of research at the end of World War II.

The explosive growth of the professorate, which today consists of more than seventy thousand positions, or more than one faculty member per medical student, reflects still another striking structural change. An important contribution to this explosive growth in faculty has been the fact that patient-care income has come to be the leading source of revenue for the nation's medical schools; it accounts for 45 percent, considerably in excess of the combined contributions from all levels of government, which account for about 38 percent.

At least brief attention should be paid as well to the preoccupation of most faculties with the training of residents and fellows, which has led to the production of many more specialists and subspecialists than generalists, with a current ratio of approximately 80:20.

The other changed boundary conditions that continue to have pronounced effects on faculty, medical students, and residents are the almost 80 percent increase in the physician-population ratio during the past three decades without a negative impact on physicians' earnings; the steep rise in the indebtedness of medical students; and the continuing large differentials in earnings between generalists and subspecialists, of an order of two to three times in favor of the latter.

Finally, in accounting for the principal structural changes that have affected medical education, particularly since World War II, we must pay attention to the rapid growth of medical knowledge and technology and the potentials that this growth has had for the practice of medicine and for the care and cure of patients.

Pressures for Reform

Although there were a number of innovations and reforms of medical school education between the end of World War II and the time a report was issued by the Association of American Medical Colleges in 1983,[1] in the last decade the United States has witnessed a marked acceleration in new efforts to make medical education more responsive to the needs of the physicians who will be practicing in the twenty-first century. The pressures for reform come from a number of different sources including the complaints of students, who object to being stuffed like turkeys during their first two years of medical school. They are taught about the most recent advances in the basic sciences, all of which they cannot possibly absorb and much of which they will forget after they enter clinical training. A growing current of criticism is also being voiced by members of the public, who complain that the physicians they need to care for them are not available or, if they are, they cannot communicate effectively and thus cannot provide the counsel and help that their patients need. And the payers for health care—both government and employers—are making the point that the out-of-control trend in medical care expenditures appears to be closely related to the faulty preparation that medical students (and residents) have received during their long periods of training.

Proposed Reforms

Because they are concerned about the disgruntled students and the disenchanted public, a growing number of medical educators have begun to make their voices heard, supported by sizable grants from the major health care foundations, which have encouraged them to undertake in-depth reassessments about what is right and what is wrong with medical education.[2]

There are five substantive components of the conventional wisdom that the reformers are disseminating:

1. *Integrate basic sciences and clinical instruction.* The reformers maintain that the sharp separation between instruction in the basic sciences during the first two years and the clinical training in the third and fourth years is faulty and needs early correction by a radically re-

vised curriculum in which instruction in the basic and clinical sciences is more integrated throughout the entire four-year sequence.

2. *Look to developmental biology to serve as the integrator.* There is a widespread assumption, or presumption, that developmental biology and genetics offer the intellectual basis for an effective integration of the four years of medical school instruction.

3. *Recognize the importance of population-based medicine.* A number of reformers are convinced that a paradigmatic shift from deterministic prognosis to clinical epidemiology is called for, with the attention shifting from the presenting patient to population-based probabilistic evaluations and treatment modalities. In this view, when genes, cells, or organs malfunction, they often indicate directions for physicians' therapeutic interventions. But patients' life histories and the socioeconomic factors that condition their lives may be omitted in diagnostic and treatment decision-making only at great cost to them, their families, and society.

4. *Make room in the curriculum for considerations of ethical principles at every stage of decision-making.* Some reformers go so far as to insist that whatever the "scientific" pretensions of medicine, the role of the physician and physician-patient interactions must be guided by ethical considerations, and any medical school curriculum that is unresponsive to this reality is malfunctioning and requires urgent attention.

5. *Inform all clinical decision-making with an awareness that dollars are scarce and will become scarcer.* In order not to extend the list of priorities for reform unduly, let me mention just one more that has attracted the attention of some thoughtful medical educators, namely, the need to train medical students and residents to use cost-benefit analysis in selecting among diagnostic and therapeutic modalities. The era of practicing medicine without regard to economic considerations that dominated the U.S. scene between 1965 and 1983 is definitely not the wave of the future. The on-coming generation of physicians needs instruction about the role of economics in patient care at every stage of their education.

Implementation Issues

How do these five reforms strike an outsider? From my vantage point as a political economist who has had and continues to have on ongoing involvement in health sciences research, let me briefly share my thoughts on each proposition.

Since no medical educator has challenged the desirability of a closer coordination of the basic and clinical sciences, the difficulties of accomplishing this objective must lie not with intent but rather with execution. How is it to be accomplished, and by whom? Because only a small proportion of the basic science faculty are physicians, they are ill-suited to take the lead. Though some professors of clinical medicine have an in-depth knowledge of one or another of the basic sciences, that is not their central interest and concern; frequently their knowledge is not deep enough for them to carry out a successful integration even in the area of their specialization. In short, we may be dealing on the integration front with an idea whose time has not yet come or, conceivably, with one whose time may already be past.

Most of those who favor integration have gone further and have identified the integrating principle that should be used. They maintain that developmental biology and genetics provide the ideas and linkages that can bring the biomedical and the clinical sciences together. Again the outsider asks, If matters were so simple and straightforward, what is holding up the action? Once again, execution may be lagging behind consensus. The hard work that would be required to develop and implement a four-year curriculum for medical education based on genetics and developmental biology would require a significant investment of talent and time from competent and interested physician-scientist-educators, the old triple threats, who, in the judgment of most informed persons, are an extinct species. If they are extinct or almost so, they cannot be looked to as the builders of the new curriculum.

What about the third priority of making room in the new curriculum for clinical epidemiology and population-based approaches to the study of medicine? The number of enthusiasts for such an innovation is still relatively low, and there are few new resources being invested to transform what many believe to be a good idea into a reality. But in the absence of a substantial and sustained investment of new resources, both for research and teaching, not much progress is likely to occur on this front in the near- or midterm.

Over a quarter of a century has passed since I recommended to Margaret Mahoney, who at the time was senior staffer at the Carnegie Corporation, that the United States should establish departments of social medicine at ten or twenty of the leading medical schools in the United States, with sufficient funding to launch and carry through substantial and sustained programs of health policy research. Without such a substantial investment, I saw little prospect for clinical epidemiology to have a place in the medical school curriculum. My view has not changed; it has been reinforced from that day to this.

How does one improve ethical perspectives throughout all aspects of medical education? Many medical schools introduced a number of lectures and small-group discussions focusing on ethical issues in medical decision making. These innovations are of sufficiently recent date that in-depth evaluations would be premature. From the scattered evidence, there is no reason to believe that either faculty or students have been greatly affected by these innovations, but it would be premature to write them off at this early point in time. I think we can say that so far they have been only a marginal influence in the reshaping of the medical school curriculum.

This brings us to the last of the substantive recommendations, which is focused on the desirability of introducing economic considerations at every stage of medical decision making. A few observations: In the first place the new physicians who were trained when the dominant view was "money doesn't count" have not bought into the new doctrine of constrained resources, and it is doubtful that they will do so until the total dollars flowing into the health care sector, in general, and into medical education, in particular, force the issue. The forcing may be long delayed, and if past is prologue it will be some years before the teaching of medical students will be framed by a curriculum that is resource-sensitive. We must first await the emergence or conversion of the faculty to such an ideology—and that conversion will not come easily.

If the foregoing observations by an outsider on the substantive recommendations for the reform of medical education have some pertinence and relevance, then it behooves the protagonists of reform to look again carefully at their agenda items and consider what needs to be done, by whom, and with what kinds of resource commitment, to speed the arrival of the "brave new world." For without such a serious and continuing effort at implementation, it appears questionable, at least to me, that reforms can make their own way.

So much for the substantive aspects of the reformers' recommendations. But the proposals they have advanced also include a number of far-reaching parallel suggestions, predicated on opportunities opened up by advances in pedagogical technology or by a critical reassessment of preexistent pedagogy. For instance, most of the reformers recommend that the heavy reliance on lectures during the first two years of the medical school curriculum be radically reduced in favor of more small discussion groups.

Next, many are enamored by what they call "problem-oriented" instruction, in which the attention of the student is redirected from the accumulation of discrete pieces of new knowledge in favor of asking and answering "What kinds of knowledge do I need to make a diagnosis and suggest a mode of treatment?"

Closely related to the foregoing is the enthusiasm of many reformers for directing more time and other resources to instructing students in retrieving information from large computerized data sets on the assumption that once students have acquired these skills, they are on the way to taking control of their future educations through "self-study." Students can effectively engage in self-study, however, only if medical schools cut back their conventional programs with their many corresponding requirements, thereby enabling every medical student to have significant blocks of uncommitted time to use according to his or her own lights. Finally the examination and evaluation issue comes to the fore, because the ways that medical students, like all other students, will invest their time and energy will be heavily influenced by the evaluation hurdles that they must surmount to demonstrate competence and to position themselves to move into the next stage of their professional training. As one might anticipate, the reformers are by no means agreed about the directions and specifications that the new evaluation procedures should take. But the more committed they are to deep and far-reaching substantive reforms involving the introduction of new educational techniques, the more likely they are to recognize that preexisting evaluation approaches need to be reassessed and redesigned, even to the point of eliminating externally set examinations.

Instruction Issues

What can an outsider who started teaching at a major research university in 1935 and who has continued to the present to instruct graduate students offer concerning the forms of instruction that should go along with the proposed reforms in content? On the basis of a two-year stint of lecturing to the second-year class at a distinguished medical school in the early 1980s, I am reasonably certain that any and all actions that are taken to reduce the number of lecture courses that students are forced to attend in the first two years of medical school constitute a move in the right direction. However, if some discussion groups are to be used as a substitute, a word of warning must be added: The instructional costs cannot be ignored when one shifts from one class for 150 students to ten discussion groups!

The emphasis on problem-based instruction and data retrieval are sufficiently closely linked to be commented on simultaneously. It is difficult for a student with limited basic sciences or clinical knowledge to make much progress in problem-solving unless and until he or she masters the art and science of data retrieval, and even then the student will be handicapped by an insufficient knowledge base. We know that there are many enthusiasts for a problem-based approach, and it may turn out that the misgivings outlined above are out of proportion and that the problem-based approach is definitely the way to go.

No one is likely to object in theory to medical schools remitting some time, even considerable blocks of time, to medical students. The difficulties arise when one asks the different departments and divisions to voluntarily reduce the number of hours they require students to devote to the curriculum. At that point, free time for students runs headlong into a conflict with what the departments consider to be the minimum hours needed to communicate to the students what they need to know to advance to the next stage in their education and training. This struggle between the perceptions of the faculty and the preferences of the students is easier to recognize and appreciate than to resolve.

On the question relating to examinations and evaluations I have little to contribute other than to point out that one of the strengths of American medical education has been the role of external examinations in helping to set and maintain a minimum national standard of professional qualifications, even though the responsibility for licensing continues to lie with the fifty sovereign states. This has been no small achievement, and it should not be jeopardized unless the putative gains loom large.

Neglected Aspects of Reform

I offer here a few observations about the reforms of medical education that are gaining strength among the medical leadership and concentrate on selected aspects of reform that I think have been neglected or minimized.

First and foremost is the substantial disregard of the length of time and the costs that medical students face in acquiring an M.D. degree and, in particular, in completing their residency and fellowship training before they are ready to practice their profession. This neglect is the more striking because of the often-expressed conviction of many, if not all, of the reformers that U.S. medical schools should make a contribution to regulating the current imbalance between specialists and generalists by producing larger numbers of generalists.

Robert Ebert and I proposed in the late 1980s that the minimum seven-year cycle of professional preparation from entrance into medical school to first certification could be reduced by two years, or 28 percent. Although a few schools picked up on our suggestion, for the most part it has been ignored, despite the fact that conservatives and reformers alike agree that the current fourth year of medical school must be restructured. The majority of the reformers appear to favor using the fourth year to revisit the basic sciences after the third-year clerkship. One does not need to argue against this view to make the point that it may prove more efficient and effective to combine the two years of clerkship and the first three years of residency training into an integrated four-year clinical training program.

The preoccupation of the reformers with altering the four-year curriculum of the medical school is understandable; nonetheless, it can be challenged. There is no possible way of making room in a four-year program for all of the important new departures in medical education, including probabilistic decision-making, clinical epidemiology, cost-benefit analysis, ethics, health education, genetics, and much more, without considering the entire span of physicians' training, from their preparation as future medical students during their four years in college to their extended years of residency training. The reformers' primary focus on the medical school curriculum makes sense, but their exclusive preoccupation with this restricted four-year period does not. It represents only a minor part of a postsecondary school experience that at a minimum exceeds one decade and that often approaches two decades.

The reformers appear to pay little attention to the economics of medical educational innovation. There is pronounced enthusiasm for small-group discussions, for more training in ambulatory-care settings, for giving students the opportunity to follow a panel of patients for an extended period of months and years, and for exposing students to different types of treatment environments, from nursing homes to home care. Each of these innovations involves additional costs, the payment for which reformers usually ignore. Clearly, recourse to ever-higher tuition is not the answer. Moreover, ever-greater reliance of the medical school on resources from patient care can only worsen the existing dilemma that many faculty members confront, that of spending so much time supporting themselves through patient care activities and contributing to their departments and the medical school that they have little or no time left to interact with medical students.

Conclusion

Medical school reform is long overdue. But an effective reform program that is not anchored in sound economics can result in things becoming worse, not better. Improving the preparation of medical students for a more effective practice of medicine involves more than a rebalancing of medical school disciplines, important as this may be. It requires much more attention than has as yet been focused on such issues as the core size of the medical school faculty, the economics of alternative instructional modes, and the close attention to the total cost of training that must be anticipated by the undergraduate student who is preparing to embark upon a medical career.

Notes

1. S Muller, "Physicians for the Twenty-First Century: Report of the Project Panel on the General Professional Education of the Physician and College Preparation for Medicine." *Journal of Medical Education* 59, p. 2 (November 1984).

2. *Future Directions for Medical Education: A Report of the Council on Medical Education* (Chicago, Ill.: American Medical Association, 1982); CP Friedman, and EF Purcell, eds., *The New Biology and Medical Education: Merging the Biological, Information and Cognitive Sciences* (New York: Josiah H. Macy, Jr. Foundation, 1983); *Adapting Clinical Medical Education to the Needs of Today and Tomorrow* (New York: Josiah H. Macy, Jr. Foundation, 1988); *Healthy America: Practitioners for 2005* (Philadelphia, PA: Pew Charitable Trusts, 1991); and RQ Marston, and RM Jones, eds., *Medical Education in Transition* (Princeton, N.J.: Robert Wood Johnson Foundation, 1992).

PART TWO

Health Care and the Market

6

The Limits of
Health Reform Revisited

The United States and South Africa are the only developed nations that do not provide a comprehensive system of health insurance for all of their citizens. Approximately 150 million Americans have some form of employer-sponsored private insurance, a large majority of them with coverage of at least a million dollars or with no limits.[1] Thirty million citizens are Medicare beneficiaries, most with supplementary Medigap policies. The remaining eighty million people (almost one-third of the population) have inadequate private health insurance (often excluding maternity benefits) or are Medicaid beneficiaries, and thirty-two million individuals have no health insurance at all.[2]

Special groups in our society, such as dependents of the military, veterans, native Americans living on reservations, and the retired military, have access to designated federal medical facilities and health care systems. Nevertheless, the special provisions made for these groups do not satisfy critics who fault the United States for failing to assure medical coverage for all Americans.

In the event that individuals with nonexistent or inadequate health coverage require emergency medical care, they are generally served in one of a large number of publicly supported and operated acute-care hospitals situated throughout the urban and rural United States. These institutions are required to provide emergency care to all patients. Teaching and community hospitals, usually operated as nonprofit institutions, likewise have a philanthropic obligation to provide emergency care.

Why don't the American people enjoy access to adequate health care as a right, not as an act of public welfare or charity? National health insurance (NHI) has been on and off this country's political agenda since 1912, when Teddy Roosevelt, running for the presidency on the Progressive ticket, first advocated its enactment.[3] Support for NHI has reemerged periodically—in the mid-1930s, the late 1940s, and the mid-1970s—yet it has never come close to winning popular or congressional support.[4] In the 1990s, the defects of the health care system in the United States—costliness, inefficiency, and inequitable provision to the population—have prompted health care specialists and the public to turn their attention once again to NHI. To understand the current debate, it is necessary to recount the last eight decades of health reform in the United States and to identify the issues that an NHI proposal must address if it is to remedy the defects of the health care system in the 1990s.

History of Health Reform

The United States was a latecomer to social welfare legislation. Franklin D. Roosevelt's New Deal programs appeared fifty years after the initial social welfare reforms of the 1880s in Western Europe. Why was the United States so far behind European nations in enacting national social welfare legislation? First, the federal-state structure of the American government has historically reserved for the individual states primary jurisdiction over most spheres of social welfare. In addition, the territorial expanse of the continental United States and the regional differences in demographics, economic vitality, political ideology, moral standards, and social mores made it difficult to enact congressional legislation responsive and acceptable to this heterogeneous population. Finally, there often was little popular support for national legislation, even among those groups whose support might have been expected. For example, the labor movement did not commit itself to a broad-based program of social welfare including health insurance and did not support federal unemployment insurance until the New Deal reforms of the mid-1930s.[5] To this day, labor leaders are far from unanimous in their advocacy of NHI.

Yet if one development must be singled out as responsible for the continued lack of support for NHI in the United States, it is the spectacular growth of private health insurance that occurred during and after World War II. In this period, the vast majority of American workers bargained with employers for an increasingly broad set of health care benefits for themselves and their dependents. The federal government provided a major stimulus for this process: taxes. Since the Internal Revenue Code of 1939, employer contributions to voluntary health insurance plans have been recognized as tax-deductible business expenses, and the value of employee coverage provided as a fringe benefit has been exempt from personal income taxation (and has been excluded, as well, from the base for the computation of Social Security taxes). This was followed in 1942 by the War Labor Board's ruling that fringe benefits were not inflationary and were, therefore, negotiable, notwithstanding a wage freeze. The nation's tax system thus provided a major and irresistible subsidy for the purchase of private medical coverage.[6]

By the mid-1950s, however, inherent shortcomings in the private insurance system became apparent. Once workers retired, most of them lost their health care coverage. In addition, the average cost of an acute-care hospital admission rose so precipitously that increasing numbers of uninsured elderly faced serious financial consequences in the event of an illness requiring hospital care. Federal appropriations in the late 1950s and early 1960s to assist the states in covering the hospital costs of the uninsured elderly were not sufficiently responsive, since these programs were conditioned upon demonstration of poverty. By and large, elderly persons were reluctant to apply for means-tested benefits administered by the welfare system, a stigmatized source of support that they had steadfastly avoided throughout their working years.[7]

Many conservative members of Congress had serious reservations about the adoption of a federally funded and administered system of medical insurance for the elderly. However, President Lyndon B. Johnson's overwhelming victory in 1964 enabled him to push legislation through Congress in early 1965 establishing federally funded medical insurance programs for the elderly (Medicare) and for the impoverished (Medicaid).

The Medicare program had two parts. Part A, its major component, provided financing for acute-care hospitalization for all elderly persons eligible for Social Security (about 99 percent); the key resource was federal payroll taxes contributed by employers and employees. Part B, which covered physician services, was a voluntary supplementary program; 50 percent of it was initially financed from premiums paid by Medicare enrollees and 50 percent from general federal funds.

Medicaid was a federal-state program, jointly funded and administered by the states, to which the federal government contributed between 50 percent and 78 percent, depending on the state's per capita income. The program mandated coverage for all recipients of Aid to Families with Dependent Children (AFDC) and other federal-state categorical assistance to the poor. In addition, as finally amended, the program offered the states the option of including medically indigent individuals not on welfare whose incomes did not exceed 133 percent of the federal poverty line. Five basic medical services were covered: hospital inpatient and outpatient care, physicians' services, laboratory services, X rays, and skilled nursing home care (for those over twenty-one). In addition, fourteen discretionary services were eligible for federal matching funds. The 1972 amendments redefined the skilled nursing home benefit to provide broadened levels of extended care in nursing home facilities.

The long-term advocates of NHI perceived Medicare as the breakthrough that would pave the way for the establishment of a system of universal health insurance. "Kiddicare" was envisioned as the next step—a national, federally financed program that would provide coverage for children under age eighteen and their mothers. Since Medicaid already included various categories of welfare recipients, NHI advocates believed that coverage would ultimately be extended to adult men and women not enrolled in private plans or Medicaid, thereby ensuring basic health care coverage for all American citizens.

The passage of Medicare and Medicaid went a fair distance in enabling the United States to correct deficiencies in the system of private health insurance. The new legislation responded to the needs of the elderly for coverage for acute-care hospitalization and physician services. However, even in the first decade of Medicare's implementation, it became evident that important needs of the elderly were still unmet or not adequately met. For example, the program did not cover multiple hospitalizations within a single year, long-term hospital stays, chronic nursing home care, and expensive drugs for ambulatory patients. After 1972, Medicaid provided a source of public payment for nursing home care for many of the impoverished and institutionalized elderly, while others became eligible for benefits through the program's "spend-down" provisions (many nonindigent individuals qualified by the simple expedient of transferring their assets to their children). Thus, some of the more egregious deficiencies were brought under control.

As for the poor, by the mid-1970s about two-thirds of all persons with incomes below the federal government's poverty line were enrolled in Medicaid.[8] However, there was serious "underenrollment" in some states, mostly in the South. The failure to extend Medicaid eligibility beyond the poorest of the poor reflected a reluctance to raise additional revenue from taxpayers to finance what some considered to be too rich a range of services for persons whose standard of living (based on local standards) did not warrant state support.

In sum, the elaboration of private insurance, Medicare, and Medicaid were instrumental over a short span of time in assuring most Americans reasonable access to acute care. After 1972 Medicaid provided a mechanism for many of the elderly poor to obtain needed long-term care in nursing homes. At the same time, serious systemic problems became increasingly evident.

Issues Facing an NHI Proposal

At the beginning of the 1990s, in addition to the lack of universal coverage, the U.S. health care system suffers from numerous inherent defects: uncontrollable costs, administrative waste, questionable quality and efficacy, and a shortage of primary-care physicians to treat the rural and urban poor. Despite the failed record of legislative initiatives in the past, NHI is again commanding attention from health policy specialists and the public. They believe that one or another version of NHI—an exclusively federal program financed by income taxes or a federal-state program that is more flexible in its method of raising the needed revenues—promises to be the most feasible solution to these deficiencies. In order to determine the likelihood that NHI will provide a partial, if not total, response to the problems of the health care system, an assessment of the ability of such a basic financing reform to address the issues of excessive expenditure, administrative waste, ineffective professional practice, and access for all is needed. If, upon assessment, a NHI program shows a reasonable likelihood of correcting these shortcomings, then its claim to public support, passage, and implementation would be much advanced.

Excessive Expenditure

Now, more than a quarter of a century after the enactment of Medicare and Medicaid, the national health care system confronts serious challenges that were barely recognized as recently as a decade or so ago. For example, health care expenditures have risen from $133 billion in 1975[9] to about $675 billion at the end of 1990.[10] Even after adjustment for the strong inflationary pressures during the first half of this period, the growth in *real dollars per capita* amounts to almost 30 percent.[11]

Although Medicaid was designed to provide coverage for all of the nation's poor, this objective has yet to be realized. In fact, the proportion of the poor enrolled in Medicaid declined precipitously from a peak of 65 percent in the mid-1970s to as low as 40 percent in 1985,[12] as a result of increased tightening of eligibility criteria and the decertification of large numbers of beneficiaries by the states in efforts to economize in their Medicaid outlays. Since 1984 the trend has been reversed through a series of congressional mandates that have extended coverage for pregnant women and children. The steep increase in expenditures, combined with a marked increase in the number of uninsured persons over the same period, now poses an unprecedented dilemma.

There is no doubt that it would be easier for a single provider-buyer-purchaser of health care to control the rate of increase in annual expenditures than it is for the present pluralistic system to do so. Would a NHI system be able to control its expenditures? If one considers the limited case of hospital reimbursement, there is evidence that the largest purchaser, the federal government, has had some success in containing its expenditures since the implementation in 1983 of a system of prospective payment for the care of Medicare beneficiaries. However, NHI alone will not solve the problem of rapid acceleration of health care expenditures as long as the public demands that advances in knowledge and technology be automatically translated into increases in the quality and quantity of accessible health care services. The United States in 1993 invests about $30 billion annually in biomedical research (half by the government and half by big business), whose productivity has contributed to a level of high-tech medicine unrivaled anywhere on the globe.[13] With a continuing investment in research and development at this rate, scientific and technological advances will be limitless. Physicians, hospitals, and patients will demand to benefit from them—the increased dollar costs notwithstanding. Thus it is difficult to see how and why replacement of the present system of pluralistic health care financing by a NHI system would result in a significant retardation in the rate of annual outlays, unless NIH can be directly linked to a lower rate of investment in the health care sector or lower intensity of treatment for patients. Both of these, however, are antithetical to the ethos of the medical profession and American society.

Administrative Waste

A second challenge to the existing health care system involves the growing complexity and administrative cost of running a multilevel system financed by four different sources: the federal government, employers, individuals, and state governments. Excessive costs of marketing private insurance, excessive record keeping, malpractice insurance (with the consequent resort to defensive medicine), and swollen hospital bureaucracies all contribute to administrative waste. Although there is no agreement on the amount of administrative waste, estimates run from a minimum of $30 billion to as much as $60 billion annually.[14]

NHI should be able to reduce the excessive costs connected with the financing and administration of our pluralistic system. There is little reason to doubt that savings of at least 5 percent might be realized by the introduction of a unified system of financing and a universal system of coverage. The protagonists of NHI in the United States repeatedly note the substantially lower costs of the Canadian system, which provides universal coverage under a tax-supported provincial budget to which the national government makes a sizable, though declining, contribution. Canadian hospitals operate within a fixed annual budget, and physicians' fees are determined by negotiation with the medical societies of the individual provinces.[15]

Other circumstances, however, should not be overlooked when adducing the experience of Canada to support the U.S. adoption of NHI. The entire Canadian population could fit into the state of California, with room to spare; unlike Americans, Canadians have confidence in government as a capable agency for social change; they are less concerned with maintaining scope for private enterprise—witness their elimination of any role for the private sector in the sale of coverage for those physician and hospital services that are included in public plans. Unless the American electorate is willing to take the extreme step of eliminating private insurance and unless the federal and state bureaucracies develop expertise in the delivery of services to the population far superior to those they have demonstrated thus far, it is problematic for us to use Canada as an appropriate model for the United States.

Ineffective Professional Practice

A third problem is posed by the performance of a growing number of unnecessary medical procedures. It is worth noting that none of the European countries with a system of NHI has focused any attention on this issue, which is frequently cited by the proponents of basic structural reform as an inherent fault of the U.S. system. Studies conducted by the RAND Corporation and Dartmouth University, among others, have revealed that many medical and surgical procedures performed by physicians are of little or no value to their patients and may, in fact, be life-threatening or fatal.[16] The growth of these wasteful and dangerous interventions accounts in part for the rise in national medical expenditures from 8.3 percent of the gross national product in 1975 to 12.4 percent in 1990.[17]

The substantial differences among regions, institutions, and physicians in the criteria for and frequency of performance of specific procedures (principally surgical) suggest the need for systematic studies of clinical outcomes. An increasing number of interest groups have joined the "outcomes research" bandwagon in the belief that this is one of the most promising paths to cutting costs and improving the quality of health care. The findings of these studies are intended to be translated into practice guidelines which, in turn, are expected to eliminate many ineffective and counterindicated procedures.

In 1989, Congress established the Agency for Health Care Policy and Research in the Department of Health and Human Services (HHS). The agency was charged with providing government support for outcomes studies. At the same time, the RAND Corporation joined the American Medical Association (AMA) and selected academic health centers (AHCs) to undertake a set of cooperative investigations that promised to yield definitive information about the effectiveness of critical high-cost medical and surgical interventions.

Initial RAND findings have suggested that between one-sixth and one-third of selected costly surgical procedures may prove to be of questionable value.[18] If this is found to be true of medical interventions in general, the application of such studies to the development of wide-ranging performance protocols for the health care sector should effectively contribute to improved medical care, health and well-being, as well as cost reduction. However, before outcomes studies can be applied, the information gathered must be as accurate, as complete, and as precise as possible. Dr. Robert Brook of RAND and the UCLA Center for Health Sciences, a pioneer in this work, has observed that in the current reimbursement environment, with its incentives for superficial and restricted treatment, systematic outcomes monitoring is likely to uncover evidence of underutilization of needed and beneficial services as frequently as the overutilization of redundant and counterindicated services.[19] Thus there is reason to temper the optimism about the potential for simultaneous reductions in cost and improvements in the quality of health care evoked by initial studies.

When will the benefits from outcomes studies be realized? Those who have studied consumer preferences, practice guidelines, physician education, and physician behavior suggest that it will take some time for the research findings to be reflected in altered physician practice.[20] Paul Ellwood, an early advocate of outcomes research, cautioned that it would be five to ten years before outcomes management will take effect.[21] Given a decade or more, it is not unreasonable to anticipate that outcomes research will yield valuable benefits, but in the near future it is not likely to serve as a major check on costs or a major contributor to quality improvement. Conceivably, NHI could be used as an effective framework to institute clinical guidelines aimed at reducing inappropriate professional practice.

Access for the Underserved

Another major problem of the United States health care system is the lack of access for the urban and rural poor. For generations, the preferred method of providing essential health care to the urban poor has been through teaching hospitals, where physicians in residency training perform ambulatory and inpatient services. In rural areas, the federal government and some state governments have sought to encourage—at least as an interim arrangement—the placement of recently graduated physicians in remote locations that for years have been without a practitioner. Such service is usually a quid pro quo for the forgiveness of educational debt. Another adjustment mechanism for the rural, underserved populations has been the establishment of rural health clinics, sometimes staffed by nurse practitioners under the supervision of a nearby physician. In addition, the federal and state governments have indirectly mitigated the problem through improved highway and transportation systems, which enable rural populations to utilize more distant regional medical facilities and resources.

Over the past twenty-five years, Congress has made an effort to improve access to health care by making sizable appropriations available to medical and other health professional schools as an incentive to increase their output of physicians and allied health personnel. In addition, in 1970 the National Health Service Corps (NHSC) was established, followed in 1971 by the provision of special funding for the support of residencies in family practice. Both were intended to expand the annual output of medical schools and to ensure that a larger percentage of their graduates would be available for assignment to low income rural and urban areas. The medical educational sector has responded; by the early 1980s, U.S. medical schools had doubled the number of M.D.s they produced two decades earlier.[22] However, this substantial increase in the nation's output of physicians, supplemented by the influx of foreign medical graduates following liberalization of the immigration statutes in 1965, proved disappointing to the health care reformers and Congress, who had expected that an enlarged supply of health professionals would improve access to medical care. Physician concentrations in attractive practice sites intensified, and the plight of underserved areas was unchanged, if it did not worsen.

Since the 1970s, attention has turned to the redistribution of medical school graduates between primary (general) care and specialized fields of practice as a possible means of improving access of the poor. An increase in the generalist-specialist ratio from 4:6 to 5:5 or even 6:4 would, over the longer term, probably make it easier for underserved rural and urban populations to obtain primary-care services from designated physicians in their communities. However, the problem of access for these disadvantaged populations goes beyond the question of generalist-specialist imbalance. Most physicians—generalists or specialists—will avoid establishing a practice in low-income communities with little medical infrastructure as long as they have any prospect of pursuing a career in a more lucrative, professionally attractive environment.

The governmental sector has been unable to assure, through compulsion or incentives, an adequate supply of practitioners to deliver primary care to the rural and urban poor. Nor has it made a serious commitment to train and employ significant numbers of alternative health care personnel who could, in the absence of physicians, provide first-contact and routine care. There is no reason to expect that generic changes in the financing of the health care system as a whole through the introduction of NHI would address, much less resolve, this problem.

In sum, this is how a trial balance sheet looks. NHI, in whatever guise, could moderate the annual increase in health care expenditures. Likewise, it should be possible to reduce administrative waste. NHI might even make it easier to institute clinical guidelines aimed at reducing inappropriate professional practice. And it should help the uninsured and underinsured to gain access to the system. Alone, however, NHI will probably not influence the locational and specialty preferences of physicians sufficiently to improve the availability of primary care for the rural and urban poor to any substantial degree.

The improvements in the delivery of health care that may be expected from NHI will not be cost free. At a minimum, NHI would act to depress biomedical research. It would also vastly expand the role of government bureaucrats, probably both federal and state, and affect the performance of physicians and hospitals and the care that patients receive. Policymakers must determine whether the benefits of NHI justify biomedical slowdown and greater bureaucratization.

A Look Back and a Look Ahead

There is no question that the U.S. health care system suffers from serious shortcomings, primarily sizable numbers of uninsured or poorly insured persons and steeply rising expenditures. There is also no question that the United States has periodically debated and rejected the adoption of NHI. The rejection of NHI has conventionally been ascribed to the militant opposition of the medical profession and private sector interests, particularly the health insurance industry. A more sophisticated view, however, would note the absence of any broad voter constituency in favor of NHI, its dire budgetary implications for the federal government (a potential increase of over $200 billion annually),[23] and public skepticism about the ability of government to provide a quality service to the population (consider how inefficiently it has performed in the fields of education, welfare, criminal justice, and public housing).

Currently, most Americans who are in urgent need of medical care are able to gain access to the system, regardless of insurance coverge, although many encounter serious barriers in obtaining primary care of reasonable quality on a continuing basis from a personal physician. However, the majority of the population have good insurance coverage and are unlikely to favor NHI unless their present situation deteriorates appreciably. Moreover, most physicians continue to earn a good living and most voluntary hospitals remain solvent. As long as this stability persists, each of these powerful constituencies will resist the adoption of NHI.

That leaves the overarching issue of cost acceleration. It is worth recalling that more than twenty years have passed since President Nixon declared that the United States faced a medical and economic crisis because it was spending $75 billion annually on health care, 7.5 percent of the GNP. The figures for 1990 were roughly $675 billion, or about 12.4 percent of GNP, and are expected to rise by $1.7 trillion over the decade, reaching 15 percent to 20 percent of GNP.[24] Whether and how long the United States can continue on its present trajectory and sustain such an increase in its investment in health care is highly questionable. This will depend largely on the rate of growth of the nation's economy. It will also depend on whether the public's "taste" (the economists' term) for medical care begins to moderate. If these factors are adverse, as economic forecasts suggest, change will be inevitable and NHI will be an option.

Where do we come out? Achievement of the political consensus required to pass one or another variant of NHI is contingent upon the extreme erosion of the present system—a large-scale increase in the number of uninsured, the closing of many hospitals, and a serious deterioration in the earnings of physicians. Should these dire events occur and NHI is enacted, the elimination of excessive expenditures, administrative waste and ineffective professional practice, and the enhancement of access for the underserved would be possible. However, these results are not assured.

What about costs? If NHI were adopted, the nation may have found a way to contain *public* outlays for medical care but not necessarily total *national* outlays. It is worth remembering that now about one-third of all elective surgery in Great Britain is performed in the private sector. Margaret Thatcher, when she needed surgery, did not join a queue to await her turn for a bed in the National Health Service. The wealthy and the well-to-do may not be satisfied with the services provided under NHI. If they seek more services from the private market, the pluralistic system would continue. In addition, without compulsion of powerful incentives, physicians will not practice among large concentrations of the poor. But most importantly, the prerequisite for slowing health care expenditures would be a slowdown, not necessarily in biomedical research, but in the introduction of new technology and new drugs in order to be sure that they are cost-effective, that is, that the additional expenditures that they entail will be reflected in substantial, not marginal, therapeutic gains. Unless there is support for a significant deceleration in total health care expenditures, the adoption of NHI would be unresponsive to the nation's health care problems.

Notes

1. J Gabel et al., "Employer-Sponsored Health Insurance, 1989," *Health Affairs* 9(3)(Fall 1990):161.

2. Health Insurance Association of America, *Source Book of Health Insurance Data, 1990* (Washington, D.C.: Health Insurance Association of America, 1990), 13.

3. P Starr, *The Social Transformation of American Medicine* (New York: Basic Books, 1982), 243.

4. TR Marmor, *The Politics of Medicare* (Chicago: Aldine, 1970), 8–14. During the 1970s, Jimmy Carter had supported national health insurance throughout his campaign and had indicated that it would be an important goal of his administration. However, subsequent deterioration in the budgetary situation precluded any action regarding NHI.

5. Starr, *Social Transformation*, 266.

6. JR Hollingsworth, *A Political Economy of Medicine: Great Britain and the United States* (Baltimore, M.D.: Johns Hopkins University Press, 1986), 116, 151.

7. Marmor, *Politics of Medicare*, 16–20.

8. CN Oberg, and C Longseth Polich, "Medicaid: Entering the Third Decade," *Health Affairs* 7(4)(Fall 1988):83, 90.

9. Office of National Cost Estimates, "National Health Expenditures, 1988," *Health Care Financing Review* 11(4)(Summer 1990):1, 27.

10. U.S. Department of Commerce, International Trade Administration, *U.S. Industrial Outlook, 1991*, 32d ed., (Washington, D.C.: Government Printing Office, 1991), 44–1.

11. Office of National Cost Estimates, "National Health Expenditures, 1988," 24.

12. U.S. Department of Commerce, Bureau of the Census, *Statistical Abstract of the United States 1990*, 110th ed. (Washington, D.C.: Government Printing Office, 1990), 98.

13. U.S. Department of Health and Human Services, Public Health Service, National Institutes of Health, *NIH Data Book, 1990* (Bethesda, Md.: National Institutes of Health, 1990), 2.

14. DU Himmelstein, and S Woolhandler, "Cost Without Benefit: Administrative Waste in U.S. Health Care," *New England Journal of Medicine* 314(7)(13 February 1986):443–44.

15. RG Evans et al., "Controlling Health Expenditures—The Canadian Reality," *New England Journal of Medicine* 320(9)(2 March 1989):572–75.

16. CM Winslow et al., "The Appropriateness of Carotid Endarterectomy," *New England Journal of Medicine* 318(12)(24 March 1988):725–26.

17. Office of National Cost Estimates, "National Health Expenditures, 1988," 24; U.S. Department of Commerce, International Trade Administration, *U.S. Industrial Outlook, 1991*, 44–1.

18. MR Chassin et al., "Does Inappropriate Use Explain Geographic Variations in the Use of Health Care Service? A Study of Three Procedures," *Journal of the American Medical Association* 258(18)(13 November 1987):2533.

19. AL Siu, and RH Brook, "Allocating Health Care Resources: How Can We Ensure Access to Essential Care?" In *Medicine and Society: Clinical Decisions and Societal Values*, edited by E Ginzberg (Boulder, Colo.: Westview Press, 1987), 30.

20. J Lomas et al., "Do Practice Guidelines Guide Practice? The Effect of a Consensus Statement on the Practice of Physicians," *New England Journal of Medicine* 321(19)(9 November 1989):1306.

21. PM Ellwood, "Shattuck Lecture—Outcomes Management: A Technology of Patient Experience," *New England Journal of Medicine* 318(23)(9 June 1988):1549, 1554.

22. "Medical Education in the United States: 1984–1985," *Journal of the American Medical Association* 254(12)(27 September 1985):1553, 1568.

23. Senator JD Rockefeller IV, "Special Report: The Pepper Commission Report on Comprehensive Health Care," *New England Journal of Medicine* 323(14)(4 October 1990):1005–1006.

24. U.S. Department of Commerce, International Trade Administration, *U.S. Industrial Outlook, 1991*, 44–1.

7

Health Policy:
The Old Era Passes

There are some important points about health policy that I do not think are well understood. My old friend, Milton Friedman, recently wrote a long piece in the *Wall Street Journal* in which he explained the reasons that our health care system is having such difficulties. To paraphrase his answer: With the government putting a lot of money into the health care system, what would you expect? Friedman is a gifted economist and deserved the Nobel Prize that he received, but his recent article proved to me that he doesn't know much about the origins of governmental involvement in health care.

Federal Programs

The federal government is in health care not because it *wanted* to, but because it *could not* stay out. When Lyndon Johnson rode roughshod over Senator Barry Goldwater in the presidential campaign of 1964, he set the stage for Medicare to be passed. It did pass, by a substantial majority, because the Congress decided that the elderly had to have access to hospital care, and since they had retired from employment, and not many employers at that point offered their retired employees continuing insurance coverage, there was no way that most of the elderly who needed hospital care could pay the out-of-pocket expenses involved. That was the origin of Medicare. Medicaid was largely an afterthought. There were many poor people who had no insurance, particularly mothers who were raising children without the benefit of a husband to help, and both the women and their children sorely needed coverage.

Private Health Insurance

Starting shortly before World War II and expanding rapidly during and after the war, we expanded our reliance on private health insurance. Today, roughly 75 percent of all dollars paying for personal health care are covered by private health insurance or the government, and that is an unique system of financing for any basic consumption good or service. There is little point in saying that the government is responsible for all our troubles. We have no parallel situation in which a person can face a bill for $10,000 as a result of requiring hospital care. There are relatively few Americans who have $10,000 in their checking or savings accounts to cover a bill of such magnitude. That is why we rely on third-party coverage. It is not an accident; it is a fact of life.

In 1970 we spent $75 billion on health care, or 7.5 percent of the gross national product and President Nixon warned that we could not continue on such a spending trajectory. In the early 1990s, however, health care expenditures exceeded $750 billion, but neither the health care system nor the economy had blown up. Caution is required in forecasting health care costs. Nixon was one of the more intelligent presidents of the nine under whom I served, but time proved him wrong when it came to forecasting the future of our health care system. Our outlays for 1992 were close to 14 percent of the national product, not far from double the 7.5 percent spent in 1970.

Nixon saw in Health Maintenance Organizations (HMOs) a way to slow the rate of health care cost expansion. But as the election of 1972 approached, the AMA persuaded him to retreat, and it was the Democratic Senate in 1973 that took the lead in sponsoring federal support for HMO expansion. Since that time, in addition to HMOs we have had PPOs, prepayment plans with point-of-service (POS) opportunities which enable the enrollee to opt for a provider who does not belong to the prepayment system for an extra charge; and most recently, corporate-insurance company risk networks. From my study of these efforts over the last twenty years, I am impressed with their limited success in controlling health care cost inflation.

Medicaid was passed to take care of poor people who did not have money to pay for their own care. I regret to say that even allowing for my pessimistic evaluation of the sensitivities of the Congress and the public toward the poor, I would never have believed that in the mid-1970s Medicaid would cover three-quarters of all Americans under the federal poverty level but in the mid-1980s, only 50 percent. At the very time the country was pouring increasing amounts of money into the health care system, we were making it more difficult for the poor to obtain essential care. My colleagues and I completed a book on changing health care delivery in the four largest metropolitan centers in the United States: New York, Chicago, Los Angeles and Houston.[1] At an early stage in our research, it was clear that care for the poor had worsened although billions of new dollars were pouring into the system.

For-Profit Hospitals

Given the strong belief in private enterprise in this country, Americans became delusional about the efficiency of for-profit hospitals during the 1970s and the beginning of the 1980s. These hospitals were going to cure everything, since American management had the answers. I wrote an article in the *New England Journal of Medicine* that ridiculed this belief.[2] A distinguished health policy analyst, however, prophesied that there would soon be ten or fifteen "supermeds" in this country that would soon control the whole health care delivery system. That, of course, did not happen. Three out of the four biggest for-profit hospital chains have been through bad times and the fourth, Humana, may not be far behind.

Another point: Just about the time that Medicare and Medicaid were enacted, the nation was suffering from a severe shortage of physicians. Ohio, for example, acted on this shortage and expanded its medical schools far beyond what was needed. In 1960 the nation had 140 physicians per 100,000 persons. I used to say to people who were worried about the physician shortage, "Do you know of anybody who ever dropped dead waiting to see a physician?" I pointed out that the odds are if you do not see a physician immediately, you will get well pretty quickly. Hence, just relax. I was willing to see only a modest increase in numbers of physicians because I knew from my army days that the worst thing one can have are large numbers of underemployed physicians. I learned very early that if you think a shortage of physicians is bad, wait until you face a surplus. Now the United States is in serious trouble.

The second error Americans made was to assume that if we had more physicians there would be more physicians available to treat the poor. The poor do not want to have much to do with physicians because they often have no money to pay them, and physicians surely do not want to have much to do with the poor because they cannot get paid. We are told by the AMA, and by other authorities, that we have a problem in this country because about 15 to 16 percent of the population is uninsured. The presumption is, therefore, that about 83 to 84 percent of the population is "well covered" for health care. My figures suggest that two-thirds of the American public are well covered for health care, those that have Medicare and those who have good, private health insurance coverage. Although Medicare does not finance nursing home care, Medicare recipients are well covered for physician services and for hospital care. There are three groups of people, however, who are at risk: the uninsured, the underinsured, and the people on Medicaid (because being on Medicaid is no guarantee that a competent physician is going to take care of you). So, there are real constraints on access to care for one-third of the population. That makes the issue of whether we have a real problem of coverage much more serious.

The Shape of the Future

What is going to happen between now and the year 2000? Despite my general skepticism about predictions, I feel reasonably certain that the U.S. health care system will not continue on its present trajectory until 2000 because we will not be able to extract the additional sums required to keep funding the system at the same rate as in the past. We will spend over $750 billion in 1991. Using that figure as a base, there are three estimates. Probably the soundest is that we will reach the $1 trillion level some time in 1994. Between 1995 and 2000, however, the projections diverge. David Jones, the CEO of Humana, estimates that health care expenditures will reach $2 trillion by 2000. While other estimates go as high as $2.3 trillion, the more conservative projection made by the Congressional Budget Office is about $1.6 trillion by decade's end. That would mean almost an additional $1 trillion between today and the end of the decade. It is my considered opinion that the growth rate of the American economy will not be sufficient to support such expenditures in health care between now and 2000. Nor would it make any sense to do so even if we could extract the money.

In the late 1980s, according to the *Statistical Abstract*, the average 2.7 person household spent roughly $17,000 for the four basic items of food, housing, clothing, and transportation. The foregoing projections suggest that in the year 2000 we could spend more on health care alone than we were spending in the late 1980s on all four basic items combined, so severe a distortion of the American economy that I don't believe it will occur. Rather, I believe that a shortage of additional dollars will derail our health care system some time after the middle of the decade. My preferred year is 1996, on the eve of the next presidential election. A financial crisis is probably the best harbinger of major health care reform.

Secondly: between now and the end of the decade, of our present 5,500 acute-care hospitals about 1,000 hospitals are likely to merge, adopt a new mission, or close. Part of the reason will be a shortage of dollars. But more potent than the dollar shortage or excess capacity will be the changes in medical technology that will make it possible to treat increasing numbers of hospital patients in an ambulatory-care setting (with perhaps an overnight respite), and that most community hospitals will be able to perform 75 percent of their surgery in such a setting.

This suggests that a large-scale shrinkage of the nation's hospital plant is well-nigh certain. Hospitals may retain their strategic role as the hub of the community's health care delivery system, but only to the extent that they succeed in becoming the centerpiece of a coordinated group of diversified delivery organizations.

A few years ago I co-authored a book with my associate Anna Dutka entitled *The Financing of Biomedical Research*.[3] In the post–World War II era the United States experienced an explosive growth in total and federal support for biomedical research: from $45 million (total national expenditures) and $3 million (federal expenditures for research) in 1940 to about $20 billion (total expenditures) and $10 billion (federal) at the end of the 1980s. These figures suggest that the country remains enamored of high-tech medicine and that it will continue to push the frontiers of knowledge and science at a rate that will assure that our health care delivery system will continue to be highly dynamic.

I have been surprised by the fact that we have not seen a substantial increase in the number of uninsured during our most recent recession. I would have guessed that the recession would have pushed the total number of uninsured from the level of thirty-three million to close to forty million, but the data do not indicate this. For example, California has a population of thirty million of which six million, or 20 percent of the population, is uninsured. That 20 percent is made up of two major subgroups. A large number of small business concerns do not provide coverage for their employees; and a very large number of new immigrants, who work in the marginal sectors of the economy, are without insurance.

Once again, the key point is that sometime after the middle of this decade we will run out of additional dollars for health care, and when that happens, we will face the necessity of confronting the major reforms that we will no longer be able to avoid.

Suggestions for Reform

There are, however, a few sensible things that we might do before then. There are those who believe that since the United States responds best when it faces a crisis, that there is little to be gained in urging the three principal parties — the federal government, state governments, and employers—to use the time still available to them to act before the crisis occurs since they may not do any better if they have more time to think about how to respond to the coming crisis. When Congress moved in 1983 to put the prospective payment system in place for reimbursement for Medicare, the Senate acted after forty minutes of debate. I am not sure that it would have done better if it had engaged in forty days of debate.

Prospective reforms falls into two parts: those that need to be done sooner rather than later, and those that address the longer-range problems. The reason we have been putting so much money into the health care system is that there is no mechanism in place to coordinate the total inflow which comes from four sources: the federal government, employers, state governments, and what we call households. Instead, we have four discrete streams of money and if any one flow is reduced the providers of care know how to juggle the system to extract more money from the other payers. This process of cross-subsidization goes on all the time, since whenever some payers are not contributing their part of the costs, somebody else gets stuck with the bill. Therefore, the primary objective must be the creation of a set of arrangements that will move the nation toward "global budgeting."

Since we cannot afford to keep spending an ever-higher proportion of the GNP for health care, the only way to be sure that we don't is to put in place an effective mechanism that will limit the total amount of money that the three principal payers will contribute next year, beyond what they contributed last year.

I do not believe that a nation that tolerates great differentials in income will ever prohibit the wealthy from spending additional amounts of their own money on their health care. But that becomes insignificant if the United States arranges to cap the principal sources of funding, the money provided by government and employers. A major reason that we mainly simply talk about reform is that the problems associated with putting new mechanisms in place are many and complex. But there is another reason. Even if the principal parties decided that they should start immediately on designing a system of global budgeting, it could not become operational for a number of years. Clearly the federal government could not operate a single-payer system out of Washington. It would have to involve both employers and (particularly) the states, which would have to play a leading role in administering such a system. Employers and providers would have to have a seat at the table. To complicate matters further, many medical care delivery markets cross state lines, which means that states would have to cooperate in working out the details for paying providers who treat out-of-state residents. Obviously, considerable infrastructure would need to be put in place and the data bases required to make the system operational need to be expanded.

The majority of large corporate enterprises in the United States are not yet ready to accept the idea that they must cooperate with the federal government to work out a joint solution. While there are some companies that have such large unfunded health care obligations for their retirees that they are willing to "bite the bullet," most companies continue to balk. Their dominant ideology is: "keep the government at arm's length," even if such a tactic forces them to continue covering rapidly rising health care benefit costs for their employees. Until the dollars run out, the recommendation for global budgeting will remain a promise, not a reality.

In addition to moving toward global budgeting, I consider it critically important for us to try to hold the line on the expansion of services. There are many elderly people who believe that Medicare is defective because it does not cover nursing home care. They have a point, but I don't believe that this is the time or place to act on it.

Since the funds required to maintain the quantity and quality of services covered by the extant system are increasingly limited, we must restrain our inclinations to add additional broad new services, such as long-term care or a much-expanded entitlement for home care. The most we should do is add some cost-effective preventive services, such as mammography, which we were slow to include on the list of covered Medicare services.

Access for the Poor

Improved access for the poor is complicated by the fact that such access must be local, because health care services must be delivered in close proximity to where people live. While the federal and state governments can help through offering financial assistance to low-income and minority populations, so that they may gain easier access to the health care system, most of the improvements require local leadership and local involvement. I live in a city that spends about $3 billion per year to finance public hospitals that provide health care to the poor. True, we have a lot of poor people in New York, but $3 billion is not a small figure; and I have to acknowledge that we do not deliver a good quality of care.

I suspect that in most cities, regardless of size, a first requirement to improved access for the poor to the health care system would be the establishment and expansion of community health clinics in the areas where poor people live. Next, we should seek to use more mid-level professionals, such as nurse practitioners, in order to expand essential staff at a controllable cost.

Long-term Problems

What about the problems that we need to tackle in the longer term? Earlier, reference was made to the fact that a thousand hospitals are at risk of closing during this decade. How does one educate the American public to think from a community perspective about changing requirements for hospital care so that cities close institutions that are not needed and redistribute the personnel and the dollars to areas in which they could be used more effectively? That was relatively easy to do in World War II when the military had control of all its resources. In an open society, however, in which each group is concerned about taking care of itself and has only a distant concern for the welfare of other groups, it is very difficult to do. Nonetheless, we have to begin to think hard about the numbers of hospitals and types of health facilities that will be needed in the future.

We need a supply of physicians who, in exchange for the cancellation of their educational debts, will be willing to serve at least for a reasonable number of years in low-income rural and urban areas. Unless we develop such a quid pro quo system, we will not have the minimum number of physicians required to provide care to the poor. Two figures will reinforce this point. In affluent metropolitan suburbs, the ratio is about one physician for every 250 people. True, these physicians may attract another hundred or two from out of the area. In the low-income areas of New York, Chicago, Los Angeles, and Houston, the ratio of physicians in private practice, not on hospital staffs, is one for fifteen thousand people. That is the way our health care market works: 1 to 250 versus 1 to 15,000.

Former HHS Secretary Louis Sullivan began to correct a serious error that Congress and the administration made in the early 1980s when they practically dismembered the National Health Service Corps. In addition to rebuilding the National Health Service Corps, the states need to lean much harder on the medical schools they support, redirecting the curriculum away from subspecialization to primary care, as well as insisting that the academic health centers play a larger role in providing health care to the poor. We also need to begin to cut back on the number of students admitted to and graduating from American medical schools. For such a policy to make sense, we would be required to exercise tighter control over the number of foreign medical graduates (FMGs) whom we admit and license. We are on our way to a ratio of 260 doctors to 100,000 people—up from 140 per 100,000 in 1960—and that is a sure way to make the dollar problem more difficult to solve, since physicians determine 75 percent of the total costs of the system. A physician is the only person who can admit you to a hospital, decide on the diagnostic tests you are going to have, tell you that you need to see a consultant, operate on you, and tell you when you can go home. Constraining the system requires us to maintain constant vigilance about the number of physicians in practice.

Next comes the federal government. When I recently responded in writing to an inquiry from the Council on Graduate Medical Education (COGME), I pointed out that I found it ridiculous for the federal government to subsidize for five or six years the postgraduate training of physicians who at the end of their training are going to be able to earn $200,000 or more per year. In all other professional fields—law, architecture, business, engineering—it is understood that once the university has handed the young professional a diploma, it is the profession's obligation to pay the costs involved in upgrading the knowledge and skills of the graduate, not society's job. Currently we are spending annually about 5 billion federal dollars and probably another 5 billion in nonfederal dollars for graduate medical education.

I acknowledge that radical changes in the ways in which graduate medical education is financed in the United States will unsettle the academic health centers, the medical schools, their major teaching affiliates, and the physicians in training, but, as the Prospective Payment Assessment Commission (ProPac) has pointed out in its reports to HHS and Congress, changes are long overdue.

Health care, like other facets of American life, is subject to fashions. Currently outcome studies are very much to the fore. I agree with those who believe that it is important that we learn more than we now know about what does and does not work in health care. But I doubt that outcome studies will save us much money. I think we will be able to improve health care because we will discover that some people are being overtreated. In fact, we may be able to save some people's lives by becoming more restrained in using high-risk interventions. Alternately, we will likely find a large number of persons who are not getting the amount and quality of service that they need.

A few more dicta. There are many observers who believe that they have a simple answer to the problems facing our health care system. Most of them favor Canadian-style national health insurance, overlooking the fact that Canada is an underpopulated country and, further, a country that respects and has faith in its government.

But we cannot afford to continue to ignore the health care problems of the poor. My considered view is that while the system is likely to be derailed sometime soon if we fail to act, there is no single bullet that can solve all our problems. It seems to me, therefore, that the better part of wisdom is to avoid the major crisis that lies ahead by moving expeditiously toward a system of global budgeting and universal coverage.

There are two lessons that we should have learned over the last quarter century. First, insurance is not the equivalent of access. Medicaid was to have brought the poor into mainline medicine. It failed conspicuously. Second, one cannot spell out on paper the essential services that all Americans are entitled to because delivery on this specification will depend on where they live and on the physicians, hospitals, and clinics to which they have access. The challenge that we face is to be sure that the nonpoor—the two out of three Americans—who have access to good care remember their less-fortunate neighbors and act to help them.

There is nothing easy about our meeting the challenges that lie ahead to preserve the great strengths of the U.S. health care system–to control the future trend of expenditures, which we must do, and to improve health care services to the poor, which is also surely within our capacity to do.

Notes

1. E Ginzberg, HS Berliner, and M Ostow et al., *Changing U.S. Health Care: A Study of Four Metropolitan Areas* (Boulder, Colo.: Westview Press, 1993).

2. E Ginzberg, "For-Profit Medicine: A Reassessment," Special Article, *The New England Journal of Medicine* 319(12) 22 September 1988): 757–61.

3. E Ginzberg, and A Dutka, *The Financing of Biomedical Research* (Baltimore, Md.: Johns Hopkins University Press, 1989).

8

Health Personnel:
The Challenges Ahead

This chapter explores some policy issues affecting physicians, nurses, and allied health workers—the three critical groups of health care personnel—and identifies the challenges that shifting trends imply for health care managers in the decade ahead. The analysis concludes with some speculative considerations on how the health personnel sector will affect, and in turn be affected by, the changing flows of funds into the health care arena.

To provide a point of departure for assessing likely developments that lie ahead and alternative policies that may be pursued in response, I start by calling attention to some of the major trends in health care employment during the 1980s.

First, the health care sector employs a very large number of people. If one uses the restricted standard industrial classification of the Department of Commerce (SIC 80), this work force amounted to roughly 7.5 million in 1989.[1] If one adds the health workers who are employed by insurance companies, pharmaceutical companies, and government, the total exceeds nine million—an increase of about 50 percent since 1980.[2]

Few people realize that the health sector is the nation's third-largest employer grouping, following only local government and retailing. The figure of more than nine million means that the health sector provides jobs for almost one out of every thirteen members of the U.S. labor force.

Most analyses of the remorseless growth in health care expenditures have paid insufficient attention to the large numbers of individuals who earn their livelihood by working in the health sector. In many small communities the hospital is the major anchor of the economy, one that local, state, and national politicians will seek to protect. In metropolitan centers, especially those with large concentrations of minorities and immigrants, hospitals and home health care services provide critically important employment opportunities for local residents, many of whom would otherwise be without a regular job.

A corollary to the fact that health employment in the 1980s grew by almost half is that the growth was relatively painless. Only in nursing, and only in the years since 1986, has the health labor market shown any significant stresses and strains. Thus the health labor market responded with great flexibility over the 1980s, as it took on more than three million new workers.

Given this striking flexibility at every level, from managers and professionals to service support personnel, what is the rationale for my using the subtitle "challenges ahead"? One reason has already been alluded to—the sudden appearance of a nurse shortage, which may turn out to be chronic, not simply cyclical. Moreover, the nation's demographic profile is undergoing change as the proportion of young people entering the work force declines, and it will not rebound during the 1990s.

Despite the increased level of health care expenditures, evidence abounds that many insured and uninsured persons encounter difficulties in gaining access to the health care system. Whether they are pregnant women on Medicaid—a group frequently shunned by obstetricians—or local or inner-city minority populations, they are hard put to obtain ambulatory or in-patient care because of shortages of health care providers in their neighborhoods.

The most important reason for examining the supply of health personnel for the decade ahead is that the priority issues on the nation's health agenda—broadened access, improved quality, effective cost containment, and greater equity—are those that first and foremost involve the more effective development and utilization of health personnel. Health care is heavily labor intensive, and personnel costs account for about 55 percent of all hospital expenditures as well as the expenditures of other institutional settings, such as nursing homes. Personnel costs account for an even higher percentage in medical, dental, and other professional practices.

Let's take another perspective: The 1980s saw the publication of three prestigious national reports dealing with physicians, nurses, and allied health workers, respectively. The report of the Graduate Medical Educational National Advisory Committee (GMENAC) in 1980 projected a surplus of 70,000 physicians in the year 1990 and double that number in the year 2000. It was followed in 1983 by the report of the Institute of Medicine, National Academy of Sciences, on the future of nursing, which came to the conclusion that supply and demand in the nursing profession were in substantial balance and would remain so in the years ahead. Some years later, in 1989, the same body issued a report on allied health workers, entitled *Allied Health Services: Avoiding Crises*. Based on a detailed analysis of ten allied health fields, it too concluded (with some minor exceptions) that the required numbers were available and the supply would continue to be sufficient to meet future needs.

Mention of these three reports should serve as a reminder that emphasis on the centrality of health personnel for the operation of the health care system is not the same as assessing, much less correctly forecasting, future developments. The principal objective of the analysis that follows is to contribute to a greater understanding of the complex interrelations among health personnel, money flows, and an effectively functioning health care system, primarily in the 1990s.

Physicians

Reference to GMENAC underscores the centrality of the issue of the physician supply, a theme that has recently preoccupied three of the nation's leading health policy journals—*The New England Journal of Medicine*,[3] *Health Affairs*,[4] and the *Journal of the American Medical Association*.[5] Let me oversimplify a complex debate and opposing approaches. Some thoughtful analysts, notably William B. Schwartz, Frank A. Sloan, and Daniel N. Mendelson,[6] argued that the rising demand for physician services consequent to advancing medical technology and the aging of the population had been underestimated by the GMENAC studies; hence surpluses projected by the report have not and will not materialize. In response, Alvin Tarlov,[7] the chair of GMENAC, countered that the demand-based approach underlying the Schwartz-Sloan-Mendelson position was seriously flawed.

As an active participant in the physician supply debate for over a quarter of a century, I have maintained a consistent position that a surplus of physicians should be avoided on grounds both of protecting the public's health and of avoiding the excessive health care costs that a redundant supply of physicians would generate.[8] When physicians are in oversupply, patients are in danger of being overtreated. And in terms of competence, surgeons are vulnerable to the erosion of their skills when they fail to perform an optimal number of operations. Busy physicians, alternately, are the most reliable triage agents: They generally opt to treat the seriously ill before spending time with the worried well.

It would be unfair, however, to overlook at least two major benefits yielded over the past three decades by the steep increase in the ratio of physicians to population. First, it has enabled high-tech medicine to penetrate into the hinterlands to the point that any community of fifty thousand or more has access to tertiary care of good quality.[9] Second, the surplus of physicians has facilitated experimentation with new modes of health care delivery. Absent an ample supply, too few physicians would have been available to support the many innovations in the delivery of care, from ambulatory surgery to the explosive growth of HMOs.[10]

A simple arithmetic exercise will help to make the point. Suppose that the physician supply had increased in the period following 1960 from about 144 per 100,000 to 180 per 100,000, rather than to 240 per 100,000, as it actually did. The calculated "excess" physician supply (240 minus 180) equals 25 percent. On the stipulated assumption that physicians are responsible for the decisions that govern about three-quarters of all health expenditures, an excess supply of 25 percent in the year 1990 with total estimated expenditures of $675 billion, translates into a possible outlay of an additional $123 billion. It is difficult to imagine another factor that is more critical for the quality and costs of our health care system than the physician supply (or to think of a factor that has been treated so cavalierly).

However, the dimensions of the problem go beyond these astounding figures. Consider the following unarguable trends that have elicited little public awareness and less deliberation. First, the ratio of applicants to admissions to medical schools declined from around 2.8 in the mid-1970s to 1.6 in 1989; in the case of first-time applicants the current ratio is even lower. Particularly noteworthy has been the declining interest in the profession among white males. The number of applicants from this pool nationwide was almost 40 percent lower in 1989 than it had been in 1983, just six years earlier.[11] Until the recent expansion in the number of applicants, it appeared that the nation would soon have to make some hard choices: whether to merge or close some medical schools or compromise standards in order to maintain class size. Even now, state legislatures may consider shifting some dollars appropriated for medical education to programs that would increase the output of nurse practitioners and physicians' assistants.

Further, the "feminization" of medicine proceeds apace. In the late 1960s, women represented no more than 8 percent of the nation's physicians,[12] the second lowest percentage in the Western world. Today, women account for just under 40 percent of new entrants into medical school. This transformation warrants greater attention than it has elicited since the gender shift affects specialty distribution, hours of work, availability of students, young physicians seeking a career in biomedical research and development, and still other aspects of medicine.

Aside from its consequences for medical practice and organization, what are the economic implications of this rapid penetration of the profession by women? From the point of view of a labor market analyst, the advancing femininization represents a downgrading of the career prospects of medicine as perceived by those workers traditionally considered to be the best-positioned workers—white males. Next, we know that, on average, women physicians practice fewer hours a week and see fewer patients per hour than do their male colleagues. Women also earn somewhat less per hour of work, specialty by specialty. I know of no sound analysis of the influence of these gender-related differences upon average per-physician visit costs and their long-term societal effects. I suspect, however, that the differences in practice will narrow and in time disappear, except for a residual small discriminatory factor.

Among the beneficial by-products of the civil rights movement of the 1960s was the awakening of the conscience of many leaders of American medicine to the gross underrepresentation of minorities in the medical profession and the leadership's determination to take corrective action. Yet, although the number and proportion of minority physicians have increased threefold, shortages persist that, it is widely believed, are responsible for much of the continuing difficulties of minority populations, particularly low-income urban and rural residents, in gaining access to the health care system. It is understandable that Dr. Louis Sullivan, the former secretary of the Department of Health and Human Services, has identified the shortage of minority physicians as a target of opportunity.

An ideological struggle has been underway for many years within the medical profession and among the general public (including its elected legislators) as to the appropriate division of labor among generalists and specialists and the optimal distribution of the physician supply. The simplistic formulation goes as follows: The American people need more generalists and fewer specialists and subspecialists. This proposition is buttressed by reference to the superiority of the medical systems of Canada and the United Kingdom, which have much higher proportions of generalists, and that of the United States.

I am skeptical of this proposition because of the extent to which the generalist-specialist issue is subsidiary to the ways in which physicians practice medicine. If HMOs eventually become the dominant mode of physician practice in the United States, one could anticipate a major expansion of primary care physicians, with a corresponding decline in the proportion of specialists and subspecialists. One way in which HMOs attempt to contain their expenditures is by monitoring patient referrals to specialists as well as by monitoring hospital admissions. Although enrollments in HMOs will continue to expand (though probably at a slower rate than in the mid-1980s), in my opinion it is unlikely that they will become the prototypical mode of practice in the near or even the distant future.

A major reform of medical education could produce a significant shift in the respective proportions of generalists and specialists. Here again, given the influence of the specialists on residency review committees, medical school faculties, and the staffs of the major teaching hospitals, any significant shift in favor of producing significantly greater numbers of generalists seems, at least in the near term, improbable.

Like most simple comparisons, however, the difference in the ratios of generalists to specialists in the United Kingdom, Canada, and the United States, when unrelated to the distinctive organization and practice of medicine in each country, implies little other than the need to evaluate the causes and consequences of these differences. It is now almost two decades since Congress first intervened by providing federal funding for family practice residency programs. Despite continuing congressional interest and support, however, U.S. medical care has been and remains specialist-oriented. The leading institutions—the research-oriented academic health centers (AHCs)—have not been seriously influenced by federal support for the training of generalists, and—even more important—the public has also given little evidence of relinquishing its preference for specialist care. It appears that although health reformers will continue to advocate generalism, the medical educational establishment will continue to produce more specialists.

There are those who believe that the newly enacted fee system for physicians who treat Medicare patients, the resource-based relative value payment scale that favors physicians who provide cognitive treatment (diagnosis, consultation, and evaluation), will redirect medical students' and residents' career choices toward family practice. I remain dubious.[13]

Thus far, I have identified a number of basic issues affecting physician personnel that should be on the nation's health agenda for evaluation and action but that, nevertheless, languish. Why are issues of physician personnel so difficult to deal with? The answers lie not so much in their substance, but rather in the nature of our society. There is a well-recognized tendency in a democracy not to intrude into professional matters, but rather to delegate them to the profession for study and action. The leadership of the medical profession in the United States has been loath to move decisively on issues of a physician surplus for fear that it will be accused of antitrust violations—not a totally unjustified fear in light of court findings of recent decades.

When it comes to issues such as the recent shrinking pool of applicants to medical schools (recently reversed), the feminization of the profession, the shortage of minority physicians, and the imbalance between generalists and specialists, even a leadership that had reached consensus would be hard-pressed to alter the underlying dynamics

Three other observations are relevant:

- In our governmental system, most physician supply issues fall within the jurisdiction of the states, not the federal government, and the individual states have distinctive problems that determine the adequacy of their supply. All states, even those with the highest ratios of physicians to population, contain pockets of underserved populations and are therefore reluctant to cut back on the capacity and output of their state-supported medical schools.
- Second, there is no decision-making mechanism in place that would enable the states to take early and meaningful action to alter the extant mix of physicians, physician assistants and nurse practitioners, even if a different mix might result in better patient care and lower costs.

- Finally, in a democracy in which individuals are free to pursue the careers of their choice, state legislators are hesitant to reduce the opportunities for their residents to apply (with a reasonable likelihood of admission) to an in-state medical school. Clearly, the rationalization of the physician supply in terms of numbers and specialty is not imminent. In manpower planning as in many other aspects of a democratic society, rationalization may not be a meaningful criterion for formulating public policy.

Nurses

The only alarming development in the health personnel sector during the 1980s was the post-1986 nurse shortage that has seriously affected almost every region of the country. The shortage was precipitous and unexpected; witness the confident assessment of the Institute of Medicine study[14] of only three years previous that the nurse supply would continue to satisfy a rising demand. This conclusion was reinforced by the experience of the first part of the decade when the number of nurses per 100,000 population, the number of nurses per 100 hospital admissions, the number of students enrolled in state-approved schools of nursing pursuing the registered nurse (RN) degree, and the annual number of newly licensed nurses all peaked in the mid-1980s. Shortly thereafter, however, reports of nurse shortages became increasingly frequent, and by 1987–1988 it was generally agreed that the nation's hospitals faced a serious nursing shortage that would at best prove recalcitrant and at worst become endemic.

What combination of circumstances can explain so sudden and so drastic a change in the short-term and, more alarming, the long-term supply of nursing personnel? The following developments may illuminate, even if they do not satisfactorily explain, this unexpected turn.

The nurse market became softened in the early 1980s by the severe economic recession that resulted in a declining number of days of hospital care, economic pressures on many nurses to return to work or to increase their hours of work, and the availability of large numbers of recent graduates—all of which encouraged hospitals to replace many of their licensed practical nurses (LPNs) and nurses aides with RNs. Upgrading their nursing staffs would be advantageous, they believed, in two respects: RNs offered greater flexibility and efficiency in the provision of patient-care services, and their relatively low wage rates would reduce the hospital's total personnel costs. The advocacy of all-RN nursing staffs by many nurse leaders gave added impetus to the substitution move. Linda Aiken (1987) has observed that the narrow differential between RN wages and the wages of subprofessional nursing personnel intensified the speed and rate of the substitution.

Of the many factors that have contributed to the current imbalance in the nurse labor market, perhaps the most ominous is the precipitous decline in the number of students enrolled in nursing schools, from a peak of 250,000 in 1983 to 184,000 in 1988. Clearly, the striking reduction in the number of young people reaching working age had serious implications for the RN profession that has long been overwhelmingly female (97 percent) and white (92 percent).

A closely related determinant was the level of nursing wages relative to that of comparable occupations in a labor market offering expanded career opportunities for college-educated women. In the 1980s more women college students expressed a career preference for medicine than for nursing, reversing a preexisting ratio of from 5 to 10 in favor of nursing.

The argument is frequently advanced that hospital administrators in the same community are reluctant to resort to significant wage increases in dealing with nurse shortages since they realize their competitors will do the same to the detriment of all, that is, wages will have risen without having significantly increased the local supply. Nevertheless, a recent study of four metropolitan areas—Boston, New York, Los Angeles, and Houston—experiencing nurse shortages in 1988–1989, found that local hospitals moved vigorously to raise salaries across the board, offering a starting annual wage of $30,000 or more and wages of $40,000 to $45,000 for a staff or clinical nurse with a decade of experience.[15]

It would be difficult to convince even a skeptical economist that such a radical improvement in nurses' salaries—especially when accompanied by improvements in scheduling practices, efforts to reduce stress levels, and better support services—will not have a beneficial effect on future recruitment, once the new labor market realities become broadly known. Not many other occupations requiring completion of two or two and a half years of training in a community college offer $30,000 as a starting wage.

However, important as the three S's—salary, scheduling, and stress reduction—are for improved recruitment into nursing, they will probably not suffice, by themselves, to restore an early and reasonable equilibrium between nurse supply and nurse demand. The increasing proportion of elderly persons with a predictable increasing prevalence of acute illnesses will generate a vast demand for intensive nursing care. At the same time, there is not a sufficiently large pool of young capable people interested in obtaining an RN degree. Nursing schools face major challenges in redirecting their recruitment efforts in the future toward groups that they have long ignored, if not avoided—members of minority groups, men, older persons seeking a career change, and nonprofessional health care workers seeking upward mobility.

It should be noted that the nurse educational leadership was not necessarily more discriminatory than other sectors of American society in failing to recruit extensively among minorities. Moreover, since the mid-1960s, the profession has set its sights on establishing the baccalaureate degree as the uniform prerequisite for entrance into professional nursing. It was perceived, quite correctly, that this goal could not be achieved if attention were focused on the recruitment of larger numbers of minorities. Until the current shortage, however, the nurse leadership avoided the implications of nursing educational trends. At peak, no more than one of every three RN students has pursued a baccalaureate degree in preparation for licensure. About 57 percent of current new licensees are graduates of community colleges, over 30 percent have completed a four-year college program, and another 12 percent or so have been trained in hospital (diploma) schools of nursing.

Recruiting among minorities by even the most motivated nurse educators is handicapped by the fact that many inner-city youth—those who have earned a high school diploma to say nothing of those who have not—cannot cope with the nursing curriculum because of deficiencies in language, mathematics, or science. This educational impediment is a fact. However, it is an impediment that can be overcome through cooperative efforts of state and local educational authorities to develop remedial bridge programs. Many, if not all, of the prospective candidates for admission to nursing education could meet the requirements if afforded access to remedial programs of six to twelve months.

Success in recruiting not only minorities but also experienced workers desirous of making a career change and lower-level health workers seeking upward mobility will require adaptations and innovations with respect to curriculum offerings and financial support for students. Many older workers must continue to earn while they learn, which means that they can attend school only after working hours or on weekends. Moreover, many will need scholarship assistance, service pay-back arrangements, or other financing plans that will provide them with a steady stream of basic income while preparing for their RN license. Many hospitals have moved to expand educational benefits and pay-back provisions for health care employees who wish to pursue an RN degree. Some states have taken initial steps to broaden financial support for needy students, but more needs to be done through joint planning and coordination among schools of nursing, health care employers, and state governments.

Admittedly, once corrective actions involve multiple parties, the process is more difficult to design and to implement. However, progressive market corrections are taking place—through significant salary advances—and current recruitment and educational stumbling blocks should gradually be resolved. Although the secretary of the HHS's Commission on Nursing[16] anticipated a long-term disequilibrium in the nurse labor market, the authors of the Commonwealth Fund report, *What to Do About the Nursing Shortage*,[17] concluded that the outlook was more favorable in view both of economic corrections that are making nursing a more attractive career and of potential changes in hospital organization and procedures to utilize expensive and scarce nursing personnel more effectively.

Allied Health Workers

Unlike physicians and nurses, allied health personnel do not constitute clearly distinguished occupations that are defined by uniform, mandated training standards and licensure. Accordingly, there is no generally accepted list of employment categories or a census of employees included under the rubric of allied health workers. One way to define this amorphous area is to subtract the number of physicians, circa 585,000, and the number of licensed nurses, 2.03 million, from the estimated total number of health care personnel—7.5 million; the remainder, some 4.9 million, would then comprise the complement of allied health workers. This figure is an upper bound since it includes substantial numbers of individuals classified as allied health personnel who have had no formal occupational-specific education beyond on-the-job training.

Irrespective of definition, the simple fact, reported by the Institute of Medicine, is that thus far the area has been poorly studied and reliable statistical information is sparse. Faced with the congressional mandate to report on this heterogeneous field in the absence of sound data, the Committee to Study the Role of Allied Health Personnel proceeded to select ten well-established allied health occupations and to assess the factors likely to influence demand and supply in these areas between the years 1986 and 2000. The ten fields and the 1986 employment estimates for each developed by the U.S. Department of Labor's Bureau of Labor Statistics are shown in Table 8.1.

The committee cautiously concluded that "for some fields such as physical therapy, radiologic technology, medical record services, and occupational therapy," decision makers need to improve the market so that imbalances in demand and supply may be prevented. Clinical laboratory technology and dental hygiene were identified as possible areas of instability. The committee was sanguine that the labor market for the remaining fields would experience smooth self-adjustment.

As one might expect, parallels are found between the wage structures and working conditions of nurses and allied health workers. In fact, one of the reasons that hospital administrators have traditionally resisted the use of wage increases to ease their nurse shortages is the link between the salary levels of hospital nurses and those of allied health workers. In 1986, the mean starting rate for allied health workers who had acquired a baccalaureate was in the $1,700 to $1,800 monthly range, not very different from the starting wage for accountants, auditors, and computer programmers. The mean maximum rate, however, was about 25 percent higher, indicating the same compression that has long characterized the lifetime salary scales of nurses.

TABLE 8.1   Major Allied Health Occupations and Employment Estimates, 1986

Allied Health Field	*1986 Employment Estimates*
Clinical laboratory technology	238,000
Radiologic technology	114,000
Dental hygiene	87,000
Emergency medical services (paid)	65,000
Physical therapy	56,000
Respiratory therapy	56,000
Speech-language pathology and audiology services	42,000
Dietetic services	40,000
Medical record services	40,000
Occupational therapy	26,000

Source: Institute of Medicine. *Allied Health Services: Avoiding Crises*, Washington, D.C., National Academy Press, 1989.

There are other parallels between allied health workers and nurses. With a few exceptions, in particular emergency medical care, allied health workers are predominantly female, white, relatively young, and are employed predominantly in hospital settings. Their training has similarly shifted progressively from a hospital-based quasi-apprenticeship to academic preparation.

The relatively consistent balance between demand and supply in the case of allied health workers (physical therapists are the principal exception) must be attributed to the responsiveness of the nation's higher educational system, which has succeeded in producing a continuing output of most types of allied health workers adequate to meet local and regional demands. To be sure, the alignment between training and employment has not been flawless; nevertheless, the educational system has demonstrated an impressive order of response. Among the principal failings is the extreme specificity of many of the training programs so that few graduates have the benefit of cross-training that would provide them with multiple competencies and greater career mobility.

Other labor market pressures and distortions also operate. They include tensions between physicians and allied health workers with respect to supervision and payment mechanisms, malpractice exposure, and efforts to tighten and extend state licensing as a vehicle of both quality control and "turf" protection. Restricted opportunities for continuing education and career progress are other impediments to a well-functioning occupational environment.

All things considered, however, the education-market relationships for allied health workers operate with a high degree of efficiency. The key to their success is found in the responsiveness both of the community college system to local opportunities for employment of a wide spectrum of health care technicians and of the four-year colleges which produce most types of health care technologists. The most serious problems found by the Institute of Medicine's Committee to Study the Roles of Allied Health Personnel were the inadequacies of the data base and the intrinsically fragmented nature of the allied health market as the result of the decentralization of responsibility among the fifty states for the rules and regulations governing competence testing and quality control, as well as the diversity of employers, with hospitals being the principal employment setting.

What Lies Ahead

Now that we have examined the multiple dimensions of health personnel at the present time we must consider the likely issues that will command attention and action in the decade ahead, recognizing that some issues will be temporized or treated with indifference because there is little likelihood of achieving a consensus on how best to respond to them.

Let us turn first to physicians. The three critical issues involving physicians in the decade ahead are whether they will be forced to relinquish many of their traditional practice prerogatives, whether they are likely to suffer a serious deterioration in their relative earnings, and whether the medical educational system will be so significantly altered as to affect the future flow of entrants into medicine. There is widespread discontent among physicians, with the everpresent malpractice suits, excessive paper work, and bureaucratic interference with professional autonomy in the practice of medicine, in particular by third parties such as insurance companies and Medicare. However, if things remain more or less as they are during the decade ahead, physicians will have beaten the odds.

What are the prospects for the medical profession to avoid a major decline in power, prestige, and income? Much is made of the fact that fee-for-service medicine is in fast retreat and that managed care is the wave of the future. I see no unequivocal evidence that staff-model HMOs or other types of salaried employment will dominate the physician landscape by the year 2000. In the past few years, advocacy has been growing for outcome studies as the basis for the specification of standards of medical practice.

What about physicians' earnings—will they decline in relative, possibly even in absolute terms? A relative drop in earnings is not an unrealistic expectation in view of the combined influence of continuing increases in the physician supply and continuing efforts to moderate total health care spending. However, it is far from certain that this will occur. The nation may not be able to get its health care financing system in order before the year 2000, and in that case the day of reckoning for physicians may be postponed.

What about the flow of new entrants into medical schools and the reform of medical education? The steep downward trend in the ratio of applications to admissions to medical schools has begun to reverse. Moreover, there has been some modest response to the Ebert-Ginzberg[18] proposition that the length of generic medical education (from enrollment in medical school to first certification) could be reduced by as much as two of the present total of seven years through the improved alignment among colleges of their undergraduate and graduate training. If this reform were adopted, the diminishing flow of students into medicine might be reversed as a consequence of the almost 30 percent reduction in the time preparing for practice.

The ascendance of high-tech medicine and its proliferation throughout the United States implies that there is little likelihood of a significant shift in the short term in the direction of more generalism and generalists. Although I would support a reapportionment of medical educational expenditures in favor of the production of larger numbers of nurse practitioners and physicians' assistants, serious moves toward this goal in the decade ahead are also unlikely. Unfortunately, we lack the consensus and the mechanisms to effect such a shift in a ten-year span.

There will be much turmoil in the physicians' world in the 1990s: Morale will continue to decline, relations between patients and physicians will worsen, but the extant institutional structures are likely to remain substantially unaltered. Nevertheless, a serious erosion of physician morale is not conducive to a well-functioning health care system.

As for nursing, there are two ways to read the future of the profession. The Secretary's Commission on Nursing[19] projected a continuing serious disequilibrium in the supply-demand balance for nursing personnel. The report of the Commonwealth Fund,[20] which was released at about the same time, arrived at a more positive outlook, concluding that shortages in both the current supply of nurses and the pool of nursing students would be corrected through the combined effects of economic adjustments, educational flexibility, and managerial improvements. Among these are: the growing recognition of the nurse leadership that the baccalaureate degree could not become the uniform requirement for RN licensure; that new sources of recruits, especially among minority groups, could provide a steady stream of nursing students; that the radical changes in starting salaries and in the salary potential of experienced nurses would strengthen the retention of hospital nurses; and that there were many opportunities for managerial improvements in the utilization of hospital nurses through job redesign, greater reliance on support personnel, and labor-saving capital investments.

Analysis of the large pool of allied health workers revealed relatively few acute problems at the beginning of the 1990s. There is little reason to anticipate worsening in the decade ahead, except for possible short-term imbalances among particular occupational groups or locations. If the states and the localities maintain a vital higher educational system with curriculum flexibility at the community college level, the allied health care market should be able to function with reasonable efficiency.

The employment of over nine million persons in health care attests to two fundamental facts: the commitment of most Americans to ready and broad access to quality health care and the willingness of society—employers, government, and households alike—to foot the bill. The continuing increases in spending for health care since World War II fueled the dramatic expansion in the numbers of physicians, nurses, and allied health workers. With thirty seven million Americans uninsured at present and with many demands for service (nursing homes and home care) unmet or inadequately met, it is more than likely that the health care sector will continue to expand. Of the ten occupational groups identified by the U.S. Department of Labor's Bureau of Labor Statistics[21] as having the greatest potential growth in the 1990s, seven are health care occupations.

One must consider, however, a potential spoiler of the above forecast—the widespread and mounting discontent among all health care payers with the continuing upward spiral of total health care expenditures. If the economy remains on a more or less expansionary trend, the level of discontent may rise without evoking early corrective action. If, however, the economy should falter and, more particularly, if federal and state governments should find themselves in a severe budgetary crunch, then the dollar flows into health care may be seriously curtailed, with corresponding disruption in the growth of health personnel.

Notes

1. U.S. Department of Labor, Bureau of Labor Statistics, *Employment and Earnings* (Washington, D.C.: U.S. Government Printing Office, 1990).

2. M Freudenheim, "Job Growth in Health Care Soars," *New York Times*, 5 March 1990.

3. WB Schwartz, FA Sloan, and DN Mendelson, "Why There Will Be Little or No Physician Surplus Between Now and the Year 2000," *New England Journal of Medicine* 318(1988):892–97; EP Schloss, "Beyond GMENAC—Another Physician Shortage from 2010 to 2030?" *New England Journal of Medicine* 318(1988): 920–22.

4. E Ginzberg, "Physician Supply in the Year 2000," *Health Affairs* 8(2)(1989):84–90.

5. AR Tarlov, Editorial. "How Many Physicians Is Enough?" *Journal of the American Medical Association* 263(4)(1990): 571–72.

6. Schwartz, Sloan, and Mendelson, "Why There Will Be Little or No Physician Surplus."

7. Tarlov, "How Many Physicians?"

8. E Ginzberg, *The Medical Triangle: Physicians, Politicians, and the Public* (Cambridge, Mass.: Harvard University Press, 1990).

9. WB Schwartz, JP Neuhaus, RW Bennett, and AP Williams, "The Changing Geographic Distribution of Board-Certified Physicians," *New England Journal of Medicine* 303(Fall 1980):1032–38.

10. JB Trauner, HS Luft, and SS Hunt, "A Life-Style Decision: Facing the Reality of Physician Oversupply in the San Francisco Bay Area." In *From Physician Shortage to Patient Shortage: The Uncertain Future of Medical Practice*, edited by E Ginzberg (Boulder, Colo.: Westview Press, 1986).

11. Association of American Medical Colleges, *Facts: Applicants, Matriculants and Graduates, 1983 to 1989* (Washington, D.C.: The Association of American Medical Colleges, 1989).

12. E Ginzberg, and M Ostow, *Men, Money, and Medicine* (New York: Columbia University Press, 1969).

13. E Ginzberg, "Do We Need More Generalists?" *Academic Medicine* 64(9)(1989):495–97.

14. Institute of Medicine, Committee on Nursing and Nursing Education, *Public Policies with Private Actions* (Washington, D.C.: National Academy Press, 1983).

15. M Roberts, A Minnick, E Ginzberg, and C Curran, *A Commonwealth Fund Paper: What to Do about the Nursing Shortage* (New York: Commonwealth Fund, 1989).

16. U.S. Department of Health and Human Services, *Secretary's Commission on Nursing: Final Report* (Washington, D.C.: U.S. Government Printing Office, 1988).

17. Roberts, et al., *A Commonwealth Fund Paper*.

18. RE Ebert, and E Ginzberg, "The Reform of Medical Education," *Health Affairs* 7(2)(Supplement 1988):5–38.

19. U.S. Department of Health and Human Services, *Secretary's Commission*.

20. Roberts et al., *A Commonwealth Fund Paper*.

21. U.S. Department of Labor, Bureau of Labor Statistics, *Employment and Earnings*.

9

Philanthropy and
Nonprofit Organizations

Perhaps the chief distinguishing characteristic of the U.S. health care system is the dominant role that philanthropy and nonprofit organizations have played, and continue to play, in the acute care area where nonprofit hospitals account for over two-thirds of all beds and admissions.[1] Though there is growing awareness among informed observers that the role of philanthropy has shrunk drastically as the costs of an acute-care hospital episode have risen, the fact remains that nonprofit ownership and management continue to dominate the acute-care hospital sector, the key arena of high-tech medicine.

A recent study, *Charity Begins at Home: Generosity and Self-Interest Among the Philanthropic Elite*,[2] reveals a serious lack of perspective regarding the continuing importance of philanthropy and the nonprofit sector in the de livery of health care. The author takes note of only three recent developments: a multimillion dollar gift to Columbia-Presbyterian Medical Center in New York for the construction of a new, off-site building (the Allen Pavilion); the fact that few rich persons make gifts to county or public hospitals; the order of magnitude of major philanthropic contributions to hospitals, came to some $65.5 million in the three years 1983–1986.

This chapter provides a historical analysis of the changing role of philanthropy and nonprofit hospitals in the structure and operation of the U.S. health care system from the early decades of the twentieth century to the present. The analysis has been subdivided into four discrete periods: *Dominance* (1910–1945); *Interdependence* (1946–1976); *Confusion* (1977–1990); and *The Uncertain Future*. In dealing with philanthropy, location is a critical factor. The cities of Boston, New York, Philadelphia, and Baltimore—from the vantage of health care, the base of the eastern establishment—account for a disproportionate number of the nation's leading academic health centers, private medical schools, and prominent health care facilities. In no other section of the country has philanthropy and not-for-profit facilities dominated the health arena to the same degree.

Since I have been engaged in health services research for the past half-century and have dealt with selected facets of philanthropy and not-for-profit hospitals in many of my earlier studies, I use my own bibliography as reference for many of the issues that are examined. I am impressed with each passing year that there is much to be learned about the unsolved problems in health, as well as other policy arenas, by mining the lessons of history. Although the future will inevitably differ from the past, the ways in which the challenges of the past were met and resolved can yield useful guides to future action.

Dominance

Shortly after the turn of the century the American Medical Association directed its attention to the then sorry state of medical education. With a major assist from the Carnegie Corporation for the Advancement of Teaching (sponsor of the Flexner report, 1910) and with the active cooperation of the state licensing authorities, the AMA took the lead to eliminate most, if not all, of the weak medical schools.[3]

The AMA, itself a nonprofit organization, was granted virtually exclusive authority by state legislatures for oversight of the rules and regulations governing the practice of medicine. Even when the states retained residual authority to act, they usually relied on the advice and counsel of the AMA and its component state societies.

The first two decades of the twentieth century also saw the accelerated decline and disappearance of many proprietary facilities as more and more members of the middle class turned to the modern hospital for medical evaluation, surgery, and obstetrics. Nonprofit community hospitals, under religious or sectarian auspices, expanded rapidly.

The large urban teaching hospitals provided much free or below-cost medical care to the poor and the needy on their wards and in their clinics. In part they were able to do so because of the substantial income from endowments and annual donations that they received from wealthy benefactors, many of whom sat on their boards; in part they depended upon voluntary services from their physician staffs; and in part they could cross-subsidize by overcharging affluent private patients to cover much of the free care that they provided the poor.

A few more references to this earlier period, which is recalled today only by a declining number of old-timers: Almost without exception, hospital staff appointments carried no financial reward. Physicians eagerly sought staff appointments at prestigious hospitals, where many of them donated the equivalent of two days of work per week for the privilege of admitting private patients. Young physicians served for years in the hospital's clinics to earn the right to be considered for a staff appointment.

The bulk of the clinical instruction in medical schools was by volunteers, physicians who had achieved reputations in their private practices and who were pleased and honored to teach medical students on their own time. Private practitioners also contributed much time and effort to patients who could not pay or could pay only part of their regular fee. It should be recalled that the average income of a physician in 1929 was around $5,000 while a full professor at Columbia earned $7,500! Today the relative economic positions of the two have been reversed, with the average income of a physician amounting to about $175,000 versus $75,000 for a Columbia professor. But one must note that in 1929 most physicians started practicing after one year's internship; currently they start to practice after their first certification, which requires that they undergo additional training for at least three to five years after graduation from medical school.

Further evidence of the extent to which hospitals were eleemosynary institutions is suggested by the fact that administrative positions and nursing staffs in Catholic hospitals were filled, by and large, by members of religious orders. Further, most hospitals attracted substantial numbers of marginal workers to provide housekeeping and other support services for which they received minimum or subminimum wages, complemented in part by free meals and uniforms and limited work demands.

Hospitals operated for the most part in a deficit position, which was liquidated at year's end by trustees passing the hat or by a fund-raising drive involving the community, or often by both. The story is told of a visit in the 1930s by George Blumenthal, then chairman of the board of Mt. Sinai Hospital and head of Lazard Frères in New York City, to the director of the hospital, Dr. S. S. Goldwater, to discuss the hospital's current deficit. On learning the amount, more than $700,000 ($7 million in current dollars), Blumenthal took out his checkbook and wrote a check to cover it in full. A point worth emphasizing is that hospital administrators and their physician staffs knew that the deficit for the year had to be kept within the bounds that the trustees were able and willing to cover. Deficit control was cost control in the pre–World War II era.

The AMA, with Morris Fishbein as its executive vice president, played a leading role in shaping national health policy in the 1930s, first by stonewalling the recommendations of the Committee on the Costs of Medical Care (1932), a plurality of whose members favored action to expand voluntary health insurance.[4] More importantly, the AMA helped to deter President Roosevelt from including health insurance in his social security reforms of 1935.

The AMA impeded the early growth of the Blue Cross movement (founded in Dallas, 1929) and, in association with the leadership of American medical schools, determined the characteristics of students accepted to medical schools in the 1920s and succeeded in reducing the numbers admitted in the depressed 1930s.[5] In the opinion of Major General Raymond W. Bliss, who served as the Surgeon General of the Army in the early 1950s, the AMA was the most powerful lobby, except for the Catholic church, in the halls of Congress in the pre–World War II years.

Table 9.1 provides the best overview of the importance of philanthropy for voluntary general hospitals in New York City in 1940.[6] What is noteworthy in this distribution is that charity accounted for more than twice the sum contributed by government.

One additional note concludes this brief account of selected events during the thirty-five years from the Flexner report to the end of World War II (1910–1945), that bear directly on the theme of philanthropy and not-for-profit facilities in health care. It was the trade unions (nonprofit organizations) that petitioned the War Labor Board in 1942 for the right to bargain with employers for health insurance without violating wage stabilization regulations. Approval of this petition set the stage for the remarkable expansion of private health insurance in the post–World War II era.

Although physicians practiced medicine on a fee-for-service basis and patient payments were the largest source of income for voluntary hospitals, the fact remains that both at the micro level of the individual's access to health services and at the macro level of state and national health care policy, philanthropy and nonprofit institutions largely determined the direction of the U.S. health care sector up to the end of World War II.

Interdependence

The best introduction to the decades following 1946 is found in a chapter written by Dale Hiestand, "Expansion of Nonprofit Enterprise: The Health Services Industry," for our collaborative volume, *The Pluralistic Economy*,[7] published in 1965.

Hiestand summarizes the findings of various discrete analyses of the early post–World War II trends as follows: "At each level of the medical and health services industry—in the provision of services and their financing, the ownership of facilities, the raising of capital funds, the training of personnel, the conduct of research and its financing—there is a reasonable sharing of responsibilities among a wide variety of private profit-seeking, nonprofit and governmental agencies."

The years following World War II saw the rapid expansion of both nonprofit and commercial health insurance; combined federal, state, and philanthropic funding for the expansion and modernization of hospital plant; the expansion of state funding for medical education; the beginning of the shift of nursing education from nonprofit hospital schools of nursing to institutions

TABLE 9.1   Income of Voluntary General Hospitals by Source, New York City, 1940

Source	Percentage
Patients	60.5
Government	11.6
Charity, total	24.0
Contributions	(15.4)
Investment income	(8.6)
Miscellaneous	3.9
Total	100.0

Source: Ginzberg, Eli. *A Pattern for Hospital Care: Final Report of the New York State Hospital Study*. New York: Columbia University Press, 1949.

of higher learning, primarily public; and the vastly expanded role of the federal government in financing biomedical research, with heavy reliance on nonprofit universities and medical schools for its performance. These and other changes still left a virile nonprofit sector, particularly in private health insurance (the Blues), in acute-care community hospitals, and in major research-oriented academic health centers.

Major increases both in the demand for and the costs of providing health care services throughout the first two decades of the post–World War II era eroded the role of philanthropy as a significant force in making essential health care services available to the American people. To oversimplify: In 1948 the average per diem cost in New York City voluntary hospitals amounted to $14.62; the comparable figure in 1957 came to $25.77. Charity as a percentage of operating income declined from 16.7 percent in 1948 to 12.6 in 1957.[8] By 1966, as Medicare and Medicaid came on stream, the average per diem cost in New York's municipal hospitals had risen to $65.25;[9] at Montefiore Hospital, not unrepresentative of the city's voluntary general hospitals, it was $85.01, and the contribution of charity had declined to 5 percent.[10]

To confound matters, the slow growth in the physician supply, juxtaposed with the rapid growth in demand for physician services, reduced the willingness of practicing physicians to volunteer large blocks of time to hospitals for care of the poor or to treat them privately for little or nothing. Most new graduates sought to recoup rapidly, via earnings, the costs of their elongated training preparatory to acquiring specialty board certification.

Further complications arose when long-established, philanthropically sponsored hospitals found themselves in neighborhoods from which their religious or ethnic clientele had relocated, replaced by other groups, primarily blacks and Hispanics, for whose welfare the hospital, its staff, and trustees had no strong obligations of kinship. This issue was central to a study conducted for the New York Federation of Jewish Philanthropies (the umbrella organization for over one hundred social agencies and hospitals) in the early 1960s, which recommended that the Hospital for Joint Diseases, located in the middle of Harlem, by then populated by blacks, be transferred to the city for the use of the local community and its practitioners.[11]

New York City is unique in the scale and scope of its public hospitals, which for generations have provided a high proportion of all inpatient and outpatient care for the city's poor and near-poor. This large public sector (currently subsumed in the New York Health and Hospitals Corporation) has served as a buffer between the nonprofit hospitals and the large numbers of poor New Yorkers who would otherwise have sought all of their care from the nonprofit sector. By the early 1960s this mutual accommodation was seriously threatened because of the inability of the municipal hospitals to attract and retain professional staff, particularly physicians. This dilemma was resolved by the device of "affiliation contracts," under which the city negotiated for physician services with leading teaching hospitals. The public hospitals were thereby enabled to expand their residency training programs and thus add to their professional resources at the same time that the contracts protected the affiliate hospitals from being flooded with excessive numbers of nonpaying patients.[12]

We have thus far considered the first part of the period of interdependence, 1946–1963; what happened during the later years, 1964 to 1976? The late 1960s conceivably represented the heyday of the nonprofit sector as the result of large infusions of new federal and state monies for medical education and research and, with the passage of Medicare and Medicaid, vastly expanded funding for care of the poor and the elderly. Throughout this period, the health insurance industry, nonprofit and commercial, reimbursed hospitals on the basis of their charges or costs, including allowances for depreciation and teaching. Medicare, in its first two years, even provided a 2 percent addition for innovation in its reimbursement formula.

It was only a question of time before the funding sluices that had been opened wide would attract the attention of payers. In 1969 President Nixon sounded a clear alarm, pointing out that the nation's bill for health care, which amounted to $75 billion or 7.5 percent of GNP, threatened the future of the health care sector and even the future of the U.S. economy. In rapid succession, Congress mandated the establishment of Professional Standards Review Organizations (PSROs), aimed at moderating hospital admissions and lengths of stay (1972); it authorized federal support for the expansion of Health Maintenance Organizations, in the belief that they could provide more and better care for less money (1973); it put in place a complex federal-state health planning mechanism as a means of controlling the expansion of hospital beds (1974); and in 1976 it declared unequivocally that the long-standing physician shortage had been resolved, thus establishing the rationale for reducing its support for the education of health professionals.

One of the little-observed and less-appreciated developments of the post-Medicare era was the substantial emancipation of nonprofit hospitals from the fiscal constraints that in earlier decades had inhibited the rate at which they could make capital investments in equipment and buildings. Operating at or close to a deficit position and unable to build up their depreciation accounts, hospitals were dependent on philanthropic contributions and governmental financing for capital investments. However, the rapidly rising reimbursements by third-party payers, which, following the implementation of Medicare and Medicaid, covered over 90 percent of hospitals' inpatient expenditures; the acceptance of depreciation as a legitimate cost that payers were willing to cover; the contributions of federal and state governments to new building projects; and the greatly improved access to the bond market, where their offerings had the benefit of tax exempt status, all created a Golden Age for nonprofit hospitals. With assured profit margins, as third-party reimbursements guaranteed virtually all their operating costs, they were able to obtain, at least for a few years, almost all the capital they wanted, as long as they came up with modest amounts of equity, which the philanthropic sector generally had little trouble in raising.

As illustrated in the study *From Health Dollars to Health Services: New York City 1965–1985*,[13] in those years an imaginative hospital administrator, who understood how to tap into diverse sources of funding, could expand his or her institution with little assistance from the trustees and with the enthusiastic support of the physician staff. The proverbial operating deficits that trustees of nonprofit hospitals had had to cover and their critical role in raising capital were no longer constraints. Strong nonprofit hospitals ceased to have worries about money. They could get all that they needed, and they could recoup all the dollars that they spent.

Reference must also be made to the changing supply of human resources, particularly nurses and hospital support personnel, in this new era. By commissioning nurses as officers during World War II and assigning them primary responsibility for overseeing inpatient care, the armed services fundamentally transformed the field of nursing. Until then nursing had mainly attracted upwardly mobile daughters of farmers and of blue-collar immigrants, who then underwent an exploitative three-year apprenticeship program leading to a marginal occupation with low earnings and little or no job security. During the Great Depression of the 1930s many nurses worked for room and board and perhaps a $25 stipend a month.

With few exceptions, the nurse leadership, the medical leadership, and the hospital leadership, individually and collectively, failed to appreciate the revolution that World War II had set in motion, and, in the succeeding decades, they were slow to appreciate the restructuring of the nursing profession and the altered medical care environment.[14]

Not a small part of the stresses and strains that have beset the health and hospital labor markets reflects the persistence of the nonprofit tradition that continued to regard nurses as "women with a mission" and hospital workers as "doing the Lord's work." Hospitals ignored the new reality until nurse associations and trade unions, with an assist from federal legislation, began to drive the point home that nurses, allied health workers, and support staff had no less interest in and concern with earnings and working conditions than other members of the labor force. Among the important by-products of the improved financial position of nonprofit hospitals in the early post-Medicare era were large-scale corrections in the reward structures for nurses and other hospital employees. In the case of the latter, the correction factor in New York City went from approximately 30 percent below the market at the end of the 1950s to 30 percent above the market in the late 1960s.

Confusion

It would be a misreading of U.S. health policy to see the post-1976 era as the only period characterized by widespread confusion. However, there are good reasons to apply this appellation to the last decade and a half because not until then were basic questions raised about the legitimacy of the nonprofit institution as a major provider of U.S. health care. It is worth recalling that the chair of the Ways and Means Committee of the House of Representatives forecast in early 1976 that Congress would pass national health insurance (NHI) in that session and, since it was a presidential election year, the incumbent, President Gerald Ford, would not dare veto it. Congress never so much as marked up a bill. During the presidential campaign, Jimmy Carter advocated NHI, but, once in the White House, he was dissuaded by the budget figures from pursuing his pledge.

Seeking a mechanism to slow health care expenditures, the Secretary of Health, Education, and Welfare in the Carter administration, Joseph Califano, Jr., commissioned Professor Alain Enthoven of Stanford University to explore alternative proposals. Enthoven produced a memorandum on universal health insurance coverage that advocated a competitive market policy, with an assist from government to help provide insurance for the poor.[15] Carter and Califano did not proceed with Enthoven's proposal. The president opted instead for a legislative ceiling on total annual capital outlays by hospitals, in the belief that controlling capacity would succeed in simultaneously controlling operating expenditures.

At this point an important nonprofit organization, the American Hospital Association (AHA), entered the fray and lobbied aggressively in favor of a voluntary cost control effort (VE) rather than a federal regulatory mechanism. It was supported vigorously as well by the Federation of American Hospitals, counterpart of the AHA in the for-profit hospital sector, and Congress adopted the counterproposal, which enjoyed only a brief period of moderate success.

Reference should be made to the rapid rise of for-profit hospital chains in the late 1960s and the 1970s and their subsequent decline. This was the first expansion of the proprietary sector since the latter part of the nineteenth century, stimulated in considerable measure by the federal government's willingness to include a return on equity. Subsequent action by Congress to reduce the rate of return and the adoption of prospective reimbursement in 1983 helped to derail the expansion of the for-profit sector.

Despite its ideological preference for a competitive solution, the Reagan administration never forwarded a complementary legislative proposal; instead it worked out a compromise with Congress to cut back on all three government fronts—Medicare, Medicaid, and other federally funded health programs.[16] In 1983, Congress and the administration adopted a prospective payment system (PPS) to replace the long-ensconced system of cost reimbursement for inpatient care provided to Medicare beneficiaries, an approach that helped to contain federal outlays for inpatient care.

It would be wrong, however, to convey the impression that competition had no influence on the health care system, even if it failed to play a major role. After the withdrawal of federal financing for HMOs (1981), which paradoxically had inhibited their growth because of its stringent criteria, HMO enrollments expanded rapidly as an alternative to fee-for-service plans. More recently, some preferred provider organizations (PPOs) have competed successfully with both fee-for-service plans and HMOs. California led the way in 1982 in putting its MediCal (Medicaid) contracts up for competitive bidding, and, subsequently, Illinois followed suit.

Probably the most intense competition occurred in the insurance area, not only between the Blues and the commercial companies but, more particularly, between the insurance industry and the increasing number of large- and medium-sized corporations that decided it would be advantageous for them to self-insure rather than continue to contract with the conventional carriers. One unfortunate by-product of these trends has been the fracturing of the insurance pool, so that many small employers and low-income individuals cannot obtain affordable, if any, coverage, a shortcoming that the industry and state governments are currently seeking to redress.

Adoption by the federal government of the prospective payment system of reimbursement for inpatient care to Medicare beneficiaries coincided with a significant decline in hospital admissions and days of care. This led to a reversal in the fortunes of the for-profit hospital chains, which for the most part were carrying excessively swollen debt at the end of the decade. The expectation a few years earlier, that a small number of for-profit "megacorps" would soon dominate U.S. health care, proved a mirage. Since the mid-1970s there has also been a proliferation of for-profit ambulatory-care establishments of every variety, but this new departure in health care delivery, too, has lost considerable steam.

It would be wrong, however, to interpret this deceleration of the for-profit sector as a strong reaffirmation of the dominant role of nonprofit facilities in the delivery of health care in the United States. True, reliance on competition and the market has not provided a major alternative to the long-ensconced nonprofit organizations. At the same time, the role of philanthropy and cross-subsidization as a means of providing for the care of the poor and the near-poor has diminished. The increase in total health care expenditures during the 1980s, from $248 billion to over $660 billion (1990), despite the greatly intensified efforts of federal, state, and local governments to rein in their expenditures, the parallel failure of employers to slow their health benefit costs, and the growing disappointment of the public with its enlarged out-of-pocket outlays, all speak to the rampant confusion of the health care financing and delivery systems at the start of the 1990s.

The Uncertain Future

Action by the federal government in 1988 to modify the corporate tax exemption status of the Blues as a consequence of their abandonment of community rating and open enrollment for persons and firms seeking coverage; parallel efforts by some local and state governments to deny nonprofit hospitals tax-exempt status on the grounds that they were not furnishing sufficient free services to the poor and the indigent; tightened regulations by the IRS to limit the tax benefits available to nonprofit hospitals on profitable undertakings not directly linked to the provision of health care services; the diminishing volume of uncompensated care provided by most, though not all, nonprofit acute-care hospitals; and the growing resort of the regulatory authorities and state and federal attorneys to antitrust action against nonprofit organizations all speak to the uncertain times ahead.

At another level of analysis, the uncertain future can be reformulated as follows: With over nine million persons employed in the provision of health care (roughly one out of every fourteen workers) and with expenditures estimated by the Health Care Financing Administration (HCFA) to total $1 trillion by 1995, there is no way for hospitals, nursing homes, and physicians (which together account for roughly seven out of every ten dollars of health expenditures) to ignore the dictates of strict financial accounting. Such dictates stand athwart the tradition and credo of nonprofit institutions, which have historically recognized their obligation to provide service to those who cannot afford to pay. However, the number of philanthropic dollars needed at present to cover a significant volume of uncompensated care is simply too large to be forthcoming, especially with the narrowing niche for cross-subsidization. A rough calculation suggests that philanthropic dollars for health care in the 1990s may come to no more than 1 percent of total operating costs and 5 percent of capital expenditures.[17]

The decades ahead require that the American people find a way of providing affordable basic care for the entire citizenry and at the same time rethink the potential and limitations of their earlier long-term reliance on philanthropy and nonprofit institutions to play lead roles in the restructuring of the nation's health care system. The recent dismal experience of the for-profit organizations, the long-term shortcomings of government-operated hospitals, and the growing pressures on nonprofit hospitals underscore that, important as the challenges to more effective cost containment are, an equal, if not greater, challenge will face nonprofit hospitals as they seek to optimize delivery of effective health care to their neighborhoods and communities.

There are many who believe that the introduction of national health insurance under federal or federal-state operation holds the answers to universal coverage, cost containment, and quality control. I doubt that it does; therefore, I make a plea that the dominant, nonprofit acute-care hospital system reassess its commitments and potential and remain actively involved in the large-scale and continuing restructuring of our health care system that will inevitably occur in the years and decades ahead.

Notes

1. U.S. Department of Commerce, Bureau of the Census, *Statistical Abstract of the United States 1990*, 110th ed. (Washington, D.C.: U.S. Government Printing Office, 1990).

2. T Odendahl, *Charity Begins at Home: Generosity and Self-Interest Among the Philanthropic Elite* (New York: Basic Books, 1990). More comprehensive and incisive explorations of the roles of philanthropy and profit status in the health care system are found in R Stevens, *In Sickness and in Wealth: American Hospitals in the Twentieth Century* (New York: Basic Books, 1989); BH Gray, ed., *The New Health Care for Profit* (Washington, D.C.: National Academy Press, 1983); and J Iglehart, *Private Foundations and Health Policy* (Millwood, Va.: Project HOPE, 1990).

3. A Flexner, *Medical Education in the United States and Canada* (New York: Carnegie Foundation for the Advancement of Teaching, 1910).

4. Committee on the Costs of Medical Care. Final Report. *Medical Care for the American People* (Chicago, Ill.: University of Chicago Press, 1932).

5. E Rayack, *Professional Power and American Medicine: The Economics of the American Medical Association* (Cleveland, Oh.: World, 1967).

6. E Ginzberg, *A Pattern for Hospital Care: Final Report of the New York State Hospital Study* (New York: Columbia University Press, 1949).

7. E Ginzberg, D Hiestand, and BG Reubens, *The Pluralistic Economy* (New York: McGraw-Hill, 1965).

8. H Klarman, *Hospital Care in New York City* (New York: Columbia University Press, 1963).

9. C Brecher, *Where Have All the Dollars Gone? Public Expenditures for Human Resource Development in New York City, 1961–1971* (New York: Praeger, 1974).

10. *Facts and Figures* (New York: Montefiore Hospital and Medical Center, 1966).

11. E Ginzberg, and P Rogatz, *Planning for Better Hospital Care* (New York: Kings Crown Press [Columbia University], 1961).

12. M Ostow, "Affiliation Contracts." In E Ginzberg, and Staff, *Urban Health Services: The Case of New York* (New York: Columbia University Press, 1971).

13. E Ginzberg, and Staff, *From Health Dollars to Health Services: New York City 1965–1985* (Totowa, N.J.: Rowman & Allanheld, 1986).

14. CR Minick, and B Haimowitz, "Nursing and the Public Good: A Conversation with Eleanor Lambertsen," *Cornell University Medical College Alumni Quarterly.* Double Issue: 50(4) and 51(1):53–62; and The Committee on the Function of Nursing. E Ginzberg, Chairman, *A Program for the Nursing Profession* (New York: Macmillan, 1949).

15. A Enthoven, "Memorandum for the Secretary of Health, Education, and Welfare, Joseph Califano, Jr.," 22 September 1977.

16. DA Stockman, "Premises for a Medical Marketplace: A Neoconservative's Vision of How to Transform the Health System," *Health Affairs* 1(1)(1981):5–18; and E Ginzberg, "Stockman's Medical Marketplace Reexamined," *Health Affairs* 1(2)(1982):118–20.

17. Office of National Cost Estimates. "National Health Expenditures, 1988," *Health Care Financing Review* 11(4):1–41.

10

High-Tech Medicine

Since the early 1970s the United States has pursued multiple strategies aimed at moderating the increases in its annual health care expenditures. In the search for causes and cures of health care inflation, high-tech medicine (HTM) is increasingly identified as the major culprit responsible for our steeply rising health care costs.

To illuminate the issue, this chapter offers an operational definition of the term HTM, examines the supporting arguments for the claim that HTM is the principal propellant of escalating health care cost and that it is often counterproductive, reviews the role of public policy in speeding the growth of HTM, and concludes with some forecasts about the probable impact of HTM on future U.S. health care costs.

High-tech medicine may be defined simply and comprehensively as the sum of all the advances in medical knowledge and technique that have been translated into improved diagnostic, therapeutic, and rehabilitative procedures during the past several decades. High tech is the driving force of contemporary medicine that is committed to continuing sophistication and change as a result of ongoing basic and clinical biomedical research and its application through new technology to the treatment of patients.

Since the end of World War II, and more dramatically in recent decades, HTM has become synonymous with American medicine as perceived by mainstream society, the profession, and the world at large. The dynamism of our system of HTM is fueled by four forces: large-scale public and private investments in biomedical research (approaching $30 billion annually); a sophisticated system of undergraduate, residency, and fellowship training that produces large numbers of specialists and subspecialists; the availability of public, voluntary, and private funding for the continuous modernization of hospitals and the employment of more sophisticated staff; and business enterprises and venture capitalists seeking to exploit advanced knowledge to develop new, improved products for the medical armamentarium.

Common Fallacies

HTM is not what the American people want or need. On its face, this often cited negative assessment of HTM seems to command considerable support. Many Americans complain about the difficulties of finding a competent generalist physician who will oversee their care and the care of their family, a physician who will be available and willing to talk with and counsel them. Those who speak for the elderly contend that the chief unmet need of their constituency is improved access to long-term care facilities and treatment rather than state-of-the-art short-term care. And all of us have been bombarded with evidence that the greatest positive influence on our future health is the adoption of a healthy life-style.

One need not minimize the desire of many Americans for access to physicians who will spend more time listening, explaining, and counseling, or question the contention that lack of long-term insurance coverage and ready access to nursing homes seriously compromises the well-being of the elderly, or challenge the proposition that if people ate better, exercised more, drank less, and stopped smoking they would live longer or at least enjoy better health. But none of the above, individually or cumulatively, substantiates the claim that most Americans do not want more and better HTM. They want all of the above plus HTM.

HTM is responsible for the severe cost escalation of our medical care system. The hospital has been and continues to be the center of HTM, and hospital care constitutes the single largest component of our total health care outlays, approximately 40 percent. Physicians who treat patients in ambulatory care settings also rely on high-tech diagnostic and therapeutic procedures; their services account for another 20 percent. Drugs, appliances, and dental care, all increasingly high tech, account for 20 percent. If one adds the outlays for construction and research, both closely related to HTM, the total approaches 85 percent. Nursing home care is the only low-tech sector of importance and it accounts for roughly 8 percent.[1]

There are, however, two ways of interpreting these figures. It is commonly inferred that HTM has driven health spending from $280 billion in 1980 to approximately $840 billion in 1992.[2] An alternative and more cogent formulation, however, emphasizes that as long as the American people want access to more and better medical care, total expenditures will of necessity continue to climb. There is no low-tech, low-cost, medical care alternative available to them.

Our system of HTM is not only very costly but is also dysfunctional for many individuals and for society. In support of this contention, the critics of HTM note the number of comatose persons who are kept alive for years by virtue of life-prolonging medical devices and the many low-weight newborns of 600, 700, or 800 grams who are snatched from death and stabilized in sophisticated neonatal nurseries, many of whom, because of their birth defects, are unable to ever live normal lives.[3] The clinching argument for the critics of the dysfunctional nature of much HTM is the reminder that close to 30 percent of the nation's annual outlays for the hospitalization of Medicare patients is on behalf of those who will be dead within twelve months, the majority within six months.[4] With Medicare reimbursements in the $150 billion range, this criticism cannot be taken lightly, much less dismissed.

There are good reasons for the medical leadership and the public to engage in ongoing dialogue aimed at clarifying, if not codifying, the uses of HTM in the case of comatose patients or newborns with severe birth defects. But the basis for this concern has less to do with economics than with ethics. In the case of the very old, it is important to note that physicians who resort to aggressive measures can judge only retrospectively, not prospectively, the success or failure of their interventions. Many more Medicare beneficiaries who are hospitalized during a year are discharged, survive, and function than die within the succeeding twelve months. Among all short-stay hospital discharges, the ratio of decedents in their last year of life to survivors is roughly 1:4.[5]

There is an urgent need for our society to invest substantially larger sums in expanded technology assessment and outcome studies. The conventional wisdom holds that we do not know what we have bought for the $840 billion that we spent in 1992 for medical care. To make matters worse, many patients undergo diagnostic and therapeutic procedures of dubious benefit; some of the procedures are, in fact, harmful. Analysts remind us that there is an economic incentive for unscrupulous physicians to resort to unnecessary or questionable tests and therapies.

In the face of these serious charges, which can be substantiated, why would anyone object to investing more resources in assessments and evaluations? Clearly, the reduction of uncertainty should contribute to improved quality of care as well as to lower costs. Is there any doubt that an expanded evaluation effort would yield early and substantial benefits?

In the course of a year, Americans initiate about one billion ambulatory visits to physicians in a variety of settings—private offices, outpatient clinics, emergency departments, and ambulatory-care centers. The thirty-three million patients who are hospitalized for an average stay of some six and one-half days have another three hundred million encounters with admitting physicians, consultants, and house staff.[6] When one considers that each patient is unique and that no two have the same presenting symptoms, the inherent variability in selecting a therapeutic protocol and in assessing therapeutic outcomes is underscored.

Variability, moreover, is not limited to patients. The one-half million licensed physicians who treat patients span three distinct age cohorts: recent graduates, old timers, and those in-between.[7] They differ in their medical educations, their specialties, and the extent to which they have kept abreast of their disciplines; they practice in different areas and in different settings, all of which influences their medical decision making.

There is a further complication that stands athwart the evaluation effort. Medical innovation is a continuum, never a completed process. Since the new offers the promise of a better result, there is a need to balance the time required for data collection and definitive evaluation against the value of providing earlier access for patients who might benefit.

In light of the foregoing, more investment in technology assessment and outcome evaluation should contribute to improved quality of care, but it is not likely to retard the upward trend in health expenditures.

Propositions Counter to Common Fallacies

As counterpropositions to the common fallacies about HTM we offer the following:

- Americans want more, not less, HTM.
- High-tech medicine cannot be held responsible for rising health expenditures; there is no low-cost alternative.
- It is not true that much HTM is dysfunctional. What is true is that many elderly patients die within twelve months of hospitalization.
- More and better technology assessment and outcome studies could contribute to improving the quality of care, but it is unlikely that such studies will contain costs effectively.

How did HTM come to dominate U.S. health care? The American people have had a long infatuation with technology and innovation, and this predisposition, shared by patients, physicians, and hospitals alike, has imprinted our health care system. But there is more to the story, and much of it involves two principal actors: the federal government and the academic health centers.

In his 1945 report, *Science: The Endless Frontier*, Vannevar Bush, science adviser to President Franklin D. Roosevelt, recommended a much-enlarged role for the federal government in the support of science. He proposed an initial allocation of $5 million for biomedical research, rising in time to perhaps $25 million! The federal government, however, did more than expand its funding for biomedical research by many orders of magnitude. At the same time, it made large sums available to outlying communities for hospital construction, and in the 1960s it took the leadership in expanding the physician supply through direct financing for medical schools and medical students. Its success may be gauged by the rise in the number of active physicians from 140 per 100,000 population in 1960 to 240 per 100,000 today. A future supply ratio of 260 to 275 per 100,000 is likely. The federal government also provided, via

Medicare and Medicaid, much-expanded funding for care of the elderly and the poor, thereby supplying the dollars required for hospitals to modernize and upgrade their facilities and capacities.

One result of the vastly expanded flow of federal funds into the health care system was the increased sophistication of the modern academic health center, which set the United States on an accelerated course of high-tech development by providing ample resources for biomedical research. The leading centers of medical education shifted their focal interest many degrees from the instruction of undergraduate medical students to biomedical research.

Without much deliberation and even less conscious design, the medical education mission was transformed from a typical program of four years of undergraduate study followed by one year of internship to a minimum sequence of seven years of school and clinical training to qualify for initial certification and two to five years of additional preparation for specialization and subspecialization. No one who has observed this radical transformation will doubt that the research orientation of the leading medical schools and the approximate doubling of the time required by many specialists to become eligible for board certification has played a direct, possibly determining, role in transforming U.S. medical care into HTM.[8]

In summary, our contemporary, high-tech health care system is a consequence of over three decades of liberal federal financing for research and for services to the elderly, with the academic health center setting the pace and with the much-expanded physician supply, heavily weighted with specialists, carrying the miracles of modern medicine throughout the land, from urban centers to outlying areas.

Unless the public undertakes an unprecedented reversal in favor of reducing the resources currently available for biomedical research and opts to ration expensive medical procedures, it is inevitable that HTM will continue to dominate the health care system. Opponents of this trend must present cogent evidence to justify a severe curtailment of national funding for biomedical research and identify health care alternatives that promise Americans returns at least equal to, if not greater than, those they now derive from the advances of HTM. Failing such evidence, the only reasonable conclusion is that HTM will dominate the future as it has the recent past.

Some Cautious Projections

A look backward over the last few decades provides some guidance as to the probable course of events in the years ahead. The following are a few cautious projections:

- High-tech medicine is normative medicine in the United States, and it is evident from both utilization trends and opinion polls that the

American people favor it. Accordingly, health care costs, in all probability, will continue to increase.

- Cost-control measures, ranging from utilization reviews to managed care, have failed to slow in any significant way the rise in health care expenditures. The current enthusiasm for outcome assessments to gauge effectiveness and appropriateness of treatment may improve the quality of medical care but holds little prospect of slowing expenditures: The costs of expanding desirable services that are found to be underutilized are likely to exceed the savings from the elimination of unnecessary procedures. In 1988 the National Leadership Commission on Health Care, a body that represents heterogeneous segments of the American polity, recommended that we spend $500 million annually on health services research. Arguably, such an investment would yield useful information for clinical practice, but the commission's projection of a *savings* of $84 billion between 1990 and 1993 was unrealistic.[9]

- The steadily increasing numbers of elderly, especially those older than eighty-five years-of-age, will fuel the increase in costs, since the growth of this cohort implies disproportionate expansion in the utilization of health care services. Unless convinced by the argument that expensive, high-tech medical procedures should be rationed by age, a proposal that is unlikely to be acceptable to the American public, the nation must make its peace with continuously rising health care expenditures.

- The public is concerned with the fact that thirty-five million Americans are uninsured and that the Medicaid program fails to cover more than half of the poor for whom it was designed. On one hand, sooner or later we will take actions to broaden Medicaid coverage, and the poor and uninsured will be provided access to hitherto unobtained HTM. Inevitably, total health care costs will increase further.

- On the other hand, the public and congressional backlash over the catastrophic amendments to Medicare should serve as a warning against hasty efforts to transform unmet expectations into new commitments. Improving access for the poor and the uninsured will be a sufficient undertaking without adopting in the near future new commitments for long-term care and other costly programs.

There is nothing inherently bad about the expenditure of $840 billion on health care services by a $5 trillion economy. Nor is there any reason that a $6 to $7 trillion economy should not spend $1 trillion or more for its health care. The nub of the issue is whether the U.S. economy will grow in the decades ahead at an average rate of 1.5 percent per annum or a rate of 3 percent. At 1.5

percent, increasing health care costs could preempt most of the increment in GNP; at a 3 percent growth rate, which translates into an annual addition of $150 billion, the nation will be able to cover a rising health care bill and still have considerable remaining for other socially desirable uses such as increased expenditures for education, housing, and infrastructure. High-tech medicine is not the villain and its restraint is not a preferred strategy; slow economic growth is the challenge to meet and overcome.

Notes

1. SW Letsch, KR Levit, and DR Waldo, "National Health Expenditures, 1987," *Health Care Financing Review* 10(1989):109–22.

2. Office of National Cost Estimates, Office of the Actuary, Health Care Financing Administration. Washington, D.C. Unpublished.

3. JA Barondess, P Kalb, WW Weil, C Cassel, and E Ginzberg, "Clinical Decision Making in Catastrophic Situations: The Relevance of Age," *Journal of the American Geriatrics Society* 36(1988):919–37.

4. J Lubitz, and R Prihoda, "The Use and Costs of Medicare Services in the Last Two Years of Life," *Health Care Financing Review* 5(1984):117–31.

5. Ibid.

6. *Source Book of Health Insurance Data 1989* (Washington, D.C.: Health Insurance Association of America, 1989).

7. Department of Medical Data Services, Division of Survey and Data Resources, *Physician Characteristics and Distribution in the United States* (Chicago, Ill.: American Medical Association, 1989).

8. RH Ebert, and E Ginzberg, "The Reform of Medical Education," *Health Affairs* 7(1988):5–38.

9. *Report of the National Leadership Commission on Health Care: For the Health of a Nation* (Washington, D.C.: National Leadership Commission on Health Care, 1989).

11

Competition and Health Reform

Most Americans look to the market and competition to keep their economy functioning effectively. Small wonder, therefore, that in the late 1960s and early 1970s many academicians, as well as Wall Street operators, saw the rise of for-profit hospital chains as the harbinger of a more efficient and effective health care system. At long last, with experienced business people at the helm, new for-profit hospital chains would soon enjoy economies of scale and other efficiencies that would result in better care at lower prices. But the record belied these anticipations. The four largest for-profit hospital companies survived only after cannibalizing themselves, and the anticipated benefits from these for-profit chains remained unfulfilled.

About a decade later another version of the same optimistic expectations of what large-scale business enterprise and competition would be able to contribute to rationalizing the health care industry was encapsulated in a forecast by a sophisticated health care analyst: He claimed that within a few years most health care in the United States would be controlled and delivered by a small number of "medicorps," some ten to twenty national or regional companies. But this projection never became a reality and today is not even a memory.

When the first Reagan administration was about to take office, the director-designate of the Office of Management and Budget, David Stockman, wrote a piece in *Health Affairs*[1] in which he explained that the serious problems facing contemporary American medicine resulted from the nation having turned its back on competition to allocate resources flowing into the health care sector. In my reply,[2] I suggested that Stockman had created a historical record out of whole cloth since competition had never dominated the U.S. health care sector.

A reasonable explanation for these faulty expectations and false conclusions is that most Americans believe that the competitive marketplace assures the best results in terms of resource use and lower prices for the consumer. In fact, along with their deep-seated suspicion of government and bureaucracy, Americans have no model other than competition that they know or trust to guide the production and distribution of the goods and services that they need and want.

Alternative Models

Why, then, is competition an inappropriate model for assessing the U.S. health care system and what other models are more appropriate to the task? To address the second question first: As suggested above, the public's skepticism about governmental efficiency in producing goods and services leaves them with no alternative models ready at hand. True, the United States has a third sector—the nonprofit sector—that plays a dominant role in the provision of hospital care, which accounts for the single largest segment of health care expenditures—approximately 40 percent. In 1992 hospital expenditures came to about one-third-trillion dollars. But in recent decades, nonprofit hospitals have been forced to pay ever-closer attention to their financial viability, with a corresponding decline in their earlier concerns with providing services to the community, especially to low-income groups.

The limitations of the competitive model for understanding the evolution of the U.S. health care system since World War II is suggested by the major investments of the federal government: the Hill-Burton Act of 1946, which made substantial federal funds available for hospital construction, and large-scale and continuing appropriations for biomedical R & D, which today exceed over $12 billion annually. By the mid-1960s the federal government had started to play a significant role in further hospital construction and upgrading through various tax and financing aids to hospitals floating tax-exempt bonds.

Further, the federal government, with assistance from the states, also took the lead in doubling the number of medical school graduates after 1963; and in 1965 it passed Medicare and Medicaid, which provided broad access for the elderly and for persons on AFDC and Supplemental Security Income (SSI) to acute-care services via a federal-state system of joint financing.

The federal government also played a key role, starting in the World War II era, in stimulating the rapid growth of private health insurance by providing the subsidies to both employers and employees, which amount to $70 billion currently. Since most employed persons and their dependents are covered by private health insurance and since the elderly and many of the poor are covered by government entitlement programs, the demand for health care services is not constrained by the disposable income available to consumers. Moreover, it is not constrained by annual appropriations of the federal and state legislatures as are most "merit" goods such as education, highways, environmental protection, and defense.

It is only a slight overstatement of the facts to claim that from the mid-1960s, with the passage of Medicare and Medicaid, to the present the conventional links that exist in all advanced societies between the availability of funds and the demand for goods and services were severed in the U.S. health care sector and have not yet been reknit, despite ongoing efforts by the principal payers—government and employers.

Completing the list of institutional factors that have contributed to the greatly diminished role of competition in the operation of the U.S. health care system are the leading academic health centers, the recipients of continuing large federal research grants, which enabled them to expand specialization and subspecialization in the training of physicians to the point where generalists today account for only one out of every five new entrants into the medical profession, a ratio viewed by most informed persons as grossly inadequate on both professional and economic grounds.

The confusion about the role of competition in U.S. health care has been compounded by evidence that competition still remains an important—if not the dominant—force in many sectors of the health care market. Consider, for instance, the effectiveness with which the commercial insurance companies, by offering employers underwriting based on their firm's experience, were able to undermine the community-rating system that the nonprofit Blue Cross movement had earlier introduced.

Consider further the slow but nonetheless substantial growth of alternative health care financing and delivery systems (in comparison with fee-for-service medicine) in which staff and group HMOs, PPOs, POS arrangements, and many other variants have enrolled over forty million persons. A related development has been the initiative shown by various entrepreneurial physician groups in developing ambulatory surgical centers that later proliferated into a variety of diagnostic and treatment centers in competition with local acute-care hospitals.

Let us consider the intensive and continuing competition in most large and many smaller metropolitan areas among the leading hospitals seeking to establish and maintain their positions by attracting superior professional staff and offering a wide range of sophisticated services, rather than resorting to price competition. The price of services is, after all, a matter of little or no moment for the predominant number of patients who have good insurance coverage.

Competition has also existed in varying degrees among different groups of health professionals: between physician and nurse anesthetists, psychiatrists and other groups of psychotherapists, registered nurses with differing levels of educational preparation, and between registered nurses and physician assistants and practical nurses.

Competition has also been keen among the pharmaceutical and medical supply companies in developing and marketing their new products. With large investments required to finance the development process, they compete intensively in the marketplace to attract and retain the support of physicians, hospitals, and the public.

Contradictions

Even if we stop at this point, the unequivocal conclusion is that competition is alive and thriving in many sectors of health care financing and delivery. It is important, however, to explore various contradictions embedded in the preceding analysis. We argued at the outset that because of the prominent, if not dominant, role of the government in the financing of health care and the further fact that most Americans have good health insurance coverage that makes them largely insensitive and indifferent to the prices charged by physicians, hospitals, and to some extent even by pharmaceutical companies, competition is not the dominant force that regulates the health care marketplace. In fact, the contrary formulation would be closer to reality. The medical marketplace is dominated by the availability of funding from the two principal payers—government and employers—that enables providers to offer and patients to obtain the full array of costly high-tech treatments.

The limitations of competition in guiding the development of the health care system can be further illuminated by a brief consideration of some related factors. Even if American society is still equivocal about whether health care is a right or not, it has long since acted on the premise that persons who are injured or who are suffering from an emergency condition such as a heart attack must have access to health care, irrespective of whether they have health insurance or can afford to pay for their care. If they have a slightly above-average length of hospital stay and require more intensive treatment, their bill for a single hospitalization can easily amount to between $25,000 and $50,000. One need only consider this one example to appreciate the extent to which the American people have differentiated between the demand for health care and the demand for other scarce goods and services. There is no comparable situation where our society steps in to assure that persons of low income will be able to receive such high-cost services on the public's account.

Important as this open-ended funding arrangement is, there are a number of other distinctive accommodations that warrant at least brief consideration, all of which underscore the limitations of using the competitive model in assessing how the U.S. health care system operates. We must remember that by state law only licensed physicians have the right to diagnose and treat patients: The health care that 260 million Americans receive or fail to receive rests in the first instance on the actions and reactions of the 500,000 physicians in active practice. Since on the whole patients have access only to physicians who practice in their localities, an unwillingness on the part of physicians to locate in rural or inner-city neighborhoods precludes residents of these areas from

receiving adequate health care. This much is clear: The 80 percent increase in
the ratio of physicians to population during the past three decades has not resulted in an effective redistribution of the physician supply. The size of the
population in underserved areas is declining, but the total is still substantial. It
is highly improbable that competition will ever match up the physician supply
and the demand of these groups for improved access to care.

The "maldistribution" of physicians has its parallel in the location of hospitals. One by-product of the free flow of funds into the health care sector in recent decades was the large number of unsophisticated hospitals, which previously had provided only primary or secondary care, that transformed
themselves into tertiary-care institutions by attracting specialist staff and acquiring the accoutrements of high-tech medicine, both diagnostic and therapeutic. The consequence of this development was the creation of substantial
excess hospital capacity, leading to occupancy rates below 65 percent, as well
as rampant duplication of many high-cost services, including open-heart surgery and organ transplantations. Instead of contributing to keeping and re-
storing a balance between consumer needs and demands and productive capacity, competition has played a major role in creating and maintaining our
overexpanded hospital system.

If competition is unable to balance demand and supply in the health care
sector, how can the growing enthusiasm and support for "managed competition" that is supposed to right all that is currently askew in terms of costs, coverage, administrative overhead, and quality be explained?

The answers have to do with the failure of the enthusiasts to distinguish between reliance on a competitive approach to regulate the *entire* health sector
and the recognition that competition has survived and prospered in discrete
sectors of the market by contributing to wasteful investments and increased
expenditures, rather than by the more efficient use of total resources and the
control of prices. The second explanation derives from the earlier theorem
that since Americans have no alternative for competition, they maintain it as
the only trustworthy regulatory principle. It should come as no surprise that
the protagonists of managed competition are academic economists who know
no other truth; large health insurance companies whose underwriting policies
reflect risk management strategies that enable them to make money by not
writing or renewing policies for those most in need of coverage; and employers who after twenty years or more of frustrating experiences and excessive pa-
perwork are willing to try anything except an expanded role for the federal
government.

The directions U.S. health reform must take are clear: First, a system of
global budgeting must be established if financial turmoil and chaos with a
threat of annual health care expenditures of $2 trillion by the year 2000, less
than eight years distant, is to be avoided. Next, insurance coverage for essential care must be provided to all Americans, with special incentives put in place

to attract and retain an adequate supply of competent physicians in areas currently without them.

We urgently need more planning, not more competition, to moderate and reduce our "upstream" investments involving the physician supply, hospital capacity, and the rate and diffusion of new technological innovations. In a period of cost containment, the investment frontier needs early and continuing attention.

Finally, though managed competition is not the answer to health care reform, new arrangements must be developed for group practice, with the maximum use of midlevel personnel as well as incentives for paying physicians. Fee-for-service should be phased out, and physicians should take the lead in practicing good but cost-conscious medicine.

In sum, competition, in the sense used by economists, has never been the dominant strategy shaping the U.S. health care system. Philanthropy and, more recently, government have played important roles, abetted by private health insurance. The current crisis reflects the absence of an effective substitute for competition, which in the health care field has turned out to be an inappropriate model. The conception that "managed competition" can usher in a period of major reform is not realistic. More viable prescriptions are global budgeting, universal coverage, controls over new investments, and modifications in how physicians practice and are reimbursed. Though these and other reforms will not be easily or readily realized, valuable time and effort can be saved if we are not deflected by pursuing "managed competition," a promise of reform that cannot be broadly introduced, much less succeed.

Notes

1. DA Stockman, "Premise for a Medical Marketplace: A Neo-Conservative Vision of How to Transform the Health System," *Health Affairs* 1(1)(Winter 1981):5–18.

2. E Ginzberg, "Stockman's Medical Marketplace Reexamined," *Health Affairs* 1(2)(Spring 1982):118–20.

12

Hospitals, Doctors, and Global Budgets

"Global budgeting" is conventional shorthand for a national system to limit the funds flowing into the health care sector. In most of the approaches that have been proposed for the United States, this would be done by limiting annual increases in spending to a rate approximately equal to the growth of the gross domestic product, not a rate two or three times greater—as has been the case during the past two decades.

No matter what shape global budgeting might take, it is bound to profoundly affect hospitals, physicians, and their interrelationships. What's more, global budgeting—already well established in countries such as Canada and Great Britain—has strong support in the United States. During and after the presidential campaign of 1992, Bill Clinton emphasized the importance of global budgeting because of his conviction that without a slowed flow of resources into health care, it would be impossible to reduce the federal deficit, now or in the future. Global budgeting thus promises to reduce the resources flowing into health care, thereby helping to reduce the federal deficit and to invigorate the rest of the U.S. economy.

What else can we learn from and about the champions of global budgeting? Most of them favor the establishment of an independent board of distinguished citizens to advise Congress about the annual size of the health care budget. They also anticipate that the four principal payers—the federal government, employers and private health insurers, state governments, and households—will continue to pay their current shares into the national health-care pool, shares that have been surprisingly unchanged over the last decade or so. Furthermore, most advocates of global budgeting believe that the federal government will have to begin transferring most of its share of the funds to the states for further redistribution to the principal health care providers in their jurisdictions—in particular, hospitals, physicians, and nursing homes.

The Challenges of Global Budgeting

A troubling question bears on the limits of global budgeting. Do the proponents mean literally "all" sources of funds that will be expended for health care during the course of a year, or do they see "global" budgeting as covering all governmental funds plus all private (including employment-based) health insurance funds that benefit from a tax subsidy? Reworded, the question can be put thus: Do the proponents of global budgeting contemplate putting barriers in the path of wealthy individuals and families who, for good or bad reasons, want to spend their own money on additional health care services?

Several observations are in order: First, the National Health Service (NHS) in the United Kingdom has never interdicted Britons from spending their own money in the nongovernmental sector. In fact, one out of almost every three Britons who needs elective surgery currently goes outside the NHS. In France, the government passed legislation many years ago prohibiting the public from buying supplementary health insurance, but, in the face of voter hostility, the prohibition was speedily rescinded. It is impossible to conceive that the U.S. Congress or the courts would uphold a policy that would prohibit individuals from spending their own money for services that exceed the level of services provided the public at large.

A more critical and complex challenge that the advocates of global budgeting will have to face relates to the suballocation of the total funds, first to the states and then to sectors within the states, for further distribution to hospitals, nursing homes, and physicians. Though the federal government has had long experience in distributing congressional appropriations among the states and experience in providing federal funds directly to local and regional agencies within the states as well as to eligible individuals, it has had no experience as a collector and distributor of funds from multiple sources.

An even more critical challenge to the operation of a global-budgeting system in the United States comes from below the federal level. Success would depend on the effectiveness of mechanisms that the states put into place to reimburse providers of services and how well both the payers and the providers stayed within their respective budgetary constraints.

What happens if, in late November, all the funds available under the year's global budget have been spent and patients require treatment at their physicians' offices or their local hospitals? Clearly, they would be treated, and the fiscal adjustments would come later. Sometimes state governments would find the necessary funds in other parts of their budgets. More often, they would make providers "eat the deficit" in next year's appropriation. That is what we do *overtly* in reimbursing physicians under Medicare's resource-based relative value scale (RBRVS) and what we do *covertly* when Washington and the states reduce the amounts of money they pay out for Medicare and Medicaid when expenditures exceed their budgeted outlays.

The states, which have been the dominant payer for nursing-home care (via Medicaid) since the mid-1970s, have had considerable experience in operating a global-budgeting system. Some of the states, such as New York, have instituted more sophisticated systems for reimbursing nursing-home providers that reflect rates adjusted to the severity of the illness of patients who are admitted. A number of states also have had some experience in using a global-budgeting approach to reimburse hospitals. Although Maryland is the only state that currently controls all payments to hospitals, a number of others, including New York, New Jersey, and Washington, have had experience with a single-payer system for hospital care.

We see, then, that the United States would not be starting from scratch in introducing a system of global budgeting that requires states to reimburse hospitals according to an annual budget. This is not to say that the states would find it easy to take account of sudden shifts in the local demand for hospital services or to respond sensibly and expeditiously to various exigencies. But they have a body of experience on which they could draw. Moreover, even the largest states would be dealing with only about three hundred acute-care hospitals, a manageable number.

A more serious challenge to global budgeting by the states is presented by the need to reimburse the more than 500,000 physicians in active practice who handle about 1.3 billion patient visits per year—physicians whose current earnings vary by more than two- or three-fold from one doctor to another, depending on specialty and, to a lesser degree, on location. But once again, instituting global budgeting would not start from scratch. With the RBRVS in 1992, Medicare initiated actions to increase the relative earnings of primary-care physicians at the expense of proceduralists and to reimburse physicians just entering practice at a lower rate than their established colleagues.

Though the RBRVS sheds some light on global budgeting, there are important differences: Currently, physicians have the option to treat or not treat Medicare patients. Also under the current system, physicians have much more freedom than they would have under global budgeting to set and achieve personal income targets.

The proponents of global budgeting have never claimed that this system would be easy to introduce and implement. Rather, they have emphasized that unless the nation adopts global budgeting in the near future, our health care financing and delivery system will be derailed as it crosses the trillion-dollar mark in 1994–1995 and continues to hurtle toward a $2 trillion outlay by decade's end.

It would be an error for the proponents of global budgeting to gloss over the complicated policies and administrative rules and regulations that would have to be designed and implemented to make global budgeting operational. It would also be a mistake to gloss over the distortions that are likely to accompany the implementation of global budgeting, including critical issues such as slowing the diffusion of advances in diagnosis and therapy and in organizational and managerial innovations by its bias in favor of the maintenance of the status quo. In addition, at least initially, there would be substantial costs involved in creating new infrastructures for the planning, decision making, execution, and accountability that would be required if global budgeting is to work.

Managed Competition

The question that needs to be confronted next is: If not global budgeting, what? The current, financially uncontrolled system has only a limited number of years before it collapses. Some argue that, even with chaos on the horizon, global budgeting is the wrong way to go, since price-fixing never works. The opponents of global budgeting propose as an alternative one or another version of managed competition, on the assumption that the competitive market will be able to assure the effective allocation of resources and control prices.

These analysts miss the critical lesson that they should have learned over the past several decades: The competitive market is not an appropriate model for health care. A health care system must protect the citizens against large out-of-pocket expenditures and provide every citizen with ready access to essential services. The competitive market is incapable of meeting either test, much less both, at a cost that the United States can meet.

There is nothing inherently good or desirable about global budgeting. But contemplating the chaos that looms ahead, the question that the body politic faces and the one that it must answer sooner, rather than later, is whether it has any realistic option other than to push ahead with global budgeting to control total costs. Once the nation has introduced global budgeting, and not until then, will politicians, physicians, hospitals, and the public be able to address the second challenge: How to improve the efficiency and the effectiveness of the resources that are directed to health care and at the same time assure reasonable equity in the distribution of services. This second question must be put on hold until fiscal discipline is in place, and for that we need global budgeting.

PART THREE

The Poor and the Uninsured

13

Financing Health Care for the Poor: Second-Best Solutions

Since I prefer not to load this chapter with a large volume of data but rather to focus on conceptual clarifications and policy alternatives, I shall start by setting forth my basic preconceptions:

- Lack of money (insurance) prevents sizable numbers of poor persons from seeking health care services.
- This monetary or insurance barrier means that many untreated conditions worsen progressively. As a result, when the patient can no longer avoid seeking treatment, the costs are higher than they would have been had treatment been sought earlier.
- In most instances, health care involves a relationship between a physician, or other health professional, and the patient. Since most physicians are self-employed, they prefer to practice in locations where there is a sufficiently large concentration of middle- or upper-income families to assure that they can earn a reasonable livelihood under conditions to their liking. Hence, most physicians avoid practicing in areas with large concentrations of poor people.
- In an effort to economize in their use of public funds, many states have set Medicaid reimbursement rates for physicians who treat the poor at such low levels that many practitioners are reluctant to or refuse to treat them.
- A number of states have also placed limitations on the duration and types of hospital or ambulatory care for which they will reimburse for Medicaid patients.
- Poor people, by virtue of their inadequate incomes, often pursue life-styles that are dysfunctional for their health, and, as a result, require lengthier and more intensive treatment than the more affluent members of the community.

- Since poverty is frequent among racial or ethnic minorities, these poor are doubly handicapped. Racism and cultural and language barriers exacerbate the difficulties of many blacks and Hispanics in obtaining access to the health care system. The problem is aggravated for minorities who live in rural areas that lack an adequate health care infrastructure.
- Though I acknowledged earlier that lack of financing blocks the access of millions of poor people to the health care system when they need it, by far the major deprivation that the poor suffer is the inferior quality of the care to which they do have access.

My subtitle, "second-best solutions," requires explanation: Why second-best rather than best solutions? Let me state the basic premises for my choice of this limited objective.

- Our nation is strongly committed to a relatively weak system of government and, accordingly, is averse to expanding the responsibilities of the federal and the state governments for providing broadly needed and desired social goods or services. I see no early change in this basic orientation.
- The distribution of income in the United States is becoming more, not less, skewed. Accordingly, it is even less likely that our society will make any substantial progress in the near- to middle-term toward providing the poor with access to medical care equal in quality to that received by the well-insured population.
- Regional and subregional differences in the standard of living and in public and philanthropic infrastructures are so great that it is difficult for the federal government to legislate a single level of benefits for all beneficiaries. The best that one can hope for is that the federal government will establish a minimum standard that the more affluent states are free to (and will) exceed.
- The medical profession and the acute-care hospitals, which are greatly influenced by the medical profession, are in a unique position to determine the structuring and restructuring of health care services: how they are delivered, to whom, and under what conditions. It is wiser to elicit the cooperation of the medical profession in the processes of change than to assume that its members can be coerced into going along.
- The increasing restiveness of public and private payers for health care, with the unremitting rise in their outlays, suggests that their ability to provide more liberally for the poor or underserved is limited.

Given these realities, I believe that it is the better part of wisdom to search for second-best solutions. It will be hard enough for the United States to achieve these realities, let alone to pursue optimal solutions that appear, surely for the time being, to be beyond realization.

Current Financing

The single most important observation to be made about current financing arrangements that facilitate the access of the poor to the health care system is to emphasize the variety of mechanisms that are used to accomplish this purpose. I will call attention seriatim to the most important of these, with some reflections about their scale, scope, and importance:

Medicaid

Ever since Arizona joined the Medicaid system under a special waiver about a decade ago, all fifty states have in place a mechanism mandating that all persons enrolled in Aid to Families with Dependent Children programs must be covered for a specified number of health care services, as stipulated by federal legislation. The costs of Medicaid are shared by the federal government and state governments on a sliding scale; the states with the lowest per capita income receive up to 78 percent, the maximum federal contribution, a rate that dips to 50 percent for those at the top of the income distribution.[1]

Further, the Medicaid legislation gives considerable discretion to the states in providing coverage for persons with incomes above the poverty cutoff point (to 130 percent); for certain categories of services, eligibility may extend as high as 185 percent. In addition, the states may offer more than the stipulated services. With respect to both the number of persons and the services covered, the states enjoy considerable discretion, and the federal government has assumed what must be defined as a liberal system of expenditure sharing.

There would be no need to look closely at Medicaid if it were in fact doing what its enthusiastic sponsors initially expected it to do—namely, to provide the financing that would enable the poor and the near-poor to gain entrance into the mainline health care system and thereby bring about a single level of care for the entire population. Even in its heyday—the early to mid-1970s—Medicaid fell far short of accomplishing this goal. At that time, a few states covered from 85 to 95 percent of families in poverty, but the national average was closer to three-quarters, with a considerable number of jurisdictions covering as few as one-third or even fewer.[2]

The Reagan administration's cutbacks in 1981 and the delegation of greater authority to the states to restructure their Medicaid programs resulted in a substantial reduction in the number of individuals covered under Medicaid. Today, the number of persons in poverty who benefit is estimated to be in the range of 50 percent nationwide, a severe decline from the peak of 75 percent a decade and a half ago. In the last few years, Congress has taken a few steps, some obligatory, others optional, to expand prevailing coverage and benefits for pregnant women, mothers, and young children. However, the fact must be emphasized that almost a quarter-century after the passage of Medicaid, fewer than half of all the people who live in poverty are enrolled in the program.[3] Let us assess the other principal mechanisms that are available to help the poor gain access to the health care system.

Ambulatory-Care Programs

There are a large number and variety of publicly financed general and categorical health care programs, including community health centers, well-baby clinics, and mental health services, to which the poor and the near-poor have access free-of-charge or with only a token fee. In total, these publicly funded programs provide considerable access for poor people to needed health care services. However, the same forces that led to cutbacks in Medicaid coverage in the first half of the 1980s also curtailed the funding available for publicly financed ambulatory-care programs. The planned expansion of community health centers with large-scale federal underwriting was aborted in midstream, and the early 1980s saw substantial retrenchment by all three levels of government—federal, state, and local—in financing for general and specialized clinics and programs.

Federal Programs for Military Personnel, Dependents, and Veterans

It is not widely known that the single largest health care system in the United States is that operated by the Veterans Administration for selected groups of veterans—those with service-connected disabilities and others eligible by virtue of low income. Most of the millions of veterans who utilize the ambulatory, inpatient, or extended-care facilities of the VA in the course of a year fall below the income ceiling established by the federal government, a standard that is above the poverty level, but not far above.[4] Restated, the VA provides a wide array of health care services to poor and near-poor veterans.

The armed services have long had a tradition of providing medical care not only for servicemen on active duty but also for their dependents and for retired military personnel, to the extent that their resources permit. During the last decades the Civilian Health and Medical Program of the Uniformed Services (CHAMPUS) has provided financing for large numbers of dependents of military personnel who must be cared for in civilian facilities because of the lack of accommodations for them in many military hospitals and clinics.

The CHAMPUS program operates at an annual level of around $3.6 billion (fiscal year 1992), and it is reasonable to infer that a significant proportion of this expenditure goes for dependents of military personnel who fall within the category of poor or near-poor.

State, County, and Municipal Hospitals

A statistic often overlooked is that about one-fifth of all short-term general and special hospital beds—that account for somewhat less than one-fifth of all expenditures for inpatient acute care in the United States—are found in state and local public hospitals.[5] Admittedly, states and localities differ greatly in the extent of their public hospital commitments. New York City, for instance, has long maintained an elaborate municipal hospital system that includes no fewer than eleven general hospitals. In Chicago/Cook County, the nation's second-largest urban center, there is only a single county hospital, with a constantly diminishing number of active beds due to the deterioration of its physical plant and equipment.

The extent to which the poor, particularly those not covered by Medicaid, have access to the health care system depends in no small measure on whether they live within reasonable distance of a public hospital. One of the many disabilities suffered by the rural poor is the absence of a nearby public hospital. It does not follow, of course, that poor people who have access to a public hospital have the benefit of an acceptable level of care. Women are discharged from the Los Angeles County Hospital eight to twelve hours post-delivery, so great is the demand for beds.[6] In Cook County Hospital, patients are often held for two to three days in a general receiving ward until a bed can be found for them on the particular service where they are to be treated.[7] Notwithstanding these important quality considerations, the fact remains that access of the poor to the health care system is contingent upon their proximity to a public hospital, not only for inpatient but also for ambulatory care.

Medicare

The Medicare reforms of 1965 have accomplished in very considerable measure what they were intended to do—to enable the elderly to be treated in acute-care hospitals with the Social Security system covering most of the costs of their care. Since most of the elderly have also availed themselves of Medicare B coverage (or are covered by Medicaid), which provides insurance against physician fees in or out of the hospital, only about one percent of all noninstitutionalized persons over the age of sixty-five are without any form of coverage.[8]

This favorable appraisal must, however, be put in context. The elderly still need a variety of health care services, from drugs to eyeglasses to extended nursing-home care, that have not been covered thus far and that would not have been covered even if the provisions for catastrophic care that were enacted in 1988 had not been rescinded. Perhaps the most serious indictment of Medicare is that, in 1989, the elderly paid out-of-pocket a higher percentage of their income for health care than they did in 1965, before passage.[9] But this negative assessment must be balanced by an undisputable positive observation: The elderly today have access to a far greater number and a higher quality of health care services than they had before the passage of Medicare.

Cross-Subsidization, Bad Debts, and Charity

Until the outbreak of World War II, most poor people gained access to the health care system—to the extent that they did—through the willingness of physicians and nonprofit hospitals to treat them at reduced prices or free-of-charge, something the providers were able and willing to do by extracting a little extra in payment from middle-income and wealthy patients. Many nonprofit hospitals could also rely on philanthropic gifts of money or unrequited labor to help balance their books, which were frequently in deficit as a result of providing care to those unable to pay. The expansion of private insurance, the rapidly growing demand for physician services, and the steep rise in per diem hospital expenditures during the post–World War II era substantially undermined this system of caring for the poor through cross-subsidization. It would be a mistake, however, to assume that charity or "charity and bad debts," as hospital accountants designate the residual item, has disappeared. Not at all. On average, charity accounts for something like $15 billion a year out of a total hospital expenditure of about $250 billion.[10] There are no reliable data about the free or less-than-full-charge services provided by physicians, but it would be hard to believe that they would amount to less than 5 percent of billings; this would represent another $6 billion of contributed care.

In summary, the major facts of current financing for health care for the poor are these:

- Medicaid is the only national mechanism in place, but it falls far short of providing access for all of the poor because many states have not put up the matching monies required to obtain their full federal allowance. Further, the severe limits imposed by many states on reimbursements for providers, both physicians and hospitals, have caused additional difficulties for the poor in obtaining care, and more particularly, adequate care.

- There are other sources of financing—federal, state, local, and philanthropic—that enable different groups of the poor to gain access to inpatient or ambulatory care. However, many public hospitals are seriously overcrowded and underfunded, and this leads to an inadequate quality of care for a considerable number of the poor.
- Because of their freedom of choice with respect to location and type of practice, physicians avoid practicing among concentrations of the poor or in isolated communities. This explains the existence of large numbers of underserved populations. The phenomenon is exacerbated by racial prejudice and ethnic differences (language and culture), which compound the problem of access for poor Hispanics and blacks.

Proposed Financing for Health Care

A few introductory remarks are needed to set the parameters for a discussion of proposed financing. Some policy analysts believe that our health care system has currently enough money to provide access to an acceptable level of care for all. They argue that the system operates with considerable waste—the estimates run as high as 25 percent[11]—that needs only be reprogrammed to cover all of the poor and the underserved. The reprogramming approach can be seriously entertained only on the condition that its protagonists explain how the sources of waste can be identified, the waste eliminated, and the "saved" money redirected to cover the costs involved in expanding access of the poor and underserved. Since they have not faced up to this challenge and, in my view, will never be able to do so, we can safely put the reprogramming approach to one side.

It follows that any serious proposals for improving access will involve new money, even though there may be disagreement about the amount required. But the need for new money must be tempered with the realities of political and economic life in the United States. Congress is disinclined to take any new action on the health care front that is not "budget neutral." This term means that whatever the additional costs, they will not fall on the federal treasury but will be carried by others—employers, the states, taxpayers, beneficiaries—but *not* the federal government.

Without making the case in extenso, one can add that most of the states also find themselves in a severe budgetary bind, and since by law they are not permitted to operate with unbalanced budgets, they too are cautious about buying into new legislation that will raise their expenditures unless they see a way of imposing new taxes on the electorate.

As for employers, they are increasingly and understandably restive, with the unremitting double-digit increases in the costs of their health care benefits and with the fact that no relief is in sight. The strike by the Communications

Workers of America (CWA) against the "Baby Bell" companies is a potent reminder of the determination of management, even in profitable utilities, to find some protection from their open-ended liabilities by shifting more prospective health care costs to its work force.

When it comes to beneficiaries, there was the classic case of the uprising of the more affluent elderly against the federal government's inclusion of coverage for catastrophic benefits under Medicare, enacted in 1988. With people in the highest income brackets facing an eventual added tax liability of $1,300 per couple annually, the opposition succeeded in persuading Congress to rescind the legislation in late 1989.

That leaves only one source of new revenue—income, sales, excise, or other taxes, particularly at the state level—that individuals and corporations would be willing to consider in order to support societal goals that they recognize to be of prime importance. I later consider the potential of these revenues when I explore policy alternatives. Now, however, I examine recent major legislative actions and proposals.

Medicaid

As noted earlier, Congress and many of the states have taken small steps since the mid-1980s to expand the number of Medicaid enrollees and to add new or broadened benefits, especially those for pregnant women and infants. Even the Bush administration, which sought to avoid expanding a deficit-ridden budget, would have liked to have Medicaid cover all women and all infants below the age of twelve months if their family incomes did not exceed 130 percent of the poverty level. However, the administration did not want to add any new dollars to its share of the pot. Rather, it suggested that states use the $1.5 billion of federal support for Medicaid administration to help cover the additional outlays.[12]

Many states initially found themselves facing a sizable new financial commitment as a result of the provisions of the 1988 Medicare amendments. These amendments would have required the states to pay all the premiums, deductibles, and coinsurance for beneficiaries with incomes below the federal poverty level, as well as to moderate the spend-down provisions (which allow families to become eligible for Medicaid by spending down to a certain level of assets and income to avoid impoverishment of the noninstitutionalized family member whose spouse is in a nursing home). The new commitments under these amendments would have involved the states in additional annual outlays of $2.5 to $4 billion, but the rescission saved them from most of these additional commitments.[13]

It is important to note that several powerful groups that are deeply concerned with health policy regard major improvements in Medicaid as the preferred mechanism for improving the access of the poor to the health care system. The Health Policy Agenda for the American People, which the American Medical Association took the lead in organizing, recommended a substantial increase in the number of enrollees—all persons with incomes below the poverty level—as well as a standardized package of benefits. The estimated annual cost ranges between $13 and $28 billion.[14]

In testimony before various congressional committees, the Blue Cross–Blue Shield Association favored expanding Medicaid through a federal requirement that the states adopt a minimum income eligibility level, eliminating the linkage between welfare and Medicaid in the determination of eligibility, and exploring the feasibility of permitting low-income persons to buy into Medicaid.[15]

The Health Insurance Association of America (HIAA), which represents the commercial insurance industry, has also recommended that Medicaid be expanded so that all persons below the poverty level are eligible; that opportunities be provided for people between 100 and 150 percent of the poverty level to purchase on a sliding scale first-dollar coverage for primary, preventive, and ambulatory care; and that full Medicaid eligibility be provided for persons above the poverty level who are forced to spend down to the poverty level.[16]

Once one recalls that the current level of Medicaid coverage protects only about 45 percent of the population living in poverty,[17] that the foregoing proposals are aimed not only at covering all people living in poverty but also at opening opportunities for considerable numbers above the poverty level to receive benefits or buy into Medicaid, and that 1988 expenditures for Medicaid amounted to over $54 billion,[18] it is obvious that using the Medicaid route to improve access for the poor is not inexpensive. The odds are that the AMA's high estimate of $28 billion is in fact a low figure.

Federal Mandating Proposals

To confront the pressing dilemma of a constrained federal budget and millions of adults and children lacking health insurance, two major proposals have appeared in the congressional hopper. The Basic Health Benefits for All Americans Act (S.768; H.R. 1845), introduced by Senator Edward Kennedy (D-MA) and Representative Henry Waxman (D-CA), and the Employee Health Benefits Improvements Act of 1988, written by Representative Fortney Stark (D-CA), would require employers to cover all workers who are employed for more than 17.5 hours a week. Although these bills have distinctive financing mechanisms, their respective provisions are not dissimilar with respect to coverage for dependents, benefits specified, employer premiums (set at 80 percent), and the inclusion of stringent financial penalties for noncompliance. A waiting period is allowed for small businesses.

It should be noted that of the estimated thirty-five million persons currently without health insurance, only about 30 percent have incomes below the federal poverty level.[19] Although the federal mandate to cover the uninsured may have much to commend it on the ground of greater equity in spending and paying for health risks, the significant point is that it would not contribute much to improving access for the poor and the underserved, a great many of whom are out of the labor force or work fewer than 17.5 hours a week.

It is also far from clear that a major mandating effort would not result in severe roiling of the labor market and in additional costs to the federal and state governments for subsidies and administration so that the total costs might exceed the benefits. Employers would find good reason to offer employment to many part-time workers at a level below the cut-off point; a large number of low-income workers currently prefer cash income to health benefits; and, in an economy that is relying increasingly on "contingent workers," other unanticipated consequences must be considered.

State Mandating Plans

With considerable fanfare, the Commonwealth of Massachusetts, through a complex political bargain involving the employer community, the hospitals, and other interested parties, sought to put in place a state-mandated system of coverage for all workers, except seasonal workers, employed at least 30 hours a week. This system would impose penalties on firms—with five or more workers—that do not offer health insurance and would provide tax incentives for firms with less than five workers that do offer insurance. Under the plan, all uninsured residents would eventually be able to buy insurance from the state pool. The enrollment objective for 1992 was estimated at 600,000 people.[20] Given the state's severe budgetary problem, it is clear that Massachusetts will not be able to accomplish its ambitious plan, surely not within its original time frame.

The state of Washington has taken a somewhat different tack. It subsidizes, on a sliding scale, the premiums for 30,000 people whose incomes are up to 200 percent of the poverty level. Coverage is administered and underwritten by designated insurers. If it is successful, the state will extend the program to 720,000 uninsured persons at the end of five years.[21]

Direct State Subsidies for Hospitals that Provide
Large Amounts of Uncompensated Care

A number of states, including New York, New Jersey, and Florida, have resorted to one or another type of special levy—in Florida, a tax of 1.5 percent of hospital revenues,[22] and, in New Jersey, a 12 percent surcharge on the bills of paying patients—the proceeds of which are distributed to hospitals, mostly in the inner city, that provide large amounts of uncompensated care.[23] It should be observed that these "all-payer systems" are more directly responsive to the problems of access for the poor than are the various mandating schemes that focus on uncovered workers, the majority of whom are not poor.

California recently approved a tax on cigarettes that was expected to generate $600 million. Half of the sum will be distributed to hospitals and physicians who treat the medically indigent.[24]

Universal Access State Pools

The prestigious National Leadership Commission on Health Care has recommended that Medicaid be replaced by Universal Access State Pools, which would provide an opportunity for all persons—nonworkers, uninsured workers, and workers with incomes below 150 percent of the poverty line—to obtain coverage for themselves and their dependents at a net annual cost of some $15 billion.[25] It is noteworthy that the commission's report elicited strong dissent from several of its members on the ground that the proposal failed to take into account the possibility that many employers might find it advantageous to discontinue offering their employees health insurance and simply pay the required premiums into the state fund.[26]

National Health Insurance

After a relatively long period of quiescence since 1976, when the issue was last prominent, national health insurance has once again been placed on the nation's health agenda. This was done not only by liberal members of the medical profession, such as the Physicians for a National Health Plan, but also, surprisingly enough, by the chief executive officers of some of the nation's large corporations, who see no resolution of the crisis that confronts health care financing except for government to assume greater responsibilities. Many large corporations are not only concerned about the continuing double-digit inflation in their annual health care expenditures but are also threatened by the adoption of a new accounting convention. Hitherto, a company that had an obligation to provide health care to retired workers was not required to show that liability on its balance sheets. Now corporations face a federal requirement to divulge such information. The General Accounting Office estimated the total as over $200 billion; the Blue Cross–Blue Shield *Environmental Analysis for 1989* set the amount as high as $400 billion.[27]

Since NHI has only recently returned to the nation's health policy agenda, there are neither carefully articulated plans nor sufficient financial data that would permit one to judge whether the estimated costs would be matched or exceeded by the expected returns. We do know that the Physicians for a National Health Plan recommended that the system be financed entirely by the federal government by means of federal income taxes and that private insurers be excluded from underwriting.

A few comments about the financing proposals that I have just reviewed:

- Medicaid currently covers fewer than half of all persons in poverty; some of the coverage is quite thin (providing for a limited number of hospital days and physician visits), and payments to providers are often below cost or market prices. Accordingly, it is difficult to see how anything short of a doubling of Medicaid outlays would be sufficient to provide adequate coverage to the poor and the underserved. Currently, that would amount to an additional outlay of some $50 billion.

- There is little justification for the expectation that either the Kennedy-Waxman or the Stark proposals mandating that most employers provide health insurance for members of their work force will win congressional approval in the near term. Among the reasons are possible serious adverse consequences for employment, wages, and federal and state budgets.

- The outlook for state-mandated health insurance has worsened by virtue of the slow start in Massachusetts, the bellwether in this approach. There, the budget is so strained as to undermine the viability of the entire effort.

- A number of states on the East Coast, recently joined by California, have resorted to special taxes or surcharges to yield pools of revenue with which to reimburse providers that are burdened with disproportionate amounts of uncompensated care. This approach has had considerable success in New York, New Jersey, and Florida.

- There are several far-reaching proposals aimed at providing insurance coverage for the entire population. These run the gamut from federally financed NHI to Universal Access State Pools, the latter a plan recently advanced by the National Leadership Commission on Health Care. In the absence of demonstration efforts and results, it is too early to assess their potential.

Policy Directions

Before coming to the principal objective of this review of current and proposed methods for improved financing of health care for the poor and the underserved, it is important to step back and view health within the larger framework of essential goods and services to which people require access, such as to income, food, housing, education, and welfare. The following observations are pertinent:

- The health of the population is undeniably affected by the extent to which individuals are able to work and be self-supporting (and have health insurance); can purchase or otherwise obtain the amount and variety of foods that are necessary for their physical well-being; have adequate housing, defined as not overcrowded and offering essential amenities such as running water and indoor toilets; and have access to schooling that will provide their children the requisite skills for becoming self-supporting adults in a democratic society.
- The foregoing list is a potent reminder that the poor and the underserved lack not only access to adequate health care but also, in varying degrees, lack access to the other prerequisites for effective functioning in our society. I postulated some years ago that the most important health reform in the last quarter century was neither the passage of Medicare nor of Medicaid but rather the expansion of the food-stamp program. Along these same lines, I would argue that since health insurance for the mainstream in the United States has been linked to employment, the nearer the United States comes to running its economy at full or near-full employment, the smaller the numbers who would lack access to the health care system. There are other examples of the interaction between health care and the basics cited above. It is, or should be, clear that the ravages to health from crack addiction and from AIDS can at present be best controlled through education, not medical intervention. It should also be clear that when people are homeless and without work, do not receive welfare, and have not been certified for food stamps, improving their access to health services, though important, falls far short of the range of public services that they require.
- The third observation that is critical for the delineation of policy alternatives relates to the uncertain future of private health insurance in the United States because of its dependence on employment. The U.S. economy is moving strongly from traditional manufacturing to the production of services, much of it concentrated in small enterprises, which for a variety of reasons find it difficult or impossible to

provide health insurance for their workers. Moreover, the growth of the contingent work force continues apace. This suggests that the population without health insurance is likely to rise from its current level of 35 million persons, conceivably to a point at which the link between jobs and health insurance will no longer be sustainable. For the time being, however, I will put aside this threat in the exploration of preferred ways to improve access to services short of a major overhaul of the extant health care system.

One more salient observation: it is unlikely that the United States will attempt a large-scale restructuring of its health care system primarily to improve access for the poor and the underserved. That is not the way national policy is formulated. The current needs of the poor may play a role in strengthening the forces for reform, but the poor by themselves are unlikely to develop the leverage required to bring about fundamental structural changes. Such changes will occur only if the principal payers for health care—the federal and state governments and employers—decide to press for radical change. An additional or alternative condition is that the principal beneficiaries of health care insurance, the elderly and the employed population, become seriously dissatisfied with the access and quality of services to which they currently have access.

Second-Best Suggestions

In light of the foregoing limitations and constraints, my second-best suggestions for improving access to health care for the poor and the underserved rely primarily on the following:

- The federal government should take specific actions over the next few years to establish national criteria for Medicaid eligibility that would bring the present level of enrollment from around 45 percent of persons in poverty to 100 percent; to stipulate a uniform national set of benefits that would include essential preventive services, particularly for pregnant women, infants, and children; to decouple eligibility for Medicaid from AFDC enrollment; and to experiment with varying approaches that would permit individuals and families with incomes up to 150 percent of the poverty level to buy into Medicaid or otherwise benefit from it.
- The federal government should continue to formulate differential reimbursement policies for hospitals that are responsible for providing large amounts of uncompensated care. These policies might include higher reimbursement rates for rural hospitals and the provision of an override for inner-city hospitals that care for large

numbers of poor people. The closure of a substantial number of financially stressed hospitals would in many areas deprive large numbers of persons of services and should be avoided.

- States that have not yet established a revenue pool for distribution to providers of large amounts of uncompensated care should do so. California's special tax on cigarettes for this purpose indicates the willingness of the electorate to accept the societal need for additional tax resources.

- Because of the growing financial vulnerability of many inner-city and rural hospitals, each state needs to establish a mechanism that enables it to assess, ahead of time, whether special state funds may be required for capital or operating subsidies to maintain critical institutions that provide access to the poor until alternative arrangements can be instituted. Some years ago, the New York state legislature appropriated special funds for the rehabilitation of a needed hospital in the Bronx because of the large numbers of poor who were dependent on it.

- Since I do not believe that any financing reforms, not even NHI, will attract adequate numbers of competent physicians and other health professionals to areas that they customarily avoid—that is, areas with concentrations of low-income and minority groups—improved access for the underserved must go beyond financial reforms to focus more specifically on the education of health professionals and their choice of practice location following completion of their training. In this connection, I strongly urge the federal and state governments, as well as foundations and other private-sector parties, to increase their funding for the education of larger numbers of minority physicians. Next, I see merit in the expansion of the National Health Service Corps and other programs of subsidized medical education that would induce larger numbers of recently trained physicians to practice for a period of years among underserved populations. Finally, I would recommend that the states take the lead in expanding the training and employment of nurse practitioners. At an annual salary of $40,000, the total earnings of nurse practitioners would represent only one-quarter that of physicians in private practice. The deployment of larger cadres of nurse practitioners based at nearby or more distant facilities could improve initial and continuing access of underserved populations to the health care system.

Conclusion

I stipulated early in this chapter that although lack of finances blocks a small minority of the nation's population from gaining access to the health care system, the more serious impediment that the poor face is the quality of the health care services available to them. Because large numbers of the poor are treated in public hospitals, one way to enhance the level of care accessible to them would be to ensure that these hospitals are better staffed, equipped, and managed and that they should not have to operate at excessively high occupancy rates. This is a challenge in the first instance to state and local governments, in the second, to federal reimbursement policies for Medicare patients.

The other serious shortcoming affecting the quality of health care for the poor is that large numbers lack an ongoing relationship to a physician and must resort to emergency rooms and clinics for most or all of their ambulatory care. The earlier recommendation for a much-expanded cadre of nurse practitioners might provide a continuing source of advice and guidance for poor people who face serious hurdles in negotiating our splintered health delivery system.

It may turn out over time that some type of Health Maintenance Organization, particularly one that treats privately and publicly insured persons in the same organization, might assure the poor access to a higher quality of care. That is an inference from the inpatient care that the poor have long received at the nation's teaching hospitals.

Having reached the end of my analysis, I am as restive as I assume most readers must be with the modest and constrained recommendations that I have advanced to improve the access of the poor and the underserved to our health care system. I am not sure, however, that deep unease and dissatisfaction are justified. If one is not convinced of the proposition that it is feasible through a single legislative initiative, even the introduction of NHI, to resolve all or even most of the barriers that confront the poor in gaining greater access to an acceptable level of health care services, the proposals that have been advanced are moves in the right direction. The real cause for disquietude is that the majority of the population and the majority of federal and state legislators faced with severe budgetary constraints and a long list of pressing demands—from improving the nation's physical infrastructure to improving the efficacy of our educational system—will not come up with the resources required to expand significantly the access of the poor to improved health care services. Beyond this hurdle lies one other: In a society predicated on a money-making ethic and committed to the belief that those who make more money are entitled to dispose of it as they see fit, there are inherent constraints on any public policy aimed at improving the lot of the poor. It may be true—and I believe it is—that we have done better in providing access to health care for the poor than in providing them with opportunities for jobs, decent housing, and effective education. We still have a long way to go on each of these fronts.

Notes

1. BO Burwell, and MP Rymer, "Trends in Medical Eligibility: 1975 to 1985," *Health Affairs* 6(4)(1987):31–45.

2. CN Oberg, and CL Polich, "Medicaid: Entering the Third Decade," *Health Affairs* 7(4)(1988):83–96.

3. D Chang, and J Holahan, *Medicaid Spending in the 1980s*: The Access/Cost Containment Trade-Off Revisited (Washington, D.C.: Urban Institute, July 1989).

4. U.S. Department of Veterans' Affairs, *Annual Report, 1988* (Washington, D.C.: July 1989).

5. U.S. Department of Commerce, Bureau of the Census, *Statistical Abstract of the United States 1989* (Washington, D.C.: U.S. Government Printing Office, 1989 [Table 158, p. 101]).

6. ER Brown, and G Dallek, "Changing Health Care in Los Angeles: Poverty Amidst Affluence, Competition Leading to Crisis." "Report to Metropolitan Health Delivery Systems Monitoring and Assessment Project" (Conservation of Human Resources, Columbia University, March 1990). Unpublished.

7. JW Salmon, "Report to Metropolitan Health Delivery Systems Monitoring and Assessment Project" (Conservation of Human Resources, Columbia University, 1990). Unpublished; and Health Insurance Association of America, *Source Book of Health Insurance Data 1989* (Washington, D.C.: Health Insurance Association of America, 1989).

8. D Rowland, "Financing Health Care for Elderly Americans." In *Health Services Research: Key to Health Policy*, edited by E Ginzberg (Cambridge, Mass.: Harvard University Press, 1991).

9. "National Health Expenditures 1988." *Health Care Financing Review* 11(4)(1990). Also, U.S. Department of Commerce, International Trade Administration, *U.S. Industrial Outlook, 1990* (Washington, D.C.: U.S. Government Printing Office, 1990).

10. "National Health Expenditures 1988."

11. Blue Cross–Blue Shield, *Environmental Analysis 1989* (Chicago, Ill.: Blue Cross and Blue Shield Association, 1989).

12. Ibid.

13. American Medical Association, "The Health Policy Agenda for the American People." *Final Report of the Ad Hoc Committee on Medicaid* (Chicago, Ill.: American Medical Association, February 1989).

14. Ibid.

15. Blue Cross–Blue Shield, *Environmental Analysis*.

16. Ibid.

17. Chang, and Holahan, *Medicaid Spending*.

18. Blue Cross–Blue Shield, *Environmental Analysis*.

19. Ibid.

20. Ibid.

21. Ibid.

22. Ibid.

23. Ibid.

24. Report of the National Leadership Commission on Health Care. *For the Health of a Nation* (Washington, D.C.: National Leadership Commission, 1989).

25. Blue Cross–Blue Shield, *Environmental Analysis*.

26. Ibid.

27. DU Himmelstein, et al. "A National Health Program for the United States," *New England Journal of Medicine* 320(1989):102–10.

14

Restructuring Health Services in New York City

The title of this chapter is something of an oxymoron. No individual or agency—neither the mayor of New York City, its Health and Hospitals Corporation (HHC), the health commissioner, the Academic Health Centers, the voluntary hospitals, nor the community health clinics—has such a charge; and if it had, it could do little about it. I have reached this conclusion in part as a result of my participation on the recent New York City Child Health Commission—my first direct exposure to local government agencies—which convinced me that the reform of the bureaucracy, though in theory possible, will in practice turn out to be largely an exercise in frustration.

If we were living in different times, when money was available in large amounts, I might have concluded otherwise, because money, especially lots of new money, can help to unfreeze frozen interdepartmental relationships. But in the absence of new money I seriously question that structural reforms can be introduced on a sufficiently broad scale and within a reasonably contained period for outcomes to be improved significantly. The commission found that New York City spends annually $1.2 billion of public funds to provide health services for 1.2 million poor children, and yet many of the recipients get indifferent, if not poor, care, and many others slip between the cracks. That is sufficient cause for pessimism.

I come to the subject of improving primary care services in low-income neighborhoods with perceptions informed by direct experience with this topic. Specifically, in the mid-1980s the Conservation of Human Resources (CHR) project that I direct at Columbia University published two books, each of which has something to contribute to the inquiry. The first, entitled *Local Health Policy in Action: The Municipal Health Services Program*,[1] was a thorough, concurrent evaluation of a five-year five-city demonstration, sponsored by the Robert Wood Johnson Foundation with a grant of $15 million. The aim of the project was to strengthen local community health centers so that low-income residents could obtain more and better health care than by crowding the emergency rooms and clinics of munici- pal and voluntary hospitals. For a variety of reasons we concluded that the concept, though sound, was difficult to implement and that, on bal- ance, the outcome was no better than a draw.

The other work of the CHR project relevant to the theme of this chapter is the volume entitled *From Health Dollars to Health Services, New York City 1965–1985.*[2] Although the city lost 10 percent of its population during these two decades, its total expenditures for health care increased by about 250 percent in *real* dollars. Our study traced who got the money and who got the additional services. It is not necessary to recount in detail the principal findings; the most important one is that relatively little of the siz- able new funds actually went to improving the quality of ambulatory care for poor people.

In this chapter, I first set forth the realities that determined the availabil- ity of neighborhood health care services in New York, and then advance a limited number of modest suggestions that might help to improve service delivery to groups most in need of more and better care.

Availability of Services

In brief review: In many neighborhoods in New York most of the residents have sufficient income to obtain the ambulatory care they want and need from private practitioners. They confront no special difficulty in finding prac- titioners who are willing to treat them. In short, both patients and physicians are more or less satisfied with each other. These more affluent neighborhoods need no special attention or action. However, other areas, chiefly those with concentrations of low-income residents, have a severe shortage of practitio- ners. If my recollection is correct, some years ago there was not one pediatri- cian left in full-time private practice in Harlem.

There are about thirty-five to forty community health centers still operating in New York City, but no more than ten function in a way that they and their patients consider fully satisfactory. Most have serious difficulties in attracting and retaining staff, and the staff they have is often unable to follow its patients when they are admitted to local hospitals, among other reasons because of lack of adequate liability insurance. Moreover, many of these clinics are in seri- ous physical disrepair and lack critical equipment. The emergency rooms and the clinics of most of the Health and Hospitals Corporation facilities are se- verely stressed in terms of volume, staffing, physical surroundings, poor equipment, inadequate data systems, and many other deficiencies.

Finally, the ambulatory care services of the voluntary hospitals provide large amounts of care for poor people who live in the immediate neighborhood.

The worsening financial outlook of these voluntary hospitals is attributed to the large volume of uncompensated ambulatory care.

The combination of weakened health clinics, a stressed municipal hospital system, and many voluntary hospitals that are racing toward bankruptcy because of the volume of unreimbursed ambulatory services that they provide has serious consequences for the care received by the poor and the needy. Many individuals fail to enter the system before their conditions have become seriously aggravated as the result of prior neglect; there is a lack of continuity and comprehensiveness in the care that they receive, which is particularly dysfunctional for the health of children; there is considerable slippage with respect to referrals, so that many patients who should be evaluated and treated by specialists fail to be seen promptly, if at all; and preventive services are neglected as institutions and personnel are overextended in trying to cope with patients who present with emergent conditions.

Ways to Improve Service

The foregoing are not minor deficits. They are serious and warrant attention and correction. As a contribution to the improvement of health care for the poor, I offer several modest suggestions.

Since I postulate that most of the poor will continue to seek care from their neighborhood hospitals, the first challenge is to upgrade the operations of the emergency rooms that are currently the principal sites of care. It would seem that what is needed are walk-in clinics for those presenting with minor symptoms. Strengthening the hospital information system so that the physician on call can be informed promptly about the patient's prior history would contribute significantly to an improvement in the quality of care.

Voluntary hospitals should explore the approach adopted by New York's Presbyterian Hospital of establishing an ambulatory-care network in the surrounding community. The state should support such efforts and offer hospital reimbursement rates to participating physicians.

More of the Health and Hospitals Corporation hospitals should follow Harlem Hospital's decentralization program, which has established off-site clinics readily accessible to the local population. And the Health and Hospitals Corporation should assess the strengths and weaknesses of its pioneering efforts to establish a modified HMO at Coney Island Hospital to assure continuity and comprehensiveness of care for children and other family members.

The state of New York should explore different mechanisms that might be used to facilitate borrowing by established community health centers in need of capital investments to modernize their facilities. State officials should explore the potential for providing improved malpractice coverage for physicians on the staffs of community health clinics to enable them to treat clinic patients who have been hospitalized, and the state should act promptly on its plan to increase the per-visit fee for qualified practitioners from $11 to $40.

Since a growing number of the poor and needy in New York City are recent immigrants, many with little or no knowledge of English, the commissioner of health should explore opportunities to reach these groups through the schools, churches, and other neighborhood organizations with educational materials informing them of the range of medical services available to them.

The state of New York should review its present scholarship and loan programs for low-income students who study medicine and should aim to broaden the opportunities available to those who commit themselves to join the staff of a community health center or other type of practice in an underserved area on completion of their training.

Finally, the advocacy community for improved health care for the poor should press Congress and the Department of Health and Human Services to maintain (preferably expand) their funding for existing community health centers that provide effective care. Another step is to lobby Congress to expand the number of entrants into the National Health Service Corps, whose members currently account for a significant proportion of the staffs of community health clinics.

My concluding observations may be summarized as follows: There is a need to improve ambulatory care in low-income areas of the New York City. Such improvement must take into consideration that, in general, physicians avoid establishing practices in poor neighborhoods. Accordingly, the main object of the reforms must be to improve the ambulatory care currently provided by the municipal and voluntary hospitals located in or close to low-income neighborhoods. Some effort should be directed to maintaining and improving the viability of community health clinics currently meeting significant needs in their areas. Efforts to improve the quantity and quality of health care services for the poor and the needy must never lose sight of the fact that more jobs, more income, more security, and more hope can also make major contributions to the health and well-being of the poor.

Notes

1. E Ginzberg, M Ostow, and EM Davis, *Local Health Policy in Action: The Municipal Health Services Program* (Totowa, N.J.: Rowman & Allanheld, 1985).

2. E Ginzberg, and the CHR Staff, *From Health Dollars to Health Services: New York City 1965–1985* (Totowa, N.J.: Rowman & Allanheld, 1986).

15

Access to Health Care
for Hispanics

Over the years, the United States Census Bureau has used a variety of classification schemes to determine who should be designated a Hispanic. Reliance on a single criterion, such as self-designation, or multiple criteria, such as language and country of origin, yields ambiguous results. In current practice, the twenty million Hispanics in the United States are classified by country of origin. The subgroups of the Hispanic population and their proportional representation are as follows: Mexican-Americans (62 percent); Puerto Ricans (13 percent); Cubans (5 percent); Central and South Americans (12 percent); other Hispanics—the Spanish-Mexican-Indian population in the Southwest (8 percent).[1]

Although some Hispanics live in every state, the vast majority, over 70 percent, reside in six of the nation's most populous states—California, Texas, New York, Florida, New Jersey, and Illinois.[2] Compared to the non-Hispanic white majority, Hispanics are more heavily concentrated in metropolitan centers, particularly in the inner cities.

Several links can be made between these geographic characteristics and the growing needs and pressures among Hispanics for improved access to health care services. Their concentration in six states indicates that the health policies of these states are first-order determinants of the availability of health care to the Hispanic poor through their Medicaid programs, public hospitals, and special programs such as compensatory reimbursement to providers of uncompensated care.

The overrepresentation of Hispanics within the inner cities of metropolitan areas suggests that most of them live relatively close to hospitals and clinics. The critical question of the ease or difficulty with which low-income Hispanics obtain treatment in such facilities is assessed below.

Socioeconomic Status

Health care analysts have long understood that the quality of health care available to different groups is influenced by their socioeconomic status, specifically their level of education, occupational achievement, and income. Persons with low income frequently have greater-than-average need for health care because of the differentially high birth rates, below par health status, and above-average prevalence of specific diseases associated with these populations.[3] Let us examine the major groups of Hispanics to assess the extent to which socioeconomic status influences their access to health services.

A particular disadvantage of the Hispanic population, many of whom are the first generation in the United States, is the large gap between their level of educational achievement and that of the white majority. The years of school completed by whites and Hispanics, twenty-five years-of-age or older in 1987, are seen in Table 15.1.

It is noteworthy that the Cubans and "other" Hispanics (Central and South Americans as well as the Spanish-Mexican-Indian subgroup) approximate most closely the educational levels of the white majority.[4]

Below average educational achievement is reflected in less favorable occupational status and lower incomes. Among the total population, 56 percent of all employed persons fall into the two highest categories of the occupational ladder, professional and technical;[5] among the Hispanic population the proportion is 38 percent, except for Cubans, 57 percent of whose working members are classified in these two top categories. Mexican Americans are particularly disadvantaged by virtue of the fact that about 9 percent are still employed in farming, a predominantly seasonal, low-wage sector. In comparison, only 1 to 2 percent of other groups of Hispanics are agricultural workers.[6]

The relationship between occupational status and income is confirmed by data for 1988 showing that the median family income of all Hispanics amounted to $21,800, lagging behind the median family income for whites, $33,900, by 36 percent.[7]

In addition to their low family incomes, Hispanics also face difficulties in obtaining health care because a large proportion of them are employed in low-wage sectors of the economy in which employers fail to provide health insurance benefits.[8] Hispanics have lower rates of coverage by private or government health insurance than do whites or blacks. In 1987, 30.1 percent of Hispanics were not covered, as compared with 20.4 percent of blacks and 12.6 percent of whites.[9] Medicaid coverage varies widely by state of residence. As a result, Hispanics in New York and California are more likely to be enrolled in Medicaid than Hispanics in Texas or Florida, a reflection of differential eligibility criteria and administrative practices in these states.[10]

In sum, many Hispanics are poorly positioned to access the health care system by virtue of below-average family income, above-average employment in

TABLE 15.1 Comparison of Educational Level of White Versus Hispanic Students in the United States (1987)

	Percentage Attending Less Than Five Years of High School	Percentage Attending Four or More Years of High School
White	2.0	77.0
Hispanic	11.9	50.9
Mexican	15.4	44.8
Puerto Rican	10.3	53.8
Cuban	6.1	61.6
Other	5.7	61.5

Source: U.S. Department of Commerce, *Statistical Abstract of the United States*, 1990. Washington, D.C.: GPO, 1990.

establishments that do not regularly provide private health insurance, and because sizable numbers live in states with low Medicaid enrollments.

Demographic and Epidemiologic Determinants of Need

The influence of demographic and epidemiologic factors on Hispanics' need and demand for health care services must also be assessed. On the favorable side, Hispanics, other than Cubans, have a younger age profile than the population at large; this means that they are concentrated in age groups that characteristically need and use fewer health care services. Alternatively, their disproportionate representation in the lower-income brackets points to an above-average need for health care services because of the association of lower socioeconomic status with poor health status.

A similar favorable-unfavorable balance is suggested by the differentially high birth rates of Mexican-Americans, indicating a greater need for access to prenatal and postnatal care for women and children.[11] On the favorable side, it should be noted that the birthweight pattern of Mexican-Americans resembles that of upper-income, non-Hispanic whites, rather than that of comparable lower-income blacks. Distinctive cultural factors, such as less-frequent smoking and lower alcohol intake by Hispanic women, probably contribute to this counterintuitive finding.[12]

Mexican-Americans and Puerto Ricans have a much higher incidence of Type II diabetes, approximately two to three times that of the non-Hispanic population. Moreover, this disease strikes a younger age group and often leads to complications that have been attributed in part to the difficulties encountered in obtaining adequate health care.[13]

The health status of Hispanics, by subgroup and by gender, has thus far been insufficiently analyzed because of the late start of federal and state bureaucracies in collecting health data based on ethnic background. However, there is evidence that a considerable number of Hispanic women are obese, perhaps as many as one third of all Mexican-Americans and Puerto Ricans.[14] Other data point to differentially high rates of cancer of the cervix among Hispanic women, which may be caused, in part, by their inadequate access to and use of preventive services.[15] On the positive side, there are statistics indicating that Hispanics have lower-than-average rates of other varieties of cancer.

Data in 1989 from the Centers for Disease Control reveal that of the 15,763 reported cases of AIDS among Hispanic adults and adolescents, 50 percent are directly or indirectly related to intravenous drug use. Of the 419 reported Hispanic pediatric AIDS cases, 72 percent are children of mothers who had been infected by sexual partners who were drug users.[16] Among selected groups of Hispanics who are heavily addicted to intravenous drug use, the rising trend of AIDS cases is a serious threat. In New York, this threat is compounded by the fact that there are serious deficiencies in the addiction treatment capacity of the state.[17]

Obviously, the foregoing does not provide a comprehensive view of the morbidity trends of different Hispanic groups; rather it is a reminder that, in addition to problems of access that result from low income and lack of insurance, epidemiological factors underlie the needs of some Hispanics for above-average utilization of health care services.

Locational and institutional factors also influence the ease or difficulty that Hispanic groups experience in obtaining access to health care. Since Mexican-Americans constitute the largest group, about three out of every five, I will examine their problems first.

The Mexican-Americans most at risk are the approximately one million farm workers who have both above-average accident rates and the most limited access to health care providers. A second subgroup is the large number of Mexican-Americans who live along the U.S.-Mexico border, stretching from Southern California to Brownsville, Texas. The population on both sides of the border is estimated to be about ten million this year. In Texas alone, over 110,000 Mexican-Americans live in *colonias* or unincorporated areas. These settlements often lack septic tanks, sewers, and running water.[18]

Water and air pollution and the dumping of hazardous waste threaten residents on both sides of the border. In a recent article, David Warner pointed out that health care entitlements are extremely thin and that, along the entire border, there is only one fully supported public hospital (in El Paso) that serves as a facility of last resort for the poor. Many Mexican-Americans cross back into Mexico when they have to buy pharmaceuticals or need to obtain health or dental care.[19]

Another example of how Hispanics fare in the Texas health care system is seen in a report on Harris County, which includes the city of Houston. A recent draft report from the School of Public Health of the University of Texas Health Science Center states:

Chronic illness as a health problem is less important than are the problems of younger people: poor pregnancy outcomes, growth and development of children, drug abuse, AIDS, and other infectious diseases. The proportion of users of the district [public] services that are Hispanic has been steadily growing during this decade. ... A high proportion have low incomes. Overcrowding of patients stresses this system. ... A disproportionately large amount of resources is directed to emergency or otherwise delayed and serious admissions. Elective or tardy admissions are crowded out.[20]

Paradoxically, Houston has the greatest concentration of health care facilities of any metropolitan center in Texas.

The Mexican-American immigrants in Southern California are the largest group of Hispanics involved in the amnesty program. For the most part, this population consists of younger people, a great many of whom are classified as "working poor," implying that most of them do not have private insurance. The Immigration Reform and Control Act of 1989 has placed constraints on this group's access to need-based health service programs. Many new aliens were not eligible for Medicaid services until 1992—even during the period when they become permanent residents.

If we shift our focus from the West Coast to the East Coast, the situation in New York City clearly illustrates the influence of location on the health care services that are available to different Hispanic groups in the metropolis. For the most part, Hispanics are dependent first on the clinics and emergency rooms of public hospitals that are operated by the New York City Health and Hospitals Corporation and, second, on the ambulatory care services of selected voluntary hospitals. In some neighborhoods Hispanic citizens have access to local community health centers and also obtain care from group practices and private practitioners. Since there are substantial differences in the availability and quality of ambulatory care and of inpatient care among the hospitals that Hispanics use, any overall generalization about the health services available to them would be unjustified. However, their concentration in low-income areas of the city carries a presumption of a lower quality of care than that available to persons living in higher-income neighborhoods.[21]

The Paucity of Hispanic Health Professionals

One of the reasons for the difficulties Hispanics experience in obtaining adequate health care is the fact that they are seriously underrepresented in the health occupations, particularly those requiring higher levels of skill. The complements of Hispanic dentists, registered nurses, pharmacists and therapists accounted in 1989 for between 2.2 percent and 3.0 percent of the totals in these professions. The proportion of physicians is somewhat higher, about 5.4 percent, reflecting the considerable number who were trained abroad and subsequently immigrated to the United States.[22]

According to the most recent data from the Association of American Medical Colleges, Hispanics comprise the following proportions of the current student enrollment in U.S. medical schools: Mexican-Americans, 1.7 percent; Puerto Ricans, 2.0 percent; other Hispanics, 1.7 percent. The trend in first-year matriculants in 1989 showed no increase.[23]

Since Hispanics will soon exceed 10 percent of the total population, a continuing gross deficiency of Hispanic health professionals threatens the degree of access of this large and growing minority to the health care system. However, to increase significantly the flow of Hispanics into health professional schools is not an easy undertaking, and the resources required far exceed those currently available. Such an effort requires early interventions to direct capable students to precollege programs that offer special educational guidance, counseling, and tutoring; the availability of financial assistance; and the provision of a variety of other supports. Effective efforts that might contribute more immediately to reducing the present and prospective gap between the needs of Hispanic users and the availability of Hispanic health care providers include intensive health educational programs conducted by community groups, and, particularly, the preparation and dissemination of preventive health materials in Spanish.

Implications of Major Health Reform Proposals for Improved Access for Hispanics

This section considers the strengths and weaknesses of some of the nation's major health reform proposals from the vantage of their probable impact on access to health care for the large, growing, and highly diversified Hispanic population.

Currently the only measure with a probability of early action is the further extension of recent federal legislation to improve Medicaid coverage by mandating or permitting the states to liberalize eligibility requirements for women and children. Despite the fact that the federal government funds from 50 to 80 percent of the costs of state Medicaid programs, 48 of the nation's governors recently petitioned Congress (unsuccessfully) to slow the pace of its liberalizing efforts because of the strain that expanded eligibility and service provisions impose on their states' finances. Given the larger proportion of Hispanic women who are of childbearing age than that of the population at large and Hispanics' above average birth rate, the new Medicaid reforms cannot have anything but a positive impact.

As has been noted earlier, two facets of health and medical care for Hispanics warrant the special attention of the federal government. The existence of the Mexico-U.S. border creates distinct health problems that exceed local and state agencies' obligations and capabilities to respond. This is also true for the large numbers of aliens included in the amnesty program who face barriers in qualifying for Medicaid services. With respect to both facets, modest actions by the federal government could measurably improve access to health care for particular groups of low-income Hispanics.

Turning to more fundamental reform, the overarching policy issues that affect Hispanics involve national health insurance, mandatory provision of health insurance by employers, new approaches aimed at reducing the costs of private health insurance, and state support to compensate providers of disproportionate amounts of charity care. I discuss each in turn, from the least to the most radical.

Several states, including New York, New Jersey, Florida, and California, have had some success in establishing a state financing pool for redistribution among hospitals and other providers that furnish large amounts of uncompensated care. There is considerable potential for extending this strategy, including recourse to "sin taxes," following the recent initiative of California. Greater state support for public hospitals directed at sustaining the extant health care system is a variant of this approach. Since a high proportion of Hispanics lack adequate, if any, insurance, such efforts, if aggressively pursued, should facilitate their access and improve the level of care they obtain.

If the private insurance industry, with the assistance of state and federal support, addressed the issue of providing catastrophic insurance to individuals, directly or through intermediaries, a considerable proportion of the presently uninsured Hispanic population could obtain coverage. This proposal reflects the fact that in 1987 over a quarter of all uninsured Hispanics had incomes that exceeded 200 percent of the poverty level.[24]

Currently, a widely debated health reform proposal is employer-mandating, either by the federal government or by the states. It should be noted, however, that except for Hawaii and the abortive effort in Massachusetts, employer-mandating initiatives are still in the planning stages.

Nevertheless, there are good reasons for Hispanics to be cautious of mandating proposals because of the potential disruption they can cause in coverage for dependents, many of whom are now included under the so-called richer policy of another member of the family. Moreover, faced with a cost that they cannot absorb, many employers may seek to escape the obligation to provide health coverage by hiring part-time employees. Even worse, there is a distinct likelihood that a considerable number of employers would be forced to close down their establishments, jeopardizing the jobs of many Hispanics.

Given the many complexities and potentially adverse consequences of employer-mandating, it is not surprising that a growing number of Hispanics favor a federal-state system of national health insurance. In principle, it looks extremely attractive to draw all of the presently uninsured individuals into a system that promises greater equity as well as the potential for effective cost control.

However, there are important negatives that cannot be ignored. So far there is no political consensus for national health insurance; the likelihood of excluding private health insurance companies from the financing of the nation's health care system is problematic; and the ability to devise a national system flexible enough to be responsive to the distinctive conditions in each of the fifty states is questionable, the more so in light of the history of declining Medicaid coverage between the mid-1970s and the mid-1980s. Further, there is little reason for confidence that a federal or federal-state-funded national health insurance system would not run into a financial-service squeeze that would lead to early and probably even tighter rationing of health care services.

Nevertheless, proposals for a national health insurance system, as they develop in the years ahead, warrant the serious consideration of Hispanics. If a national health insurance system were to move to the top of the health policy agenda, it would be responsive to many of the health and medical needs of the Hispanic population. At the same time, it would carry a great many concomitant and congruent costs that need to be assessed.

Conclusion

We know less than we should about the present and emerging health care needs of different Hispanic populations; nevertheless, we know enough to understand that Hispanics with below-average education, skill levels, and income are at risk and will remain at risk until all U.S. residents have coverage for essential health services.

We also know that broadened and improved health care services for Hispanics depend in large measure on increases in the numbers of Hispanics interested in and prepared to enter the health care professions.

Finally, a strengthened economy with associated improvements in family income, housing, and educational services would contribute significantly to the future health and well-being of the large and growing Hispanic minority.

Notes

1. U.S. Department of Commerce, Bureau of the Census, *Statistical Abstract of the United States 1990*, 110th ed. (Washington, D.C.: U.S. Government Printing Office, 1990). Table 45, p. 40.

2. Ibid. Table 28, p. 23.

3. JP Bunker, DS Gomby, and BH Kehrer, *Pathways to Health: The Role of Social Factors* (Menlo Park, Calif.: Henry J. Kaiser Family Foundation, 1989); LA Aday, R Andersen, and GV Fleming, *Health Care in the U.S.: Equitable for Whom?* (Beverly Hills, Calif.: Sage, 1980).

4. U.S. Department of Commerce, Bureau of the Census, *Statistical Abstract of the United States 1989* (Washington, D.C.: U.S. Government Printing Office, 1989) Table 215, p. 133.

5. U.S. Department of Commerce, Bureau of the Census, *Statistical Abstract 1990*. Table 645, p. 389.

6. Ibid. Table 626, p. 379.

7. Ibid. Table 716, p. 444; table 726, p. 450.

8. FM Trevino, ME Moyer, RB Valdez, and CA Stroup-Benham, "Health Insurance Coverage and Utilization of Health Services by Mexican-Americans, Mainland Puerto Ricans and Cuban-Americans," *Journal of the American Medical Association* 265(1991):233–37.

9. U.S. Department of Commerce, Bureau of the Census, *Statistical Abstract 1990*. Table 152, p. 100.

10. Ibid. Table 146, p. 97.

11. CA Stroup-Benham, and FM Trevino, "Reproductive Characteristics of Mexican-American, Mainland Puerto Rican and Cuban-Origin Women," *Journal of the American Medical Association* 265(1991):222–26.

12. D Hayes-Bautista, "Latino Health Indicators and the Underclass Model: From Paradox to New Policy Models." In *Health Policy and the Hispanic*, edited by A Furino (Boulder, Colo.: Westview Press, 1992).

13. MP Stern, and SM Haffner, "Type II Diabetes and Its Complications in Mexican Americans," *Diabetes/Metabolism Reviews* 6(1)(1990):24–45.

14. DA Dawson, "Economic Differences in Female Overweight: Data from the 1985 Natural Health Interview Survey," *American Journal of Public Health* 78(1988):1326–29.

15. National Cancer Institute, *Cancer in Hispanics* (Bethesda, Md.: National Institutes of Health, 1988).

16. AL Estrada, et al. "Risk Reduction Among Hispanic IV Drug Users and Receptivity to Community AIDS Education." In *Hispanic Health Policy Issues from Recent Research*, edited by A. Furino, Center for Health Economics and Policy and the South Texas Center for Health Research. (San Antonio, Tx.: University of Texas Health Science Center, 1989).

17. SC Joseph, "Combating IV Drug Use." In *The AIDS Patient: An Action Agenda*, edited by DE Rogers and E Ginzberg (Boulder, Colo.: Westview Press, 1988).

18. DC Warner, "Health Issues at the U.S.-Mexico Border," *Journal of the American Medical Association* 265(1991):242–47.

19. Ibid.

20. H Loe, "Final Report: Monitoring and Assessment of the Health Delivery System in Harris County, Texas." Prepared for Conservation of Human Resources, Columbia University, April 1990.

21. United Hospital Fund, *New York City Health Facts, 1989*. (New York: United Hospital Fund, 1989).

22. *Allied Health Services: Avoiding Crises*. Report of the Committee to Study the Role of Allied Health Personnel. Institute of Medicine. Washington, D.C.: National Academy Press, 1989).

23. HS Jonas, SI Etzel, and B Barzansky. "Undergraduate Medical Education," *Journal of the American Medical Association* 262(1989):1011–19.

24. FM Trevino, et al., "Health Insurance Coverage and Utilization of Services."

16

Beyond Universal Health Insurance

No one, least of all an economist, needs to be persuaded that people who lack money or health insurance are likely to encounter difficulties in obtaining essential health care services. Alternately, the economist has an obligation to explain that the adoption of a system of universal coverage will not ipso facto translate into assured access for essential, much less optimal, care for those who are currently disadvantaged. The reasons that universal coverage will not necessarily guarantee effective services to all are embedded in the nature and characteristics of the health care system.

In my development of this argument and its policy implications, I will undertake a three-fold analysis, including (1) a selective review of health care financing reforms in the United States, (2) an explication of nonfinancial barriers to effective health care, and (3) a delineation of the range of interim policy interventions required to lower the barriers to access.

Lessons from History

The first large-scale governmental reform of the U.S. health care system in the post–World War II era involved the radical restructuring of the medical services of the Veterans Administration, now renamed the Department of Veteran Affairs. In recent years, the Department of Veterans Affairs, the nation's largest medical system, consisting of about 170 hospitals and significant numbers of adjunct facilities, including ambulatory-care clinics and nursing homes that provide long-term care, has been operating at an annual budget in the $10 billion-range. Congress has stipulated the categories of patients that the Veterans Affairs department is mandated to treat, as well as those whose care is discretionary, depending on the availability of resources.

The ease of access and the quality of treatment received by veterans with preferred eligibility depend on such considerations as the location of the nearest veterans' hospital relative to their place of residence and whether the hospital is affiliated with a medical school that has assumed principal responsibility for the operation of its professional services.[1]

For many decades New York City has operated a major health and hospital system, with a current budget of about $2.9 billion, that has been committed to delivering care to everyone, regardless of ability to pay. Accordingly, New Yorkers may be said to have had "universal coverage" for almost a century. Consider, however, the following quotation from a recent report of the state comptroller:

> HHC [the Health and Hospitals Corporation of New York] is faced with se-verely overcrowded conditions stemming from significant increases in AIDS, psychiatric and drug-abuse patients; a lack of available discharge options for patients occupying acute care beds unnecessarily; and bed closings due to shortages of key staff such as nurses and social workers.[2]

The most ambitious financial reform that the nation has undertaken dates from 1965 when Congress passed Medicare and Medicaid with the intention of assuring broad access to care for the elderly and the categorical poor (recip-ients of Aid to Families with Dependent Children). What does the subsequent record reveal? Unquestionably, the large-scale infusion of federal, state, and, in the case of Medicaid, some local governmental funds resulted in much-im-proved access of the elderly and the poor to both short-term inpatient care and ambulatory services. Furthermore, with the passage of Medicare, most of the elderly were able to turn for their short-term care needs to mainstream practitioners and voluntary hospitals.

Although it was widely believed that Medicaid would be a first step for the poor to gain access to mainstream medicine, that expectation has not been borne out. On the positive side, successive surveys conducted by the Robert Wood Johnson Foundation in the years 1976, 1982, and 1986 found that the new financing efforts contributed a great deal to increasing the number and range of health services available to the poor and the uninsured.[3] However, there are important negatives that should be identified in the context of the resurgent belief that financial reform by itself, possibly at last in the form of universal coverage, will result in access to effective care for all. The following have been some of the principal shortfalls of Medicaid in fulfilling the expecta-tions of its proponents:

- Despite the willingness of the federal government to cover up to 78 percent of the Medicaid costs of low-income states, many states have resisted the incentive. From the mid-1970s to the mid-1980s, the pro-portion of poor persons covered declined from three out of four to less than one out of two, with some reversal in the last years because Congress has forced the states to expand coverage for pregnant women and young children.[4]
- Faced with steeply rising Medicaid costs, various states have arbi-trarily limited the number of physician visits, days of hospitaliza-

tion, and number of prescriptions for which they provide reimbursement. In many states, reimbursement rates for physician visits and payment for hospital care have been set so low that a large segment of the provider community has avoided accepting Medicaid patients or has severely limited the number of Medicaid recipients treated.

Medicare came closer to fulfilling the expectations of its advocates and the legislators who passed the program, but it, too, revealed discrepancies between financing reform and effective access that are worth noting:

- No one contemplated that over 70 percent of Medicare enrollees would resort to supplemental private insurance (Medigap) to improve their coverage. Nor did Congress anticipate that Medicare enrollees would balk at covering half of the premium costs for Medicare B, placing an unexpected new burden on federal financing. In 1988 Congress sought belatedly to relieve the elderly of some of the catastrophic costs of hospital care and prescription drugs, only to have to rescind the amendments a year later in the face of a voter revolt against the higher premiums and taxes that these reforms entailed.

The burden of this review underscores that even large-scale financing reforms aimed at increasing coverage do not automatically translate into broadened access and improved services. After some years, federal and state governments often encounter budgetary stringencies that impel them to retrench in covering costs, to decertify persons who had previously been enrolled, and to place limitations on eligibility and benefits. The lessons extracted from the experience of earlier health care reforms should not be overlooked in the debate over the new agenda item known as universal coverage.

Nonfinancial Barriers to Access

This section illuminates a number of cultural, demographic, geographic, and institutional factors that adversely affect access, even in the case of individuals who have reasonable coverage or the means to buy it.

Physician Practice Preferences

Access to medical care implies access to physicians. However, it has long been evident that most physicians are reluctant to practice among the poor, the geographically isolated, and minorities. Recent studies of the health care system in the nation's four largest metropolitan centers have revealed a tenfold or greater differential in the proportion of physicians to population as between more affluent areas and low-income, minority neighborhoods.[5] Within such a professional culture, there is little reason for confidence that universal coverage by itself would effect an appreciable redistribution of the physician supply that would significantly improve access for underserved populations.

Stressed Public Hospitals

A large proportion of the urban poor and the uninsured obtain all, or the bulk, of their medical care from emergency departments, clinics, and inpatient services of public hospitals, the vast majority of which are seriously strained with respect to capacity, staff, and equipment. Even with the introduction of universal coverage, it is likely that most of these low-income individuals will continue to seek and obtain care from these neighborhood institutions. At the same time, it is not likely that enhanced coverage would enable most of the public hospitals to remedy the pressures and inefficiencies under which they have long been operating in the near- or middleterm.

Teaching Hospitals

During the first half of this century—and throughout most of the preceding century—large urban teaching hospitals were a primary source of ambulatory and inpatient care for the poor and near-poor. There was an implicit quid pro quo between the teaching hospital and its patients. Medical students, interns, residents, and fellows could learn the art of medicine only through practice, and it was the poor who provided clinical experience for the novice. In recent decades the role of the poor in the learning process has diminished, although it has not disappeared. Other things, however, have changed: The emergency department, with a cost of $140 or more per visit, is not a desirable site for the poor to receive ambulatory care. Some acute-care hospitals are forced to retain patients, usually at a high per diem cost, because there is neither an available nursing home bed nor a suitable home to which they can be discharged. It is hard to see how universal coverage would resolve these institutional "non-fits."

Immigrant Status and Language Barriers

Medical care characteristically requires an interaction between the patient seeking care and the physician or other caregiver. The United States has been admitting approximately a million legal immigrants, refugees, and illegal aliens every year for the last decade, and the inflow will increase in the years ahead. A high proportion of the newcomers take up residence in coastal cities in the West, the South, and the East, although increasing numbers are also relocating to cities in the interior such as Chicago.

Most of the immigrants do not, at least initially, understand, speak, or read English; others have entered the country illegally and generally avoid contact with institutions such as hospitals and clinics for fear that routine record-keeping may result in their detection. Although universal coverage would make it easier for many members of these groups to seek and obtain effective health services, language handicaps and the threat of deportation will continue to inhibit their gaining access to the health care system.[6]

These barriers, separate and distinct from the issue of financing, are among those that need to be addressed if the implicit promise that universal coverage will provide effective access is to be realized.

Interim Targets to Expand Access

The analysis thus far has emphasized the powerful barriers that impair access to basic medical care for various individuals and groups, even in the presence of private or public insurance. The barriers are that much greater for the approximately thirty-five million persons who are uninsured. In sum, our pluralistic health care system is failing in greater or lesser degree to meet the basic needs for effective medical care of about one-third of the American people—the uninsured, the underinsured, and the underserved Medicaid population.

The report of the Pepper Commission on Comprehensive Health Care concluded that the federal government could not take the lead to establish a system of national health insurance coverage for the entire population since the estimated cost would be of the order of $200 billion annually.[7] The difficulties that the Bush administration and the Congress encountered in 1990 in writing and enacting a long-overdue five-year deficit reduction act (which probably grossly underestimated the size of the deficit) must be the point of departure for any proposals for health care reform that are put forward in the future. In the near term, no *significant* additional financing can be expected from the federal government.

Although Congress in 1990, in the face of strong opposition from the National Governors' Association, mandated expanded coverage for pregnant women and children by the Medicaid program, no large-scale federal initiatives appear likely. There are some federal and state proposals under consideration to provide coverage for the uninsured working population through employer mandates (with some state participation), but the odds are that none of the proposals will be enacted. This suggests that additional funding for medical care must be sought from individuals and households, out-of-pocket or through payment of additional "sin," income, or other taxes.

The point could be made that an important source of potential funding has been overlooked: reform of the extant system of medical care provision to reduce its excessive administrative and malpractice costs and the elimination of many unnecessary and ineffective treatments. It has been estimated that the combined total savings from such reforms could amount to as much as $100 to $150 billion annually. In the present context, it is essential to note that although substantial savings might be recoverable over time, they cannot be spent until they have been recovered, and the lead time for implementing practice guidelines is likely to be of the order of a decade of intensive outcomes research.[8]

If one looks forward to their early implementation, all proposals for large-scale health care reform must be predicated on the foregoing pessimistic appraisal of the financing outlook. Nevertheless, it would be short-sighted to assume that the present frozen environment for health reform, as well as for other public social policy initiatives, will not ultimately thaw. The United States continues to have both the highest per capita standard of living and the lowest per capita tax rate of any advanced nation with the exception of Japan. However, it will take time before Americans reach a consensus that low taxes are not necessarily the best assurance of continuing national prosperity and progress. Hence, I present the following modest proposals for health reform, not because more ambitious goals could not be formulated or are not desirable, but because I believe that even these modest proposals will prove difficult to implement in the near term.

The Expansion of Medicaid

Despite the resistance of the state governors, I believe that Congress should continue to enact, as it has since 1984, mandates and incentives for the states to enlarge Medicaid coverage. In the recent past this effort has resulted in adding approximately 900,000 persons to the rolls. Despite federal and state fiscal constraints, I urge, at a minimum, that the present rate of expansion be continued, and, as the political and economic environment becomes more favorable, that Congress accelerate the enrollment of all persons below the federal poverty standard. This policy change has been recommended by the American Medical Association, the Blue Cross–Blue Shield Association, and the Health Insurance Association of America.

Subsidized Coverage for the Near-Poor

Some state experiments are underway to permit persons with incomes between 100 and 200 percent of the federal poverty level to buy into Medicaid. Since the federal government covers, on the average, 55 percent of state Medicaid outlays, and in low-income states as much as 78 percent, I urge the adoption of program models that, after critical assessment, have been found to be effective. This would represent, at the optimum, an addition of some eighteen million people. At an average expenditure of $2,319 per recipient (fiscal year 1989), the estimated gross cost would be $42 billion, but the net cost would be considerably less.[9]

Private Sector Catastrophic Insurance Policies

Almost 30 percent of the presently uninsured population are younger, employed persons, most of whom work for small employers or for themselves and earn in excess of 200 percent of the federal poverty level. The insurance industry, if freed from state mandates by an amendment to the Employee Retirement Income Security Act (ERISA), should be able to offer a catastrophic policy for individuals for around $1,000 per annum, perhaps less. Early action to move toward this goal is indicated.

Expansion of the Federal Community Health Center Program

Between 1980 and 1990 the federal government has maintained a reasonably constant level of funding for community health centers under the Department of Health and Human Services Migrant Health Centers Program (Public Health Service Act, section 330). In fiscal year 1990, this amounted to $459 million and supported 527 centers.[10] I recommend that Congress expand this relatively inexpensive program, which, in the areas where it exists, helps to compensate for the severe dearth, if not absence, of primary-care services.

Expansion of the National Health Service Corps
and State Educational Debt-Forgiveness Programs

As part of his budget proposal for 1991, Secretary Sullivan of the Department of Health and Human Services included funds to revive the National Health Service Corps scholarship and loan-forgiveness programs, which were allocated just $3 million in 1990, primarily for scholarships to medical students and loan repayments for physicians (federal and state). This represented a drastic decline from its peak of $79.5 million in 1980. In 1989, the National Health Service Corps placed in practice sites 215 scholars who had completed their training and about 160 physician beneficiaries of the loan-forgiveness program. However, by 1991 the pipeline will have been exhausted and virtually no National Health Service Corps scholars will be available for service. In light of the existence in the United States of 2,000 underserved areas and a requirement of 4,100 physicians in both public and private settings (in 1989, the Public Health Service sought over 1,000 NHSC graduates to fill vacancies), I urge early congressional approval of the substantial expansion of the program as well as action to extend state debt-forgiveness programs. It should be noted that the Section 330 community health centers depend heavily on the above for their physician staffing.[11]

State Subsidies for Uncompensated Care

Medicare currently assists hospitals that provide a large volume of un-compensated care through disproportionate share adjustments, special reimbursements for sole-service hospitals, and recently increased reim-bursements for rural hospitals. I recommend that more states follow the practice of New York, New Jersey, Florida, and California in creating a statewide pool for reimbursing hospitals that provide disproportionate amounts of uncompensated care. They can do so either by levying special "sin taxes," as in the case of California, by a tax on insurance premiums or hospital revenues, or by some combination of both. Since the total amount of uncompensated hospital care is of the order of $13 billion annually, and since Medicare's contribution toward meeting this deficit is considerable, state subsidies to help cover the remainder should be manageable.[12]

The foregoing six recommendations are avowedly modest. They are aimed at extending coverage for the uninsured, providing improved pri-mary-care services for the underserved rural and urban populations, and helping to assure that vulnerable hospitals, particularly hard-pressed public hospitals, have the essential financial resources to continue to oper-ate. I am aware that these proposals to expand coverage do not address the substantial variability among the states in the scope and quality of their health delivery systems. Some day, the United States will have to face up to more fundamental reforms to assure that all people have access to essential health care in a system in which the costs of health care do not outpace the growth and productivity of the economy.

Concluding Observations

This chapter is not ideologically opposed to the development of a system of universal health care coverage for the United States but rather represents an exposition—selective, not exhaustive—of the range of factors that will con-tinue to impede access to effective care for a significant segment of the popu-lation, even with the institution of universal coverage. It is at the same time skeptical of the likelihood of *early* action toward a scheme of universal insur-ance at the federal or federal-state level, or at the governmental-private sector level, in view of the resistance of the American people to further large-scale taxation and the perilous budgetary situation of the federal government and most state governments. A powerful deterrent to early large-scale health re-form is the continuing barriers to greatly expanded federal and state expendi-tures for health care and other critically important social programs.

Faced with insurmountable obstacles to the early establishment of universal health care coverage, the United States should use the next years to experi-ment with removing discrete barriers that currently impair the access of many millions of Americans to proper medical care. Such experimentation should contribute to designing a more effective system of universal coverage, if and when the opportunity arises.

Notes

1. E Ginzberg, "The VA in a Vise: An Outside Observer Spells Out the Social and Economic Realities Ahead," *VA Practitioner* 6(3)(1989):39–46.

2. State of New York, *Review of the Financial Plan for the New York City Health and Hospitals Corporation for Fiscal Years 1991 Through 1994* (Albany, N.Y.: Office of the State Comptroller, 3 July 1990). Report 7–91.

3. Robert Wood Johnson Foundation, *Access to Health Care in the United States: Results of a 1986* Survey (Princeton, N.J.: Robert Wood Johnson Foundation, 1987). Special Report No. 2.

4. U.S. Department of Commerce, Bureau of the Census, *Statistical Abstract of the United States 1990* (Washington, D.C.: U.S. Government Printing Office, 1990).

5. E Ginzberg, HB Berliner, and M Ostow, *Changing U.S. Health Care: A Study of Four Metropolitan Areas* (Boulder, Colo.: Westview Press, 1993).

6. E Ginzberg, "Access to Health Care for Hispanics," *Journal of the American Medical Association* 265(1991):238–41.

7. U.S. Bipartisan Commission on Comprehensive Health Care, *A Call for Action* (Washington, D.C.: Pepper Commission on Comprehensive Health Care, 1990).

8. PM Ellwood, Shattuck Lecture: "Outcomes Management: A Technology of Patient Experience," *New England Journal of Medicine* 318(1988):1549–56.

9. U.S. Department of Health and Human Services, Health Care Financing Administration, Division of Medicaid Statistics, *State Medicaid Statistical Report* (Baltimore, Md.: U.S. Department of Health and Human Services, 1989). HCFA publication 2082.

10. Omnibus Budget Reconciliation Act 1990. PL 101–239. December 19, 1989.

11. U.S. General Accounting Office, *National Health Service Corps: Program Unable to Meet Need for Physicians in Underserved Areas* (Washington, D.C.: U.S. General Accounting Office; 10 August 1990). Publication GAO/HRD–90–128.

12. Office of National Cost Estimates, "National Health Expenditures, 1988," *Health Care Financing Review* 11(4)(1990):1–41.

PART FOUR

Toward Health Reform

17

Health Care Reform:
Why So Slow?

Recent opinion surveys have disclosed the deepening restiveness of the American public over the shortcomings of U.S. health care, which has grown to such a point that the majority of the respondents look favorably on alternative systems, particularly the Canadian one.[1] In the face of increasingly severe and widespread criticism and discontent, why has movement toward health reform been, at best, modest and, at worst, ineffectual?

Initiatives Toward Reform

To begin with, one must distinguish clearly between actions and effectiveness. The challenge of slowing the steep rise in health care expenditures has been the focus of both public and private policy for the past two decades. To call the roll of federal initiatives: We have seen federal expenditure controls on Medicare reimbursements; federal subsidies for the expansion of Health Maintenance Organizations, born of the belief that prepayment arrangements would result in lower expenditures than fee-for-service medicine; area planning initiatives aimed at reducing the redundant expansion of hospital plant and equipment; Medicare's shift from cost reimbursement to prospective reimbursement (based on diagnosis-related groups) to encourage greater efficiency in hospital operations; and in 1989, the adoption of a resource-based relative value scale to moderate the rising payments to physicians who treat Medicare patients.

At the same time, the states have sought to limit their spending for Medicaid. Despite liberal matching funds from the federal government, Medicaid programs—even at their peak in the mid-1970s—never enrolled more than three-quarters of all those living in poverty, as defined by federal standards. In the early 1980s, many states stringently tightened their criteria for eligibility; as a consequence, the proportion of poor people who were covered dropped to about 45 percent nationwide.[2] Furthermore, many programs set limits on the number of reimbursable visits to a physician, hospital admissions and days of care, and prescriptions per enrollee.

A considerable number of states maintain very low fee-levels for physicians who treat Medicaid patients (New York pays $11 for a routine visit); a great many have adopted certificate-of-need regulations, low reimbursement rates, or both for nursing homes. The nursing home measures are meant to discourage expansion of capacity, thus protecting against the potential enlargement of state outlays, inasmuch as Medicaid covers 44 percent of all expenditures for nursing home care.[3]

Nor has the private sector been passive in the face of escalating health care costs, reflected in the virtually constant annual increases of 10 to 20 percent in industry's expenditures for employee health care benefits. After 1975, large- and then medium-sized corporations moved to self-insure, thereby avoiding some of the costs involved in using health insurance companies as intermediaries. Next, they introduced a variety of prospective utilization reviews as a way to identify and discourage the unnecessary use of health care benefits by their employees.[4]

Faced with a severe recession in the early 1980s, many employers took more radical action and persuaded their employees to accept reasonable deductibles, coinsurance (and more recently premium-sharing), or both in order to reduce the companies' exposure to continuing cost inflation. At the same time, more companies broadened the range of delivery options they offered their workers, including enrollment in health maintenance organizations or preferred-provider organizations in the expectation that managed care would cost less than fee-for-service plans.[5]

This brief listing of the varied actions taken over the past two decades by the federal government, state governments, and employers (which together account for roughly 70 percent of all payments for health care) can hardly be interpreted as passivity in the face of the marked escalation in costs. The increase in per capita expenditures from $1,026 to $1,554 (constant dollars) between 1970 and 1989, leads, however, to the ineluctable conclusion that although efforts at reform were pursued, they failed to reach their primary objective, cost containment.[6]

Attempts to Reduce the Numbers of the Uninsured

If cost containment has been the principal challenge to payers during the past two decades, the growing numbers of uninsured persons has in recent years moved to the forefront of public concern. Compared with the numerous large-scale efforts to moderate the explosion in costs, however, attempts to provide coverage for the uninsured have been modest.

A few states initiated statewide risk pools to enable small employers to obtain coverage for their workers at affordable rates. A few created opportunities for the uninsurable—those with preexisting medical conditions—to purchase insurance at a subsidized cost. Several states are experimenting with plans to extend Medicaid coverage or subsidize alternative coverage for people who have left the public assistance rolls for low-income employment. Still others have become insurers of last resort for expenditures incurred as a result of catastrophic illness.[7]

Reference must also be made to the federal Consolidated Omnibus Budget Reconciliation Act of 1985 which made it mandatory for employers to provide continuing health care insurance for workers and their dependents for a period of eighteen months after the termination (temporary or permanent) of employment.

Since 1984, the federal government has taken another step that has contributed to reducing the numbers of uninsured persons. To expand services to pregnant women, infants, and young children, the government mandated several programs that have enlarged the Medicaid rolls. Concerned about the implications for their precarious state budgets, forty-eight of the nation's fifty governors recently petitioned Congress to refrain from further Medicaid mandates that would extend their financial liability.[8]

Although the foregoing might suggest progress toward reducing the number of the uninsured, that would be a misreading of events. The two noteworthy efforts have been the extension of insurance coverage to unemployed and laid-off workers and the expansion of Medicaid coverage for pregnant women and children near and below the poverty level. The increase in the number of uninsured persons by some nine million over the past decade underlines the ineffectiveness of reforms on this front.[9]

How can one explain the contradiction between, on the one hand, the continuing and growing concerns of the American people over the issues of cost inflation and the growing population of the uninsured, and, on the other hand, the absence of successful reforms to cure these major defects in the U.S. health care system? The foregoing summary analysis indicates unequivocally that these two major challenges do not lend themselves to easy solutions. Why then have we not moved to broader and deeper reforms that offer greater promise of success? The answers cover a wide domain.

Reasons for the Caution

First, our national predilection is for modest rather than substantial interventions, in the hope that the former will prove effective at a much lower cost than would be entailed by major changes. The United States tried a federal-state financing system (the Kerr-Mills Act of 1960) for the health care of the indigent elderly before opting for Medicare in 1965.[10] It made reimbursements of overhead costs a part of grants from the National Institutes of Health for biomedical research to shore up medical school budgets before Congress moved in 1963 to finance medical education directly in order to increase the supply of physicians.[11] Taking small steps before launching major interventions is a deeply ingrained American preference.

Second, ours is a pluralistic health system with many different players and many different payers. The system's pluralism is deeply implicated in the inflation of costs, but at the same time it has many virtues: It encourages innovation, offers broad consumer choice, allows adaptation to regional and local conditions, and protects against the centralization of decision-making power in the hands of bureaucrats. These are values that the public, although increasingly disturbed by cost inflation and the number of uninsured, will not willingly jeopardize, much less abandon, until it has exhausted most reasonable alternatives.

There is an additional reason for the public's caution. True, steadily rising health care costs are burdensome and sooner or later will become intolerable, but no one can be certain of the point of no return. The same public that admires the Canadian system also expresses a deep desire for more and better health care services. Even a schizophrenic public that wants both effective cost containment and more and better health care services appreciates, at least intuitively, that effective cost controls will result in less, not more, desirable and desired services. Accordingly, Americans are slow to lobby for basic health care reforms that might result in an effective cap on the amount of money that flows into the health care system.

Similarly, although large corporations resent the fact that (through cross-subsidization) they pay indirectly for the hospital care of workers who are not covered by their employers, they are not convinced that they should support mandatory coverage by employers for all regular employees. Some corporate managers and executives nod favorably in the direction of a federal or a federal and state system of universal health coverage, but they have not moved to the head of the parade for national health insurance. Although corporations are increasingly burdened by the rising cost of health care benefits, they have not yet decided that extending government jurisdiction into the area of health benefits is the long-term strategy they prefer. Moreover, as defenders of the market, they will surely hesitate a long time before advocating that the United States eliminate the role of private health insurance companies in the financing of the nation's health care, as Canada has done.

It is no mystery that major health reforms addressing cost containment and coverage for the uninsured have been so slow in coming. The dominant interest groups—government, employers, and households—as well as the major providers—physicians and hospitals—have reached no agreement on how to change the existing system to accomplish these widely desired reforms. In the absence of a strategy that can command broad support from disparate groups, a political consensus for major reforms will remain elusive. The only reasonable assessment, as of the beginning of the 1990s, is that we are unwilling to risk the strengths of our existing health care system in a radical effort to remedy admittedly serious deficiencies. The American public, in its political inaction, has so far opted for continued temporizing.

Notes

1. RJ Blendon, and H Taylor, "Views on Health Care: Public Opinion in Three Nations," *Health Affairs* 8(1)(1989):149–57.

2. D Chang, and J Holahan, *Medicaid Spending in the 1980s: The Cost/Access Trade-Off Revisited* (Washington, D.C.: Urban Institute, July 1989).

3. SW Letsch, KR Levit, and DR Waldo. "National Health Expenditures, 1987," *Health Care Financing Review* 10(2)(1988):109–22.

4. J Gabel, et al., "The Changing World of Group Health Insurance," *Health Affairs* 7(3)(1988):48–64.

5. PF Short, "Trends in Employee Health Benefits," *Health Affairs* 7(3)(1988):186–95.

6. RH Arnett III et al., "Projections of Health Care Spending to 1990," *Health Care Financing Review* 7(1986):1–36.

7. SS Laudicina, "State Health Care Pools: Insuring the 'Uninsurable'." *Health Affairs* 7(4)(1988):97–104; CN Oberg, and CL Polich, "Medicaid: Entering the Third Decade," *Health Affairs* 7(4)1988):83–96.

8. National Governors' Association. Washington, D.C. Private communication.

9. U.S. Department of Commerce, Bureau of the Census, *Statistical Abstract 1987*; idem, *Statistical Abstract 1989* (Washington, D.C.: U.S. Government Printing Office, 1987, 1989).

10. TR Marmor, *The Politics of Medicare* (Chicago, Ill.: Aldine, 1973).

11. E Ginzberg, "The Politics of Physician Supply." In *The Medical Triangle: Physicians, Politicians and the Public* (Cambridge, Mass.: Harvard University Press, 1991).

18

Interest Groups
and Health Reform

It is first necessary to explore what is meant by interest groups in the health care arena. Who are they, how do they act, what can or should a society do about them? Second, what insights can be offered about the role of the different interested parties in the current policy arena? And finally, how can we expect the dominant interest groups to interact during the remainder of this decade.

Interest Groups

Let me begin by noting some things that struck me as I tried to think my way through the thicket of interest groups and health care. It used to be very simple: There was the American Medical Association, and everything that happened or did not happen in American medicine could be traced back to the AMA. The AMA, for instance, really played the lead role in the reform of American medical education in the early part of this century; also, the AMA was semisupportive of national health insurance between 1916 and 1919. That is a piece of history long-since forgotten.

But many decades ago the AMA had to begin to share center stage. The Association of American Medical Colleges (AAMC) became a second important interest group, especially in the post–World War II years when the federal government started to finance medical research in a big way and put much of its money into the leading academic health centers. (By way of background, the federal government spent $3 million on biomedical research in 1940, and it is spending about $12 billion today.)[1] What is more, many leadership groups in Washington are reasonably certain that the U.S. government is underfunding biomedical research.

The next development involved the proliferation of the specialty societies and residency review committees. Together they usurped control over one-half of American medical education, the critical years of clinical training.

Ever since I delivered the Martin Memorial Lecture some years ago to the American College of Surgeons I have been receiving their monthly publication, *Bulletin of the American College of Surgeons*. Looking through the April and May issues, I found that most, if not all, of the pages were devoted to the planned adjustments that Medicare was about to make in establishing a single, all-inclusive fee for surgical procedures. The articles read more like exercises in economics than medicine.

In addition to physicians, hospitals are clearly another important interest group. However, it is not easy to define the key subgroups that are involved. When we talk about hospitals, are we referring to trustees? administrators? the physician staff? the nursing staff? technicians? the other support staff? If we consider that most of the people who sit on hospital boards as trustees or directors are leaders in local business enterprises, we will realize they have conflicting interests. On the one hand, they buy health insurance for their workers, insurance about which they are complaining, legitimately, that the premiums keep going up and up and up. And on the other hand, every month when they attend the hospital board meeting, the administrator shows them that the hospital is having a hard time getting its revenues to match its expenditures. Clearly, there's nothing simple about defining the interests of at least one key group, the trustees.

To confuse the picture a little more, consider the complaints of rural hospitals that Medicare has been setting the level of reimbursements for rural hospitals too low relative to the level for urban hospitals. Further, consider that the Prospective Payment Assessment Commission (ProPac; the official governmental body responsible for reviewing Medicare rates) believes that the federal government is allowing certain urban hospitals a disproportionate share of add-ons, which the cost figures do not justify. It is easy to see that there are a great many different interests in contention.

Now let us look at the patient's side of the equation. Between 1972 and 1988 Congress did not touch Medicare entitlements. In 1988, however, Congress decided to provide catastrophic benefits for acute-care patients. But the elderly, who were the prospective beneficiaries, went out and organized, and forced the Congress, to my knowledge for the first time in American history, to rescind the new entitlements the following year. I could go on to explain that I had warned a subcommittee of the Ways and Means Committee several years earlier not to touch Medicare unless there was a lot of new money available, but they forgot that advice and got mud all over themselves. Clearly, the concept of interest groups in the health care arena is complex. One year Congress adds benefits and the next year the beneficiaries insist that they be rescinded.

Let's look next at the private health insurance sector. That is really what Americans depend on for coverage, at least most people below sixty-five years-of-age. Private health insurance is, in considerable measure, a misnomer. The federal government contributes over $50 billion of subsidies annually to make the private health insurance system work.[2] Employers can deduct the cost of health care benefits as a business expense, and workers do not have to include the value of their benefits in their reported income. Even with these subsidies, private health insurance doesn't work very well. I am disturbed that the industry devotes more time and effort in avoiding the enrollment of high-risk individuals than it does in designing and selling low-cost policies to many of the uninsured who need catastrophic coverage at an affordable price.

Once upon a time, the Blue Cross system went out of its way to enroll people on a community rating basis. In the last fifteen to twenty years the commercial health insurance companies, and many, though not all, of the Blues, have been pursuing a risk-management strategy. The United States, having decided it did not want public health insurance and having opted for private health insurance, is the only country that tolerated the major insurance companies' pursuit of a risk-management strategy that makes it much more difficult for large groups of the population to obtain coverage. That is no small trick.

We do not usually think of government as an interest group, but it must be remembered that government has a special relationship to health care. Federal, state, and local governments together contribute over 40 percent of all the monies going into health care. To give an idea of how much money this entails, total outlays for 1991 were estimated at $765 billion.[3] To put that figure in perspective, I should remind you that in 1970 the United States spent $75 billion for health care, or 7.4 percent of the GNP.[4] In 1991 the ratio was projected to be 12.4 percent.[5] Obviously, governments, as major payers, have to worry about these matters. Further, there are conflicts of interest within the governmental structure.

One more point, in order to bring to the surface still another order of complexity: National health insurance first appeared on the American political agenda in 1912. Theodore Roosevelt ran for president on the Bull Moose ticket in that year, and he had national health insurance in his platform. Few people were much interested in "TR" at that point or in national health insurance, and the latter never got anywhere. I recently read a copy of President Truman's 1945 proposal for national health insurance. Except for a few stylistic changes, the same message could have been reformulated in 1991, forty-six years after Truman's initial proposal. The question that one needs to raise is why did the proposal die aborning? I have two answers.

First, the trade unions, the primary party of interest in pushing national health insurance, remained—except for a few leaders, such as Walter Reuther—on the sidelines. The reason that they did so was very simple: After private health insurance was established, they found that their members wanted union leaders to negotiate better health benefits and that, in general, employers were cooperative. Many legitimate, and some corrupt, unions had leaders who recognized the additional power and influence they could wield if they had a decision-making role in the investment of the union's health and welfare funds.

Second, once the hegemony of the AMA was destroyed, which was surely the case by 1965, after it lost its allout effort to defeat Medicare, the organization has spoken with a soft and, I believe, a better voice. Dr. James S. Todd and I were consultants to Dr. W. C. Hsaio when he developed his resource-based relative value scale for Medicare, and I thought Todd played a constructive role in developing the new fee and value measures. But the AMA does not have anywhere near the leverage in the political arena that it had before it put all of its chips into the defeat of Medicare and lost. If you go for broke and lose, you have demonstrated your weakness for all to see. National health insurance never gained broad public support so Americans never got it.

To round out this line of interpretation, let me add a third point, which concerns the attitudes of Americans toward the poor. As a people we believe that everybody should have maximum freedom to prove what he or she can do. Consequently, anyone who does not succeed is, by definition, at fault. The "great communicator," Ronald Reagan, articulated this view not once but time and again.

Insights on the Role of Interest Groups

So much for the past. Now we come to a consideration of interest groups and health care reform today. I start with this proposition: Two-thirds of the American people with good insurance coverage, either private health insurance and/or Medicare, are satisfied, in the main, with the health care system as it is working for them. That means that they will have little or no interest in major health reform, unless and until they come to believe that their present coverage is in danger. (I used to do a fair amount of overseas consultation for the Department of State, and I always gave some thought to where I wanted to be treated in case of a medical emergency. Although I was willing to consider treatment in Switzerland, Holland, or London, my preference was always to get back to the United States. That was a guiding principle, which fortunately I never had to put to use.)

The business community is split three ways in terms of the present situation. Employers who offer good benefits would like to see those of their peers who offer no benefits forced to do so, because otherwise they will continue to cross-subsidize these avoiders. In short, many favor a mandate that would require all employers to provide coverage for their workers or pay a special tax. The small employers are complaining that they cannot afford present insurance premiums, and some say they cannot afford to provide any health benefits at all because they are working too close to the margin. If they had to pay something on the order of $1,500 per employee per year, that would tip their business into bankruptcy. Therefore, most small employers do not want to see any employer-mandating initiative.

The large employers, who could get considerable help if they invited the federal and the state governments to collaborate with them in a conjoint effort to control the total flow of funds into the health care system, have up to the present resisted the temptation. They fear, and with good reason, that if government became an active partner in controlling health care costs and benefits, it would not be long before government might decide that it should play a more active role with regard to other benefits, such as pensions. And then it would be only a small step for government to seek a voice in wage determination. Faced with these dangers, most private companies have decided, at least for the time being, to keep their distance from government.

The private health insurance sector, in my view, has performed poorly in recent decades, nor am I impressed with the overall performance of American industry over the last twenty years. However, I believe that we are doing better now, and I hope we will do still better in the middle and late 1990s. The best evidence of how poorly the private insurance companies performed is the number of large- and medium-sized employers that decided to self-insure their workers. They saw no point in continuing to advance large sums to their insurers for the minimum services they received in return.

I have read the testimony on small-group policies recently given before the House Ways and Means Committee by Bernard Tresnowski, the head of the National Blue Cross–Blue Shield Association.[6] It was a statement that he should have given about fifteen years earlier. My personal expert on private health insurance is Stanley Jones, who was the long-term vice president of Blue Cross in Washington. In a speech he concluded that he has almost given up on the capacity of private health insurance to meet its societal obligations. I have not quite given up, but I am pretty close.

As far as the physician community goes, I pointed out earlier that although surgeons and primary-care physicians avoided an open fight among themselves over attempts to influence the physician reimbursement structure, each remains very restive about the new system and spends a lot of time lobbying. Not long ago, I was in West Virginia. As might be imagined, in the mountain areas people have all kinds of problems with prenatal care and deliveries. Nevertheless, the state's medical profession managed to defeat a nurse-midwifery bill, and in discussing the issue with me they contended that it was the lawyers' fault. I have a view that these two professions—medicine and law—are likely to become more closely allied. They may get together somewhere down the road and conjointly confront the rest of society in protecting their respective spheres of action. I am by no means sure this will happen, but it may.

I noted earlier, but it is worth repeating in the present context, that the biomedical research community in the principal academic health centers is a powerful interest group. Despite the fact that the federal government spends $12 billion on basic research and industry spends another $12 billion, the leadership of medicine says it needs more for training, facilities, equipment, and grants. I am sure they can use more, but to an economist "need" is a complex concept.

At last we have reached the finale; the role of the different interest groups in relation to health care reform in the 1990s. Some preliminary speculations about the 1990s: First, President George Bush did not take any lead regarding health care, except for peripheral issues. This is my view of malpractice reform. I think we need malpractice reform; I think defensive medicine is costing us an arm and a leg, but in the broader picture of health care reform, malpractice is a peripheral issue. From my long-term experience in Washington, where I worked for nine presidents, some smart and some not so smart, I doubt that any one of them would, up to this point in time, take the lead in health care reform. It is far from clear to me that either political party could gain much from trying to take the lead because it would face great difficulty in developing a consensus on health care reform.

But there is another part to this story. The forecast for 1994–1995, which is only a short time away, is that the United States will reach the $1 trillion expenditure level for medical care. Joseph Califano used that figure in a 1991 article for the *New York Times*, and it has been used by others as well.[7] Senator Everett Dirksen used to talk about a million here, a million there; now we have to talk about ten billion, even a hundred billion extra. A trillion dollar expenditure for health care in 1994–1995 cannot fail not only to impress economists but everybody. But the more ominous estimates are the $1.5 trillion to $2 trillion by the end of the decade. I believe that $2 trillion will not be extractable from the American public. That means the system cannot continue on its present course.

I have recently looked at the data anew and thought my way through these forecasts. This is the first time that I state definitively that our present system will be derailed. It cannot continue at this level of expenditure. That's my first speculation.

My second speculation is closely linked to the derailment effect. The two-thirds of the American public that I earlier identified as being reasonably content with the quantity and quality of medical care that they are receiving will become anxious and concerned because of fears that their health benefits will be curtailed. In fact, some of the insured are currently at risk, having agreed to pay more toward their premiums or toward coverage for their dependents.

That brings me to my third speculation, which is focused on what the United States might do to salvage as much as possible of the strengths of its system while at the same time making it more responsive to the one-third of the population who need more and better care. To do this and more will require constraining total expenditures. I would say that employers, the federal government, and the state governments have very little time left to figure out how to move toward a reformed payer system with global budgeting.

I am glad to report that the comptroller general of the United States in an April 1991 presentation to the Ways and Means Committee of the House of Representatives stressed the same goals.[8] In fact he alerted Congress that he would be back with the outlines of the actions it should take to assure the realization of these goals. Specifically, he said that the United States must provide health insurance coverage for the entire population; simplify the fantastically cumbersome and wasteful administrative structure, with its hundreds of thousands of redundant personnel in middle management, in clerical roles in insurance companies, and in the costs caused by defensive medicine. A conservative estimate would suggest that a 20 percent savings should be within reach, and 20 percent of U.S. 1991 outlays came to an impressive figure, over $150 billion. The comptroller general ended with the importance of Congress establishing an annual budgetary cap on all health care expenditures.

Speculations for the Future

I now come to my forecast: I think that the pot will boil, and it will boil over surely before or after the 1996 election. The United States has only a very few years to see whether it can forestall the crisis or whether it will be overtaken by it, and thus be forced to slug it out in the political arena when crisis erupts.

I have no reason to believe that slugging it out is a preferred way to go. I was convinced in the early 1960s that we needed to reform the health delivery system to help the elderly, but I was opposed to what we got. I was a minority of one on the policy and planning committee of the New York Academy of Medicine; sixty-four voted for what we got, and I stood up and said I was opposed to the federal government paying for the medical care of Governor Rockefeller or even Professor Ginzberg! I was worried about what would happen. I thought I was better at arithmetic than President Lyndon Johnson's actuaries, and I thought they did not understand the consequences of attaching the expanded medical care financing system to the United States Treasury. I knew the lid was going to blow sooner or later; I am only surprised that the crisis has been forestalled for almost three decades.

What are my final observations? I think the United States will pass something called universal insurance, some kind of federal-state minimum coverage package for everyone. It may be good for the people who currently have no insurance and it may even be good for those who are on Medicaid. But I seriously question that it will improve the situation of the two-thirds of the population that currently enjoys good coverage. Moreover, the morning after the new legislation is passed, millions of workers who currently have better benefits than the new federal-state system will provide will start to renegotiate with their employers. Their argument will go as follows: We worked for our benefits and accepted improved health benefits in lieu of higher wages. The fact that the federal government has passed universal insurance is not germane to our position. We want you, Mr. employer, to cover our supplemental benefits so that we stay even. I am reasonably certain that this will happen.

With between 45 and 50 percent of post-tax income going to the top quintile of American households, it looks to me unlikely, to put it mildly, that this minority will not put additional money into the health care system. If additional dollars can help restore their health and improve their later years, why not?

To put this last point in perspective, let me remind you that even Great Britain, which runs a low-cost system in which equity is a key objective, has not been able to prevent the modest expansion of a second system of hospital care outside the National Health Service. About 30 percent of all elective surgery in Great Britain is performed on people who opt out of the NHS in order to get treated expeditiously. One of the ways the British system is balanced is that many people die waiting for admission to a hospital. Death reduces the numbers in the queue. Another important balancing agent is the physician who doesn't even inform the older patient that the renal dialysis he or she needs could prolong his or her life. It is simply not available in the NHS. Clearly, there are many ways of balancing a health care system.

I am always amazed when people in the United States say, "We do not want to ration in this country." Yet, we ration all the time. Although New York City spends about $2.9 billion annually on its public hospitals and clinics, many of the hospitals provide less than an acceptable level of care. The United States has many problems that need attention beyond getting its financing in order and controlling the amount of new money that it puts into the system every year.

We need to close down hundreds of hospitals. We are not only overhospitalized in terms of beds, but we have expensive services in duplicate and triplicate that inflate our cost structure. The Medicare-Medicaid reforms initiated in 1965 helped to bring superior hospital care to every community of fifty thousand, and to many smaller communities. That is what we accomplished with the tremendously enlarged infusion of new money. We had the specialists, we had the subspecialists, and we put the money on the barrelhead for many outlying hospitals to transform themselves into tertiary-care facilities, thereby making life much more difficult for the inner-city academic health centers.

I lectured recently at Children's Hospital in Boston. It is in the process of establishing clinics in the suburbs to increase the flow of patients into its inner-city inpatient facility, an action that will almost certainly lead to some counter actions by suburban hospitals and physicians. In Iowa I was told recently that the state has ninety-nine counties, ninety-one of which contain a rural hospital. I asked how long it would take for the most isolated Iowa farmer to get to a hospital; the answer was forty-five minutes. I pointed out that if I walked out of my house in Manhattan and was struck by a truck, I couldn't get into a hospital in less than fifty minutes.

Another illustration: Some years ago during a visit to Johns Hopkins, I learned that a small local hospital a few blocks away was doing open-heart surgery and competing with Hopkins on the basis of price. I submit that there is probably no other country in the world that would expose one of its great teaching hospitals to such neighborhood competition.

My associates and I did a four-metro study—New York, Los Angeles, Chicago, and Houston. In each of the four cities we found that the low-income areas in the inner city often have only one physician in private practice for ten thousand to fifteen thousand inhabitants. In the high-income areas there is one physician for every 250 people.[9] And we say we don't ration! One of these days we will have to figure out a way of enticing, persuading, or bribing physicians to work at least for a time in underserved areas.

The United States may even want to consider shifting some dollars that it now uses on therapeutics to the area of prevention. But if truth be told, I am skeptical about such a shift. The best preventive measure I know is to pick the right mother with the right genes.

In the early 1970s the minister of health in Canada issued a document that pointed out that his country could save a lot of money and, at the same time, contribute to improving the health and longevity of its people if it shifted most of its outlays from therapeutics to prevention. In discussing this proposal, I inquired what preventive measures of known efficacy Canada was ignoring. The answer, as might have been expected, was none that permitted easy implementation. Admittedly, if one could get people to change their behavior, prevention would have a big payoff. But Moses, Jesus, and Gandhi, as well as many other great leaders, have had limited success in the arena of behavioral change. All the same, it might be a good idea to move some money out of medicine into welfare and education. The federal government probably contributed more to improving the health of the American people in the 1970s through the establishment of the food-stamp program than by additional spending for health care services. At least, I am willing to defend that proposition.

Now to my conclusion: In Philadelphia the Founding Fathers directed their considerable talents to designing a unique system of government, a system of checks and balances that was aimed at protecting the people against the arbitrary exercise of power by elected and appointed officials. The Constitution that they designed was an outstanding accomplishment, but it succeeded in giving us a government that was inherently constrained from being an efficient mechanism for the governance of a people that soon spanned a continent and that later became the world's hegemonic power. Let me conclude by emphasizing that it is hard, probably impossible, to design an effective and efficient health care system in a society that has a governmental structure that, by intent, works poorly.

Notes

1. E Ginzberg, and A Dutka, *The Financing of Biomedical Research* (Baltimore, Md.: Johns Hopkins University Press, 1989).

2. A Enthoven, "Health Tax Policy Mismatch," *Health Affairs* 4(4)(1985)):5–13.

3. U.S. Department of Commerce, "Health and Medical Services." In U.S. Department of Commerce, *United States Industrial Outlook, 1991* (Washington, D.C.: U.S. Government Printing Office, 1991), Chapter 44.

4. HC Lazenby, and SW Letsch, "National Health Expenditures, 1989," *Health Care Financing Review* 12(2)(1990):1–26.

5. U.S. Department of Commerce, "Health and Medical Services."

6. B Tresnowski, "Testimony of the Blue Cross and Blue Shield Association Before the Sub-Committee on Health, Committee on Ways and Means, U.S. House of Representatives, 102d Congress, 2d Session, 2 May 1991" (Washington, D.C.: U.S. Government Printing Office, 1991).

7. JA Califano, Jr., "More Health Care for Less Money," *New York Times*, 14 May 1991, Section A, p. 19, Column 2.

8. U.S. Accounting Office, CA Bowsher, "U.S. Health and Spending: Trends, Contributing Factors, and Proposals for Reform." Statement Before the Committee on Ways and Means, House of Representatives, 102d Congress. 2d Sess. 17 April 1991 (Washington, D.C.: U.S. Government Printing Office, 1991).

9. Minister of Supply and Services, *The Lalonde Report: A New Perspective on the Health of Canadians* (Ottawa, Ontario, Canada: Information Canada, 1974).

19

Physicians and
Health Care Reform

It should be emphasized at the outset that the scope, timing, and impacts of the health reforms that many informed persons advocate cannot be specified in detail because before they become operational they must be negotiated in three different arenas—in Congress, the state legislatures, and in the marketplace. Since the introduction of any major reform will affect the operations of the extant health care system, further reforms will be required, the nature and extent of which cannot be predicted until the impacts of the initial reforms have been implemented. Because of this series of chain reactions, any serious effort to sketch the future of health care reforms, and, more particularly, to focus on how they are likely to affect physicians, must be more speculative than definitive.

Despite these inherent difficulties in dealing with the future of health care reforms, some clarifications can be made by identifying four major areas where reforms are likely to be introduced in the near- or midterm: moderating the additional dollars flowing into the health care sector; providing the entire citizenry with health insurance coverage; changing the organization and delivery of health care services; constraining capital investments. Clearly, other targets for early reform could be identified, but any listing would overlap to a greater or lesser degree the areas that I have previously identified. The more important challenge is to speculate how the reforms within each of the four areas identified above are likely to affect the present health care system and how physicians are likely to practice in the future.

Moderating the Flow of New Dollars into the System

With the passage of time, the urgency for slowing the dollar inflow increases. The United States cannot much longer tolerate adding new funds for health care at a rate two to three times as fast as the growth of its GDP. The trillion-dollar level for health care outlays will be breached in late 1994, and current

176

projections point to a two trillion dollar figure by 2000 or shortly thereafter. The future dollar flow into the health care sector must be slowed. We are, however, still far from an agreement about how this objective is to be achieved. President Clinton, and others, have recommended that Congress increase taxes for Medicare funding and establish a system of global budgeting to achieve expenditure control. Others look to reducing or eliminating federal subsidies for health insurance, which total about $70 billion a year, to help constrain consumer demand. Still others advocate intensified reliance on competitive forces by building up strong purchasing insurance intermediaries that would be able to bargain more effectively with physicians and hospitals.

What are the likely consequences of a reduced dollar inflow into the health care system? First, fewer total health care dollars will mean fewer dollars to compensate the ever-increasing supply of practicing physicians. Inadequate attention has been paid to the fact that between 1960 and today the physician supply has increased from 140,000 to 250,000, or by about 80 percent. Despite the sizable increase in total numbers, physician earnings have significantly outpaced the increase in earnings of the typical worker. This paradoxical increase in both the number of physicians and in their earnings was possible only because of the large amounts of new money entering the health care system. Since 1965, on the eve of the implementation of Medicare and Medicaid, there has been more than a five-fold increase in total national health care expenditures.

Any serious effort to moderate the inflow of total dollars into the health care system is likely to force individuals and families to cover a higher proportion of total expenditures through out-of-pocket payments, which is also likely to have a moderating effect on physicians' earnings in the future.

The more dollar-constrained the health care system becomes the more likely it will result in a reduced demand for physician services, greater reliance on midlevel health personnel, and added payer resistance to physician fee increases, foreshadowed by the recently enacted RBRVS reimbursement approach introduced by Medicare.

Although some counterforces are likely to lead to an increased demand for physician services if and when universal coverage is implemented, it is unlikely that, even in the face of an expanded total demand for health care services, physicians earnings will continue to increase at the same rate as in the past. The more likely outcome is a retardation in the rate of growth of physicians' earnings.

Universal Coverage

One reason to expect a reduced inflow of new dollars into the health care sector is the president's program presented to Congress on February 17, 1993 in which he stressed interdependence between financial reforms and the early introduction of universal health care coverage. The latter must wait upon a prior, or at least a concomitant, effort to control the total costs of operating the health care system. The increasing awareness in recent years that all advanced nations provide universal coverage and do so at a total system cost that is considerably less than what is expected in the United States has impressed, if it has not yet convinced, the federal and state governments to deal expeditiously with the uninsured. A reasonable assumption is that universal coverage will not be much longer delayed.

As noted earlier, such action would increase the demand for physician services and thereby have a favorable impact on the earnings of the medical profession. There is a second reason to view universal coverage as a boost to physicians: They will no longer have to explain to themselves, the public, and the uninsured why they avoid treating indigent patients.

But it would be a mistake for the majority of American people who currently have good insurance to assume that the introduction of universal coverage would not have important consequences for the medical services that will be available to them once the new system is in place. Health services researchers who have been at the forefront of efforts to speed the enactment of universal coverage recognize that such coverage will be limited to essential services. It is highly unlikely that coverage will be as broad as currently enjoyed by enrollees with good health insurance policies.

One of the striking features of our health care system has been the proclivity of the medical profession to undertake any and all diagnostic and therapeutic procedures that appear to hold promise for their patients without concern for the cost-benefits of successive medical interventions. In the new era of severe dollar constraints the perpetuation of such an open-ended patient care strategy will not be sustainable. Physicians have protested repeatedly about the growing constraints on their clinical freedom but the odds favor a more restrictive environment if universal coverage brings with it, as it must, a specification of the services that the system will pay for, as well as those that are not covered.

A related observation: Although rationing has always been part and parcel of the U.S. health care system, the criteria used to decide who will have access to more costly procedures, such as a heart or liver transplant, have usually been obscured. But the well-to-do have always enjoyed preferred access. In the face of dollar constraints and universal coverage, the American people will be under increasing pressure to confront the implications of overt rather than sub-rosa rationing. Such a challenge will require the active participation of the physician community, whose members are in the best position to assess the therapeutic outcomes of costly and risky procedures. But in a democracy, decisions affecting the allocation of scarce medical resources can never be left solely to the medical profession.

Organization and Delivery Reforms

There is growing recognition that the private health insurance industry has contributed to the large numbers of persons without insurance as well as to the unease experienced by still larger numbers of people that they may lose their insurance coverage if they change jobs. The Health Insurance Association of America, cognizant of the growing criticisms levied against the industry and traumatized by the recent resignation of several of its largest members, proposed at the end of 1992 that it would cooperate with the federal government to assure universal coverage. This action represents a reversal of the forty-year strategy during which the private insurance companies splintered the insurance pool in order to improve their profitability by pursuing risk-management tactics directed at identifying and covering only the best risks.

Reacting to the growing trend of employers to self-insure—about 60 percent of all employees are in employer self-insured plans—such large insurance companies as Cigna, Aetna, Metropolitan, and Prudential have developed managed-care networks, through shared-risk contracts with large employers in which they identify preferred physicians and hospitals that offer quality care at a competitive price. A correlate of such risk contracts is the willingness of physicians and hospitals to participate in accountability systems that such risk contracting requires.

Another consequence of these managed-care arrangements are the changes introduced in the reimbursement patterns for physician services. In the place of fee-for-service, physicians who join such networks may accept capitation, go on salary, or agree to still other modes of reimbursement substantially different from fee-for-service.

A likely concomitant of the changes under way in the organization and delivery of health care, especially in an era of reduced total dollar outlays, will be the rapid decline in the number of physicians who practice solo or in small groups because of the high costs and limited market power associated with such practice arrangements. Larger group practices hold promise of substantial savings in support personnel, medical technology, rent, and other office expenditures.

Capital Investments

The fourth major area in which longer-range reforms are likely to be initiated in the near- and midterm relates to capital investments affecting the number and types of physicians trained; the size of the hospital plant and equipment and personnel staffing ratios; and trends for biomedical R & D, by both the federal government and industry.

The expansion of the physician supply in the 1960s and 1970s was undertaken with little attention directed to the costs of enlarging the educational infrastructure and even less to the significant financial consequences for the health care system resulting from the large-scale expansion of the physician supply. Had we increased over the last three decades the total supply of physicians by 40 percent instead of 80 percent, our 1992 outlays for medical care might have been $200 billion lower.

Currently the AMA, the AAMC, COGME, the Physician Payment Review Commission, and still other governmental and advisory bodies are sending the same signals: Contain the future supply of physicians; decrease the relative number of specialists; and pay more attention to linking physicians to underserved populations.

With an increasing number of medical students graduating from medical school with an average debt of $50,000—or higher—it should not prove all that difficult for the federal government alone, or better, in association with the states, to put effective arrangements in place whereby the debts of young physicians are cancelled for service among underserved rural and inner-city groups.

The federal government is also likely to take early action to modify the conditions governing graduate medical education (GME) funding aimed at providing more support for residency training for generalists rather than for specialists. The more difficult challenge will be for states, particularly those with multiple medical schools, to merge or close their smaller and less-effective schools.

In the short span between 1985 and 1992 national support for health R & D increased from $13.6 billion to $28.1 billion, with industry's share growing so rapidly that it overtook the federal government's current contribution of $11.6 billion.

One must assume that if major reforms to constrain future health care outlays are introduced and implemented in the near and middle term, such efforts will inevitably be reflected in some moderation of new investments in research and development, especially in the development arena, which is the focus of industry's concern. Hospitals facing tightened budgets will move more slowly to purchase the latest (and more expensive) new pieces of equipment, and, in turn, the medical supply companies are likely to moderate their R & D expenditures.

But there are additional forces at work that are likely to slow the purchases of expensive new technology. Medicare has taken some selective actions, both to resort to technology assessment before authorizing reimbursement and to restrict high-cost procedures, such as heart transplants, to a limited number of medical centers. These actions will also slow the pace of new sales of expensive equipment.

A more controlled and constrained financial health care environment will underpin the continuing shift of treatment to ambulatory-care settings that will be reflected sooner or later in a significant decline in the number of acute-care hospitals. The combination of fewer dollars and fewer inpatients points to a substantial shrinkage in hospital capacity in the decade ahead. Clearly, such a shrinkage will have significant impacts on access of patients to health care as well as on the future earnings of physicians. The closing of a local hospital is often prelude to the relocation of physicians or to difficulties in recruiting physicians to replace those who retire or die.

An increasing proportion of all patients are likely to become members of large insured groups, which will enter into long-term relations with designated physicians and hospitals. Enrollees will be under strong financial and other pressures to seek treatment from designated providers, whose payments will depend little, if at all, on a fee-for-service arrangement. If this is the wave of the future, physicians will find it necessary to join such large-group arrangements, where they will probably have considerably less clinical and economic freedom than they presently enjoy under a solo or small-group pattern of practice based on fee-for-service. The fact remains that the best, perhaps the only real, prospect of constraining the total costs of U.S. health care involve significant alterations in how physicians currently practice, how they are paid, and how much they are permitted to earn.

Clearly, such reforms affecting the financing and delivery of health care services as have been outlined above will also have major effects on patients' choices and their satisfaction with the medical care they receive. The scale and scope of the choices available to them as to their principal physician as well as to the specialists they may want or need to consult will be largely if not totally determined by the health care plan to which they belong. Those with more disposable income, and particularly the wealthy, will probably encounter little difficulty in maintaining the high degree of freedom of choice that they now enjoy in selecting physicians and in securing expensive modes of treatment.

In 1974 the United States resorted to federal-state governmental planning in order to control capital investments in hospitals and costly technology, but the legislation was permitted to lapse after a few years because of the cumbersome machinery needed to implement "certificate of need" (CON). The fact that the nation dropped the regulation of capital investments in the past, however, does not preclude a second and broader attempt in the near future to place a lid on total health care outlays (global budgeting), an objective that will also necessitate controlling capital investments.

Finally, it is almost a foregone conclusion that decision making regarding the number, types, and deployment of physicians in the future will see enlarged roles for both the federal and state governments. Neither effective cost controls nor universal coverage can be achieved without more effective planning and deployment of health care personnel, particularly physician personnel, who are and will continue to be key to the delivery of effective health care services to the American people.

20

Where Are We and Where Should We Be Going?

After the upset senatorial victory of Harris Wofford in Pennsylvania in the spring of 1991, many political and health policy analysts prophesied that the presidential election of 1992 would revolve around reform of the health care system. My intention here is to explore where the nation stands on health care reform and to assess when the issue may move beyond rhetoric and preliminary skirmishing to substantive political engagement.

Principal Payers

A good place to begin is to identify the principal parties whose action or inaction will determine when health care reform will rise to the top of the nation's agenda. Much of the answer will depend on the directions taken by the four principal payers—the federal government, employers, state governments, and households.

The federal government, faced with a prospective annual deficit of $300 billion, is poorly positioned to take any initiative that would require significant new outlays. Several years ago, when he was director of the White House Office of Policy Development, Dr. William Roper pointed out that any effort to provide expanded access for the many millions of uninsured and underinsured citizens would require that the nation undertake serious cost containment, but that no important interest group was willing to make the sacrifices that would be entailed. Similarly, any move to put a Canadian-style solution into effect would be sidetracked because it overlooked major differences between American and Canadian political institutions.[1] More recently, Representative Willis Gradison, Jr. (R-OH), one of the best informed legislators on health issues, stated that he did not expect the federal government to assume the leadership in health reform for the years immediately ahead, given the intractable problem of coming up with the financing for any workable plan.[2]

Matters of resources aside, it would be out of harmony with U.S. political tradition to expect Congress to act on major health care reform in the face of disagreement and lack of agreement among the principal pressure groups about the direction reform should take. The legislative hopper contains a range of proposals as diverse as national health insurance and federal tax subsidies for the purchase of private health insurance by the uninsured.

Employers, the second major payer, are deeply divided. Some would welcome the opportunity to end their commitment to provide health insurance benefits to their employees, active and retired, but many others believe that the prospect of unloading this task on the public sector is doomed to failure. No government plan will match in breadth and depth the benefits that large employers currently provide, which means that they will be forced to offer their employees supplemental health benefits.

Further, many employers are disinclined to see their freedom restricted by a possible modification of the Employee Retirement Income Security Act, the federal statute governing employee benefits, which has protected them since 1974 from numerous state taxes and regulations. Moreover, they will avoid any action that might expand the jurisdiction of the federal government over employee benefits. True, employers are disturbed by the large annual increases in the cost of health benefits, but not to the point of taking the initiative to broaden federal involvement.

State governments have been protesting to the administration and Congress since the late 1980s over continuing congressional mandates to extend eligibility and broaden benefits under their Medicaid programs. In 1989 the National Governors' Association officially requested that such mandates cease, and when Congress turned a deaf ear to their pleas, the states resorted to various financial schemes to enrich federal matching grants for their Medicaid programs. These were of such dubious propriety that the administration and Congress outlawed many of them. Even with additional federal matching money, steeply rising expenditures for Medicaid will inhibit most states from initiating substantial health care reforms. It is therefore noteworthy that a few—namely, Oregon, Minnesota, and Vermont—are moving ahead with efforts aimed explicitly at providing universal coverage.

Households—the fourth source of payment—are concerned about deficiencies in insurance coverage and increases in out-of-pocket costs. The number of people with private health insurance has been dropping since 1989,[3] and people with a history of serious medical problems often find that if they lose their coverage they are unable to replace it at an affordable price. The same is true of people in good health who work in high-risk industries or for a small employer; health insurance, if obtainable at all, comes at a cost that is frequently beyond the reach of employers and employees alike. The failure of Medicare to cover long-term care, either in a nursing home or at home, is a cause of anxiety for large numbers of older people who are disturbed by their growing personal outlays.

In sum, the principal payers—the federal government, employers, state governments, and households—are poorly positioned to assume the leadership role in health reform. The four could provide coverage for the uninsured and make at least limited benefits available for long-term care, but not until U.S. taxpayers change their formidable resistance to higher taxes.

Principal Providers

Let us now shift focus to the principal provider groups, physicians, hospitals, pharmaceutical and medical-supply companies, and various types of managed-care organizations. Physicians, the key provider group, generating about 75 percent of all health care costs, are frustrated by the steady erosion of their clinical autonomy, the avalanche of paper with which they must contend, and the latest assault on their earnings by the Health Care Financing Administration, which under the current resource-based relative value scale is capping both their fees and the volume of services they provide to Medicare patients. The disruptions caused by malpractice litigation continue, though recent years have seen some reduction on this front. Despite these threats to their professional integrity and career satisfaction, physicians are not in the vanguard of health care reform. Most of them continue to prefer their current fee-for-service arrangements, which yield a mean annual income of about $165,000[4] to prospective reforms that hold uncertain promise of reducing or eliminating the drawbacks in their current practice environment.

In the late 1970s the hospitals were able to prevent the Carter administration from introducing new federal regulations aimed at capping their expenditures; since then, they have directed their political efforts at protecting their freedom of decision making as regards new investments and current operations. More recently, governmental payers have reduced their reimbursements for inpatient care, and private sector payers have applied increasing pressure to obtain price discounts, often in exchange for a guaranteed number of admissions. Although their margins for patient care and their total margins have been declining, most hospitals continue to operate in the black. With an average occupancy rate of slightly more than 60 percent, many are uncertain about the future, but for now hospital trustees and chief executive officers generally prefer the status quo to any alternative that they see on the horizon.

The pharmaceutical and medical-supply companies have had few, if any, reasons for complaint in the free-wheeling financing environment of recent decades, because of the insatiable appetite of hospitals, physicians, and households for the latest innovations spawned by research and technology. Although a few warning shots have been fired—namely the requirement by the Health Care Financing Administration that the cost-effectiveness of selected new forms of technology be assessed before payment is approved and recent legislation by Congress requiring maximal discounts to the federal government on the purchase of drugs—the large for-profit manufacturers of health care products have much to gain from continuation of the status quo. This perception still guides their behavior.

The last of the principal providers are the many for-profit and nonprofit organizations, small and large, that continue to develop new financing and delivery mechanisms, including health maintenance organizations, preferred-provider organizations, and risk-sharing arrangements between large employers and insurance companies. These entities have grown considerably since the early 1980s, from about 10 million enrollees to close to 40 million,[5] but their futures remain uncertain for a variety of reasons: Physicians prefer to practice in a fee-for-service system, large numbers of the insured prefer to retain total freedom in their choice of providers, and new risk-sharing systems for the delivery of managed care are difficult to organize. Exacerbating this uncertainty about the future is the limited success these innovations have had in braking costs—their raison d'être.[6] A reasonable assumption is that the new entities will continue to expand, but not at a rate that will significantly alter the established patterns of health care financing and delivery in the United States. In short, providers, like payers, do not currently appear to have any strong drive to assume leadership in the reform of the health care system.

Prospects for Reform

Can one conclude from the foregoing that reform is a mirage, a subject for discussion but not for action? Nothing could be further from the truth. Consider the following: It was estimated that the 1992 total health care outlays would exceed $800 billion, and the U.S. is certain to pierce the trillion-dollar level by 1995.[7] To remain on the present trajectory, the U.S. would have to find *another* trillion dollars between the mid-1990s and the end of the decade. It is my contention that at recent and projected rates of growth of the economy, a second trillion dollars to support the nation's health care system will not be forthcoming in the last half of the 1990s. Such a level of expenditures would imply an average cost for health care of $30,000 per family of four, about as much as that family will be paying for food, clothing, housing and transportation *combined*. Even if the dollars could be found, it would make no sense.

What are the implications of this spending projection for health reform? First and foremost, the current health care system, more attractive to most payers and providers than the alternatives they can anticipate, is likely to be derailed some time later in this decade. The derailment of the current system will mean the loss of private health insurance for many people; it will place many small and large hospitals at serious risk of bankruptcy; both the federal and state governments will be forced to appropriate emergency funds to assure the maintenance of critical health care services; and all the other concerned parties, particularly physicians and patients, will be seriously unsettled. When that occurs, health reform will of necessity command attention; inaction and drift will no longer be possible.

In April 1991, Charles Bowsher, the comptroller general of the United States, testified before the House Ways and Means Committee and offered the following agenda for reform: universal coverage, global budgeting, and administrative simplification.[8] The Congress listened and did nothing, taking its lead from interest groups and the public at large, which continue to complain vociferously about the current system but are not willing to pay the price of reforming it. A first challenge is, therefore, to impress on the concerned parties and the public that time is running out and that unless a reform effort begins now, the long-term costs will be horrendous.

Global Budgeting: The First Step

In terms of priorities, I believe the United States should immediately address the comptroller general's second proposal, global budgeting, which holds the greatest promise of stabilizing the increasingly unstable health care system. If global budgeting is successful, this will give the nation time to introduce the many other reforms required to assure the system's viability. Since the federal government pays for 30 percent of all health care expenditures, covers more than half of all Medicaid costs, and undergirds private health insurance through its tax subsidy, it should be able to elicit the cooperation of the key parties—employers, private health insurers, and state governments—in implementing global budgeting. Annual expenditures would be capped at the previous year's total plus a sum that did not outstrip by much the growth rate of the GDP.

The critical step in implementing global budgeting is to engage broad public support for action now, rather than to temporize until the nation has the chaos that is inevitable if it delays. What are the steps that must be taken promptly? Since the states will have the task of allocating their share of the global funding to the specific health care providers within their jurisdiction, they will need to expand and strengthen their statistical reporting systems. They will also need to design and implement the bargaining mechanisms that will guide their payments to providers. These new mechanisms will require a period of experimentation, ongoing assessment of their early operating results, and subsequent refinement and adjustment.[9]

We are not starting from scratch, however. A number of states have considerable experience as sole payers for hospital care. Because the federal government put in place a radically revised fee system under Medicare, it is accumulating experience in physician reimbursement within budgetary constraints.

Implementing a system of global budgeting will obviously not be easy, but given the alternative of financial chaos and institutional disintegration, the difficulties encountered in its implementation should not be insurmountable. With so much to lose, the key parties should be willing to cooperate in the development and institution of global budgeting. It alone offers them the prospect of protecting their present interests and providing the stability they will need to advance those interests in the future.

Notes

1. WL Roper, "Financing Health Care: A View from the White House," *Health Affairs* 8(4)(1989):97–102.

2. WH Gradison, Jr., "Remarks to the Washington Business Group on Health and the National Association of Manufacturers." Joint Meeting, Washington, D.C., January 24, 1992.

3. Health Insurance Association of America, *Source Book of Health Insurance Data 1992* (Washington, D.C.: Health Insurance Association of America, 1992).

4. Center for Health Policy Research, *Socioeconomic Characteristics of Medical Practice, 1992* (Chicago, Ill.: American Medical Assocation, 1992).

5. Group Health Association of America (GHAA), *GHAA's National Directory: HMOs 1992* (Washington, D.C.: Group Health Association of America, 1992).

6. E Ginzberg, "Managed Care Has Not Lived up to Its Promises," *New York Times*, 20 February 1992:A24.

7. J Meyer, S Sullivan, and S Silon-Carrol, *Critical Choices Confronting the Cost of American Health Care* (Washington, D.C.: National Committee for Quality Health Care, 1990).

8. U.S. Accounting Office, CA Bowsher, "U.S. Health Care Spending: Trends, Contributing Factors, and Proposals for Reform." Statement before the Committee on Ways and Means, House of Representatives, 102d Cong., 2d sess., 17 April 1991. (GAO/T–HRD–91–16).

9. SM Shortell, "A Model for State Health Care Reform," *Health Affairs* 11(1)(1992):108–27.

21

President Clinton's Design for Reform

It would be precipitous (June 1993) for any writer to attempt to predict the details of the president's health care proposal. The president has tipped his hand, not once but repeatedly, however, about many of the key proposals that are likely to be included in the recommendations that he will forward to the Congress for its consideration and action. Since this work is aimed at explaining to the American people what happened to its health care system since the mid-1960s when Medicare and Medicaid were passed and implemented, a reasonable conclusion would be that it is more sensible—and, particularly, more useful—to get the book into the public's hands as soon as possible rather than to await the release of the president's recommendations. As is true of so many political and other decisions in life, "timing is everything," and I have opted to write this concluding chapter before the details of the president's plan have been made final. It is important for the reader to remember that while the president proposes, only Congress disposes, based on its readings of what the American voters, both the influential groups and others, prefer to see enacted.

Members of the Congress, especially those who hold senior positions on the key committees, have been able during these last years to deepen and broaden their understanding of the complex issues involved in legislating significant changes in the U.S. health care system. And the many health care interest groups have been working overtime during these past months, if not years, to increase the flow of information to the Congress to insure that it does not intentionally or inadvertently take action that will be detrimental to their interests, and by extension, to the interests of some sector of the American people.

I offer a limited number of focused observations on what I believe will be included in President Clinton's proposed reforms, how the American people should evaluate them, and the major considerations that should guide the Congress when it decides to enact, modify, postpone, or reject them.

The president has indicated repeatedly that it is essential for the nation to slow the rate of growth in health care expenditures and thus enable us to reduce the federal deficit and add to the competitiveness of American industry. I consider it critical that the American people and the Congress accept this basic premise. He has also indicated on a number of occasions that he favors the institution of a "global budget," the details of which have not been spelled out. The key to the president's proposal is his belief that a system of "global budgeting" is a necessary, if not a sufficient, condition for assuring that the outlays for health care are moderated. I believe that the president is sound in reaching this conclusion about the role of "global budgeting" as an essential constraining influence.

There are many reasons that lead citizens and members of Congress, based on our history and ideology, to have a preference for market solutions rather than global budgeting. But a preference is not adequate. If these voters agree with the president that the rate of annual increases for health care must be reversed, they have the responsibility to come forward with a proposal better than "global budgeting" to accomplish this end. To date no alternative proposal backed by analysis rather than ideology has been advanced.

The president has indicated on several occasions that he favors universal insurance for essential health care services for all Americans. He has admitted some uncertainty about whether this action should be taken immediately or whether, because of the federal deficit, expanded coverage should be stretched out over a limited number of years and completed before the end of the decade. The president knows that the American people have expressed approval for developing his plan for universal coverage as soon as possible, though many of them say that they do not want their taxes to be increased by more than a small amount ($200 a year) to advance this goal.

It is hard to see how Congress can fail to go along with the president's recommendation. Congress probably will employ a phasing-in approach, an action that the American people have repeatedly supported in opinion surveys.

The president has likewise suggested that the risk-management system of private health insurance companies in selling and renewing insurance policies is seriously deficient. It must be altered so that all Americans can be assured the ability to purchase health insurance at a reasonable price and to renew their policies even if they change jobs or develop a serious medical condition that will require expensive treatment. President Clinton favors the creation of regional health alliances that will be able to meet the essential reforms that he seeks in private health insurance. Moreover, he looks to the health alliances to bargain effectively with hospitals, physicians, and other health providers to offer enrollees quality services at a reasonable price.

There is considerable evidence in public survey data to the effect that a significant and growing proportion of the American public are worried about their private health insurance and expect the federal government to play a leading role in reducing their anxiety about their future coverage. It is difficult to believe that Congress can long remain indifferent to this steadily deepening concern among growing numbers of Americans without taking some early action aimed at reassuring them.

A difficult question relates to the emphasis the president is placing on health alliances and whether that emphasis is justified by theory, history, or experience. As for theory, the president believes that strong regional health alliances will assure citizens that the federal government will not dominate health care planning and policy, since market competition will determine most relationships between the American people and their health care providers. So far so good: The federal government is in no position to take on the detailed operation of the U.S. health care system. Reliance on nongovernmental institutions for much of the decision making is necessary and desirable.

But one must add that there is little if any basis in recent U.S. history to prompt optimism about the initiative and capability of private health insurance companies to provide the American public with good health insurance at a reasonable cost. The record of the last several decades is not impressive.

What about testimony based on experience? Although it is not impossible to find a few models of regional health alliances that could provide some support for the president's reform proposal, the important fact is that regional health alliances at this point in time are more vision than reality. It would be difficult to identify a single regional health alliance with a good enough track record that would lead a cautious observer to recommend to Congress that this is the preferred way to go. Additionally, if the public does not like the president's recommendation to assign a dominant role in health reform to regional health alliances, they will shift the burden to the skeptics and will require them to come forward with alternative recommendations.

If Congress comes to share the skepticism and unease outlined above, its next assignment is obvious. It must start working sooner rather than later to design, at least in broad outline, the principles to be followed by the federal government in suballocating the total funds to the states, which in turn must suballocate them to their counties and cities. The latter will have the primary responsibility for identifying efficient intermediaries to bargain with hospitals, physicians, and other health care providers to insure that the quality of the services provided to the public is acceptable or better and that the public can afford to pay for such care today and in the future.

Another arena that the president's proposal surely addresses relates to the scale and scope of "essential services" that will be available to all Americans, as well as his recommendations on how best to pay for the expanded coverage—whether through taxes, employer premiums, or "givebacks" and ceilings on the benefits that enrollees currently enjoy. President Clinton and his staff have thus far provided mixed signals about whether the "essential services" will be narrowly or broadly defined, a difference that can imply a variation in annual outlays of $50 billion or more, if, for example, expanded services are provided for mental health and long-term care. Since coverage for the uninsured and the poorly insured has been estimated to cost $50 billion, the fiscal implications of the health care reform program, even without further specification and elaboration, involves sizable additional outlays that will have to be met by new taxes, new employer premiums, or by limiting benefits for high-income Medicare beneficiaries and persons who have good private health insurance coverage.

Whatever the combinations of benefits and payment proposals, one thing is certain: Congress is not likely to support enlarged health care benefits that require substantially more outlays from employers and the public. As noted earlier, the public has reported that it would be willing to see its tax bill increased slightly to make universal coverage a reality. There appears to be reasonable public support for the imposition of "sin taxes" on cigarettes and hard liquor. And there appears to be support for the federal government's placing a cap on the tax subsidy for private health insurance and lifting the ceiling on the income limit on which the Medicare tax is levied. The leaders of Congress played a key role in drafting and passing the catastrophic amendments to Medicare in 1988 and were forced by the revolt of the elderly to rescind most of the legislative package the following year. It is unlikely that they will forget and fail to be influenced by this earlier untoward experience. There is no reason to believe that the American public, in general, and the elderly, in particular, have changed their basic posture over the intervening years: They want the federal government to provide them with more and better health care services, but they are opposed to paying for such improved services, either through higher taxes or larger out-of-pocket expenditures.

Reform: Problems and Prospects

The foregoing is part of the broad and accurate delineation of the services and payment dilemma, and it behooves the president, the American people, and the Congress to be aware of the dangers that lie ahead. Each needs to confront reality clearly and sharply and to realize that the American people are not willing to finance much-expanded access to essential services for the entire citizenry. It will be difficult enough to persuade them to pick up the considerably expanded tab that attaches to providing universal access, which comes to an estimated additional cost of $50 billion annually.

Even if one accepts the cautionary stance above, one still has to contend with the widespread belief by the White House, various public interest groups, and some members of Congress that an expansionary approach to health reform is possible without running into a money bottleneck. Of course, it is more attractive for the president and members of Congress to provide more and better services to the American public than it is to undertake the task of raising the additional taxes required to pay for them. But in 1993, given the importance that both the president and Congress have placed on reducing the federal deficit, the realities of benefit-payment tensions cannot be sidestepped, much less avoided. The expansionists have one card left to play and they are playing it. They contend that there is so much waste, fraud, abuse, gouging, unnecessary services, and other cost-increasing practices currently in place that when even a part of these multiple sources of waste is eliminated there will be ample funding in the system to cover the expansion of needed and desirable services.

Those who have studied the U.S. health care system in depth cannot deny the existence of a great number of sources of waste, inefficiency, and inappropriate deployment of resources that in total represent expenditures considerably in excess of the more than $100 billion required to finance both the proposed additional coverage and expanded services. But the challenge the expansionists have not confronted, and certainly have not resolved, are the steps they propose to follow to recapture the wasted dollars; how they propose to redeploy them; and, finally, how long the approach they recommend will require to accomplish its highly desirable objectives. Without answers to these three questions, it would be foolhardy for the American people to pursue what may after all turn out to be a mirage or, more correctly, a reality that cannot be altered by the societal mechanisms that the country currently has at its disposal.

One can draw up a trial balance sheet about the health reforms the president should recommend and about which the American people and the Congress should debate and then enact. The nation's attention should be focused on no more than four goals: (1) putting in place a system of cost containment that will slow the rate of health care expenditures; (2) putting in place a commitment to universal coverage over the next years and taking initial action to deliver on that commitment, for instance by covering all infants, children, and young people from birth to age eighteen; (3) restructuring private health insurance to enable the entire population below sixty-five years-of-age to obtain basic coverage at a community rate and to be assured that, no matter what changes they experience in their health status or in their employment, their insurance is secure; and, (4) making sure that the reform proposals focus on providing access to essential services to all Americans, as defined by current practice, not a considerably expanded set of services.

Such a four-faceted reform program is ambitious enough without the great many additional goals that, while desirable, would jeopardize the early accomplishment of the four priority objectives. Clearly, no one could be opposed to expanding outcomes studies and the dissemination of clinical guidelines aimed at improving the quality of care available to the American people by eliminating unnecessary procedures and, in the process, recapturing resources that are currently being wasted. Clearly, the administrative infrastructure with its complex billing and paying systems needs to be simplified, which in turn should result in cost savings. The present malpractice system and the defensive medicine that it encourages should be altered.

Greater efforts addressed to health education, life-style changes, and preventive services warrant early and continuing attention because of the promise they hold of contributing significantly to improving health status without contributing to the further inflation of total health care expenditures.

There are more challenges that Americans and Congress must begin to address, such as the sizable shrinkage of the greatly underutilized but very expensive acute-care hospitals. Further, early reassessment of the educational and training system for health personnel must ensure that it produces the number of physicians the nation can productively employ—but not a great many more—and that they are prepared to meet the priority needs of the patients who will seek treatment. Further, that these systems are supported by the appropriate number and types of midlevel health professionals who will provide patients with good treatment at a controllable cost. The nation also faces the challenge, in an era of cost containment, of assuring that research and development can be funded in appropriate depth and breadth without immediate deployment of every marginal improvement in technology, irrespective of cost-effectiveness.

This brings us to the last items on the nation's health agenda, which are likely to remain major challenges for long years to come. The American people must recognize that there are gross differences at present in the access of different groups to essential health care services, based on income, education, age, residence, gender, race and other differentiating characteristics, and that there is no prospect, surely not in the short- and middle term, of assuring that all Americans will have equal access to health care services. What the nation can and must assure is that all Americans have access to an essential level of care.

As the health reform debate has begun to escalate, the criticisms directed at the various health interest groups—physicians, hospitals, pharmaceutical manufacturers, the health insurance companies—have increased to a point where a participant observer wonders whether the critics remember that our society and economy depend on interest groups for providing the output of essential goods and services and for the initiatives that will improve such future output. This reminder does not imply that the several interest groups should not be subject to ongoing evaluation or that they should not be criticized, but only that they are key parties that must be consulted as the reform program is shaped and enacted and that their opinions, however much they are embedded in self-interest, must be carefully weighed.

Finally, despite the special attention that health reform must pay to cost containment, it would be a grievous mistake for Congress to downgrade, much less ignore, the high value that Americans place on freedom of choice, a freedom that is that much more important when they face life-threatening decisions. A reform of the U.S. health care system that does not permit the American people to continue exercising a high degree of choice in selecting their physicians and hospitals would be a reform foredoomed to failure.

Credits

Chapter 1	Originally published in *Academic Medicine* Vol. 66, no. 8, August 1991, pp. 439–442. Reprinted by permission.
Chapter 2	Originally published as Special Address, *American Journal of Medical Sciences* Vol. 304, no. 4, October 1992, pp. 268–271. Reprinted by permission.
Chapter 3	Originally published as "The VA in a Vise: An Outside Observer Spells Out the Social and Economic Realities Ahead," *VA Practitioner*, March 1989, pp. 39–46. Reprinted by permission.
Chapter 4	Originally published as "A Century of Health Reform," *Society* Vol. 30, no. 1, November/December 1992, pp. 19–25. Copyright © 1992, Transaction Publishers. Reprinted by permission.
Chapter 5	Originally published as "The Reform of Medical Education: An Outsider's Reflections," *Academic Medicine* Vol. 68, no. 7, July 1993, pp. 518–521. Reprinted by permission.
Chapter 6	Originally published as "The Limits of Health Reform—Revisited," *Stanford Law and Policy Review* Vol. 3, Fall 1991, pp. 195–201. Reprinted by permission.
Chapter 7	Originally titled "The Old Era Passes—New Approaches," the second presentation in the *Midland Lecture Series* at the Fawcett Center for Tomorrow, Columbus, Ohio, November 13, 1991 (printed as a pamphlet in 1992).
Chapter 8	Originally published with "Reply," in *Frontiers of Health Services Management* Vol. 7, no. 2, Winter 1990, pp. 3–22 and p. 38, Health Administration Press, Ann Arbor, MI. Copyright © 1990, Foundation of the American College of Healthcare Executives. Reprinted by permission.
Chapter 9	Originally published as "Philanthropy and Nonprofit Organizations in U.S. Health Care: A Personal Retrospective," *Inquiry* Vol. 28, no. 2, Summer 1991, pp. 179–186. Reprinted by permission.
Chapter 10	Originally published as "High Tech Medicine and Rising Health Care Costs," Commentary, *Journal of the American Medical Association* Vol. 263, no. 13, April 4, 1990, pp. 1820–1822. Copyright © 1990, American Medical Association. Reprinted by permission.
Chapter 12	Originally published in *Health Management Quarterly*, a publication of The Baxter Foundation, Vol. 15, no. 1, First Quarter 1993, pp. 26–28. Reprinted by permission.

Chapter 13   Originally published in Proceedings of the Second National
              Conference on Health Care for the Poor and Underserved,
              Meharry Medical College, Nashville, Tennessee, *Journal of
              Health Care for the Poor and Underserved* Vol. 1, no. 1, Summer
              1990, pp. 48–62. Reprinted by permission.
Chapter 14   Originally published as "Public-Private Issues and Access,"
              Bulletin of the New York Academy of Medicine, Second Series, Vol.
              67, no. 1, January–February, 1991, pp. 55–58. Reprinted courtesy
              of the New York Academy of Medicine Library.
Chapter 15   Originally published in *Journal of the American Medical
              Association* Vol. 265, no. 2, January 9, 1991, pp. 238–241.
              Copyright © 1991, American Medical Association. Reprinted by
              permission.
Chapter 16   Originally published as "Beyond Universal Health Insurance to
              Effective Health Care," with Miriam Ostow, in *Journal of the
              American Medical Association* Vol. 265, no. 19, May 15, 1992, pp.
              2559–2562. Copyright © 1992, American Medical Association.
              Reprinted by permission.
Chapter 17   Originally published in Sounding Board, *New England Journal of
              Medicine* Vol. 322, May 17, 1990, pp. 1464–1466. Reprinted by
              permission.
Chapter 18   Originally keynote address at conference held May 17, 1991,
              "Seeking Common Ground: Law, Psychiatry, and Patient Care
              in the 1990s," *Transactions and Studies of the College of Physicians
              of Philadelphia*, Ser. 5, Vol. 13, no. 3 (1991), pp. 235–247.
              Reprinted by permission.
Chapter 20   Originally published as "Health Care Reform—Where Are We
              and Where Should We Be Going?" Sounding Board, *New
              England Journal of Medicine* Vol. 327, no. 18, October 29, 1992, pp.
              1310–1312. Reprinted by permission.

About the Book and Author

The early 1990s saw the U.S. health care system under intensifying pressures and strains as a consequence of steeply rising expenditures, an increase in the number of uninsured persons, and a range of other challenges, including increasingly severe pressures on government and employers, the principal payers for health care. As a consequence of these and other dysfunctional developments, Eli Ginzberg explored and assessed the problems and the transformations underway in the financing of U.S. health care and in the delivery of services. On the eve of an era of major health care reform, *Medical Gridlock and Health Reform* presents his findings.

Eli Ginzberg is director of The Eisenhower Center for the Conservation of Human Resources and is A. Barton Hepburn Professor Emeritus of Economics at Columbia University.

Index

AAMC. *See* Association of American Medical Colleges

Academic health centers (AHCs), 57, 70, 77, 87, 91, 103, 166, 170
   federal support, 108, 166

Acute-care hospitals, 51, 53, 87, 91, 108
   excess capacity, 26, 32, 66, 180–181, 193
   and health care reform, 97, 120
   and Medicare, 54
   See also Nonprofit hospitals

Administrative waste, 37, 56, 59, 125, 154, 172, 186, 193
   containment, 192

Aetna (health insurance company), 179

AFDC. *See* Aid to Families with Dependent Children

Agency for Health Care Policy and Research (HHS), 57

AHA. *See* American Hospital Association

AHCs. *See* Academic health centers

AIDS, 33, 131, 144

Aid to Families with Dependent Children (AFDC), 53, 107, 121, 132

Aiken, Linda, 78

Air Corps, 17

Aliens. *See under* Uninsured

Allied health personnel, 73, 81, 82, 83, 84
   employment estimates, 82(table)

Allied Health Services: Avoiding Crises (Institute of Medicine), 73

All-payer system, 129

AMA. *See* American Medical Association

Ambulatory care, 58, 66, 100, 122, 127, 138–140, 145, 153, 173, 180
   surgery, 74, 108
   See also Community health centers

American College of Surgeons, 167

American Hospital Association (AHA), 94

American Medical Association (AMA), 57, 64, 65, 88, 89, 127, 166, 169, 180

Army Services Forces (ASF) Medical Department, 7, 10, 12, 15

Association of American Medical Colleges (AAMC), 41, 166, 180

Basic Health Benefits for All Americans Act, 127

Biomedical research, 40, 55, 59, 99, 164, 166, 180, 193
   federal support, 12, 13, 16, 32, 66–67, 91, 102, 103, 107, 170

Bliss, Raymond, 7, 9, 10, 90

Blue Cross–Blue Shield Association, 16, 89, 95, 108, 127, 129, 168

Blumenthal, George, 89

Bowsher, Charles, 186

Bradley, Omar, 17

Brook, Robert, 57

Bulletin of the American College of Surgeons, 167

Burns, Arthur F., 31

Bush, George, 22, 126, 154, 171

Bush, Vannevar, 16, 102

Califano, Joseph, Jr., 28, 94, 171

Canada, 56, 71, 174

Carnegie Corporation for the Advancement of Teaching, 88

Carter, Jimmy, 1, 94, 184

Catastrophic health insurance coverage, 25, 126, 147, 156, 163. *See also under* Medicare

Centers for Disease Control, 144

Certificate of need (CON), 181

CHAMPUS. *See* Civilian Health and Medical Program of the Uniformed Services

Charity, 124. *See also* Cross-subsidization; Philanthropy

Charity Begins at Home: Generosity and Self-Interest Among the Philanthropic Elite (Odendahl), 87

Children, 22, 53, 55, 63, 122, 139, 144, 146, 154, 192

Cigna (health insurance company), 179

Civilian Health and Medical Program of the Uniformed Services (CHAMPUS), 122–123

Clinton, Bill, 3, 112, 188–191

COBRA. *See* Consolidated Omnibus Reconciliation Act

COGME. *See* Council on Graduate Medical Education

Commission on Nursing (HHS), 80, 84

Committee on the Costs of Medical Care (1932), 89

Committee to Study the Role of Allied Health Personnel (Institute of Medicine), 81, 82

Commonwealth Fund, 84

Communications Workers of America, 126